TCP/IP First-Step

Mark A. Sportack

D1279445

Cisco Press

800 East 96th Street

Indianapolis, IN 46240

TCP/IP First-Step

Mark A. Sportack

Published by:
Cisco Press
800 East 96th Street
Indianapolis, IN 46240 USA

Printed in the United States of America 1 2 3 4 5 6 7 8 9 0

First Printing   December 2004

Library of Congress Cataloging-in-Publication Number: 2003109693

ISBN: 1-58720-108-9

Warning and Disclaimer

This book is designed to provide information about the basics of TCP/IP. Every effort has been made to make this book as complete and as accurate as possible, but no warranty or fitness is implied.

The information is provided on an "as is" basis. The authors, Cisco Press, and Cisco Systems, Inc. shall have neither liability nor responsibility to any person or entity with respect to any loss or damages arising from the information contained in this book or from the use of the discs or programs that may accompany it.

The opinions expressed in this book belong to the author and are not necessarily those of Cisco Systems, Inc.

Trademark Acknowledgments

All terms mentioned in this book that are known to be trademarks or service marks have been appropriately capitalized. Cisco Press or Cisco Systems, Inc. cannot attest to the accuracy of this information. Use of a term in this book should not be regarded as affecting the validity of any trademark or service mark.

Publisher
John Wait

Editor-in-Chief
John Kane

Cisco Representative
Anthony Wolfenden

Cisco Press Program Manager
Nannette M. Noble

Executive Editor
Jim Schachterle

Production Manager
Patrick Kanouse

Development Editor
Grant Munroe

Senior Project Editor
San Dee Phillips

Copy Editor
Tonya Cupp

Technical Editors
Henry Benjamin
Ron Kovac
David Kurtiak

Editorial Assistant
Tammi Barnett

Cover and Book Designer
Louisa Adair

Compositor
Mark Shirar

Indexer
Tim Wright

Proofreader
Katherin Bidwell

Corporate and Government Sales

Cisco Press offers excellent discounts on this book when ordered in quantity for bulk purchases or special sales.

For more information please contact: U.S. Corporate and Government Sales 1-800-382-3419 corpsales@pearsontechgroup.com

For sales outside the U.S. please contact: International Sales international@pearsoned.com

Feedback Information

At Cisco Press, our goal is to create in-depth technical books of the highest quality and value. Each book is crafted with care and precision, undergoing rigorous development that involves the unique expertise of members from the professional technical community.

Readers' feedback is a natural continuation of this process. If you have any comments regarding how we could improve the quality of this book, or otherwise alter it to better suit your needs, you can contact us through email at feedback@ciscopress.com. Please make sure to include the book title and ISBN in your message.

We greatly appreciate your assistance.

CISCO SYSTEMS

Corporate Headquarters
Cisco Systems, Inc.
170 West Tasman Drive
San Jose, CA 95134-1706
USA
www.cisco.com
Tel: 408 526-4000
   800 553-NETS (6387)
Fax: 408 526-4100

European Headquarters
Cisco Systems International BV
Haarlerbergpark
Haarlerbergweg 13-19
1101 CH Amsterdam
The Netherlands
www-europe.cisco.com
Tel: 31 0 20 357 1000
Fax: 31 0 20 357 1100

Americas Headquarters
Cisco Systems, Inc.
170 West Tasman Drive
San Jose, CA 95134-1706
USA
www.cisco.com
Tel: 408 526-7660
Fax: 408 527-0883

Asia Pacific Headquarters
Cisco Systems, Inc.
Capital Tower
168 Robinson Road
#22-01 to #29-01
Singapore 068912
www.cisco.com
Tel: +65 6317 7777
Fax: +65 6317 7799

Cisco Systems has more than 200 offices in the following countries and regions. Addresses, phone numbers, and fax numbers are listed on the **Cisco.com Web site at www.cisco.com/go/offices.**

Argentina • Australia • Austria • Belgium • Brazil • Bulgaria • Canada • Chile • China PRC • Colombia • Costa Rica • Croatia • Czech Republic Denmark • Dubai, UAE • Finland • France • Germany • Greece • Hong Kong SAR • Hungary • India • Indonesia • Ireland • Israel • Italy Japan • Korea • Luxembourg • Malaysia • Mexico • The Netherlands • New Zealand • Norway • Peru • Philippines • Poland • Portugal Puerto Rico • Romania • Russia • Saudi Arabia • Scotland • Singapore • Slovakia • Slovenia • South Africa • Spain • Sweden Switzerland • Taiwan • Thailand • Turkey • Ukraine • United Kingdom • United States • Venezuela • Vietnam • Zimbabwe

About the Author

Mark A. Sportack has worked in the information technology industry for more than 20 years. Mark's experience includes everything from computer programming and systems analysis, to running a national ISP network and hosting centers, to managing the daily technical operations of small, medium, and large enterprises. During his career, Mark has had the privilege to lead large teams of technical personnel, set technical direction and long-range plans, and manage multimillion-dollar capital and expense budgets. Mark is chief information officer for Pitney Hardin, LLP.

Mark has authored numerous books including *IP Addressing Fundamentals and IP Routing Fundamentals* for Cisco Press. He has also written *High Performance Networking Unleashed*, *Networking Essentials Unleashed*, and *Windows NT Clustering Blueprints*.

Mark holds an undergraduate degree from Montclair State University and an M.B.A. degree from Lehigh University.

About the Technical Reviewers

Henry Benjamin, CCIE No. 4695, holds three CCIE certifications (Routing and Switching, ISP Dial, and Communications and Services). He has more than 10 years experience with Cisco networks and recently worked for Cisco in the internal IT department helping to design and implement networks throughout Australia and Asia. Henry was a key member of the CCIE global team, where he was responsible for writing new laboratory examinations and questions for the CCIE exams. Henry is an independent consultant with a large security firm in Australia.

Dr. Ron Kovac is currently employed with the Center for Information and Communication Sciences at Ball State University in Muncie, Indiana as a full professor. The Center prepares graduate students in the field of telecommunications. Previous to this, Dr. Kovac was the telecommunications manager for the State of New York and an executive director for a large computing center located on the east coast. Dr. Kovac's previous studies included electrical engineering and education. Dr. Kovac has numerous publications and has consulted in both the education and telecommunications field, speaks worldwide on telecommunications issues, holds numerous certifications including the CCNA, CCAI, and almost complete CCNP.

David M. Kurtiak is a principal engineer and manager of Network Computing Services for Loral Skynet, where he leads a team of technical professionals responsible for managing the company's IT and data network infrastructure. Dave has more than 17 years of experience in the IT and telecommunications industry. Prior to joining Loral Skynet, Dave was a senior data communications specialist for AT&T. David is experienced in many telecommunications technologies and is recognized as the resident expert in TCP/IP networking. He specializes in end-to-end network analysis, planning, troubleshooting, and performance tuning. David has a and a bachelor's degree in information systems from the University of North Carolina at Greensboro.

Dedications

I dedicate this book in memory of Veronika J. (Sportack) Swisher. Thank you for being my sister.

I would also like to dedicate this book to my wife Karen, my son Adam, and my daughters Jennifer and Jacqueline. I don't know how I would have made it through the last year without you. If ever there was an ill-timed project, this was it. Yet, your love, support, and patience helped me to persevere.

Acknowledgments

There are many people to whom I am indebted for their assistance with this book.

First, thanks to Jim Schachterle for his patience as I missed deadline after deadline due to the events in my personal life. I know I sorely tested your patience, but thank you for sticking with me.

I'd also like to thank my technical editors for keeping me honest and not laughing too loudly at my inevitable mistakes and typos. Special thanks to my long-suffering friend and favorite technical editor, David Kurtiak. Knob Creek beckons! Thanks also to Ron Kovac and Henry Benjamin for their contributions as technical editors.

I'd also like to thank John Kane for continuing to watch over my authoring career with Cisco Press, Christopher Cleveland, Grant Munroe, and everyone else at Cisco Press that helped to make this book possible.

Lastly, I'd like to thank Michael Simmons: my friend, fellow long-distance commuter, and surrogate for this book's target audience.

Contents at a Glance

x

Contents

Introduction

TCP/IP is the language of the Internet. As such, it has become the single-most widely used communications protocol ever. It has literally revolutionized our world by enabling the Internet to become what it is today. Yet, for all its success, it remains a shadowy mystery to all but a handful of computer geeks and network nerds.

I'll be the first to admit that TCP/IP is as complex and mysterious a protocol suite as you could hope to find. That's a shame because it doesn't need to be. TCP/IP has a rich history and offers many capabilities that the vast majority of today's Internet users don't know about. Although you could live a lifetime without ever knowing about or using these features, you would also be missing out on quite a bit!

To my twisted way of thinking, the only way to truly understand the Internet and learn how to use it to maximum advantage requires that you first understand TCP/IP. Armed with the knowledge you gain from this book, you can take the first step into your future and become more than just another point-and-click Internet user.

Goals of This Book

My goal in writing this book was to help make TCP/IP as understandable as possible for all people, not just computer science majors or network engineers. The Internet has become everybody's most powerful tool yet so much of it is hidden behind a graphical user interface. It seemed only fair and fitting that somebody should write a book for the nontechnical Internet user community to help them harness more of the power of the Internet.

Who Should Read This Book

If you use the Internet, or any other network that uses TCP/IP, you should read this book. I intentionally stayed away from technical jargon and used everyday analogies to help you understand otherwise technical material. However, TCP/IP is sufficiently complex that many a fine IT engineer can benefit from the plain English explanations and illustrations in this book.

How This Book Is Organized

This book is organized into a logical, step-by-step approach to building a comprehensive understanding of TCP/IP and the Internet. That approach is demonstrated for you in the following outline of the chapters:

Part I, "Introduction and Architecture"

- **Chapter 1, "TCP/IP: The Official Protocol of the Internet"**—In this chapter, you learn what TCP/IP is, what it isn't, and where it came from. This provides you with a foundation that the rest of the book builds on.

- **Chapter 2, "What Has TCP/IP Done for Me Lately?"**—TCP/IP literally supports everything that you do on the Internet and any other private network that uses it. When you think about it, that's a Herculean task that implies TCP/IP can support virtually any type of application anywhere around the world. This chapter shows you just how TCP/IP manages to successfully meet that challenge.

- **Chapter 3, "The Quest for Freedom of Choice"**—TCP/IP is perhaps the best example of a nonsecret technology. Unlike many companies that jealously guard their trade secrets, TCP/IP was made, and continues to be developed, in an open and public forum. This chapter shows you how TCP/IP became the best-unkept secret in the world.

- **Chapter 4, "TCP/IP: The Networking Protocol That Changed the World"**—One of the hallmarks of success is consistency over time. TCP/IP achieves consistency by having a carefully sequenced set of steps that it must perform time after time. This chapter shows you how TCP/IP manages to achieve consistency and introduces you to those sequenced steps that it needs to perform when sending and receiving your data.

Part II, "Protocols: The Building Blocks of TCP/IP"

- **Chapter 5, "Peeking Under the Covers"**—Whenever you want to see how something was made, or really works, you need to look beyond what's superficial and obvious. In this chapter, you see what's under the hood of TCP/IP so that you can see the actual mechanisms that enable it to work.

- **Chapter 6, "Pushing the Envelope"** — All data sent across the Internet or any other TCP/IP network is wrapped up in an envelope (known more properly as a packet) and pushed through the network; however, to get to where it needs to go, that envelope *must* have an address. This chapter introduces you to the seemingly arcane mathematics of the Internet's addressing system. Don't worry: It's not that bad!

- **Chapter 7, "More Fun with IP Addresses"** — One important trick that can be performed with IP addresses is taking a big block of them and breaking them down into many smaller blocks. That lets you take a block of addresses designed for use on one network and use it to provide unique addresses for many networks. That concept, known as subnetting, is demystified for you in this chapter.

- **Chapter 8, "Guaranteed Delivery: Your Package Will Get Delivered...Eventually!"** — The notion of guaranteeing the delivery of your data to a remote computer is paramount in a TCP/IP network. In this chapter, you learn how TCP/IP actually does that. In the process, you might be surprised to learn of a "gotcha" or two that lies hiding in wait.

- **Chapter 9, "Best-Effort Delivery: It's Now or Never"** — This chapter is all about a stripped-down, built-for-speed transport mechanism built into TCP/IP. You learn about this mechanism, UDP, how it is used, why it's important, and which of your favorite applications use it without you even knowing it!

Part III, "Network Services: Making Your Network Easy to Use"

- **Chapter 10, "Special Delivery for Special Messages"** — Not all messages sent across a TCP/IP network are sent by users and their computers. Sometimes, machines need to communicate and coordinate activities with each other. For such instances, there is a special delivery mechanism, ICMP. This chapter introduces you to ICMP and shows you how it works and the role it plays in a TCP/IP network.

- **Chapter 11, "How Do I Get There from Here?"** — Ahh, the universal question. You will be pleased to know that knowing how to get from Point A to Point B is quite the mathematical science in a TCP/IP network. That science is known as routing, and in this chapter, you learn more about how your data actually finds its way to where you want it to go.

Part IV, "User Services: Making the Most Use of Your Network"

- **Chapter 12, "Connecting to TCP/IP Networks"**—In this chapter, things become a bit more real; you learn how to connect to a TCP/IP network.

- **Chapter 13, "Smiling and Dialing"**—This chapter builds upon the previous chapter by showing you that there is still a place in a modern TCP/IP network for a modem and good, old-fashioned dial-up access to the Internet.

- **Chapter 14, "Taking the Next Step"**—In this final chapter, you advance beyond the first step toward understanding TCP/IP and take the next step: learning how to diagnose network problems from your computer.

Part V, "Appendix"

- **Appendix A, "Chapter Review Answers"**—This appendix contains answers and explanations to the "Chapter Review Questions" that appear at the end of each chapter.

- **Glossary**—The glossary is a tool that you can easily reference as you come across key terms throughout the book.

Stuff You'll Find in This Book

This book includes several features to help you master wireless topics. Here's a summary of the elements that you'll find:

- **What You Will Learn**—Every chapter begins with a list of objectives that are addressed in the chapter. The objectives summarize what you learn in the chapter.

- **Key terms and glossary**—Throughout this book, you will see key terms formatted with bold and italics. These terms are particularly significant in wireless and networking. So, if you find you aren't familiar with the term or at any point need a refresher, simply look up the term in the glossary toward the end of the book to find a full definition.

- **Chapter Summaries**—Every chapter concludes with a comprehensive "Chapter Summary" that reviews chapter objectives, ensuring complete coverage and discussing the chapter's relationship to future content.

- **Chapter Review Questions**—Every chapter concludes with "Chapter Review Questions" that test the basic ideas and concepts covered in each chapter. You can find the answers and explanations to the questions in Appendix A.

- **Nontechie headings and explanations**—The headings and text used throughout this book avoid the use of technical terms when possible, focusing instead on words that connote something about the underlying concepts.

The illustrations in this book use the following icons for networking devices and connections:

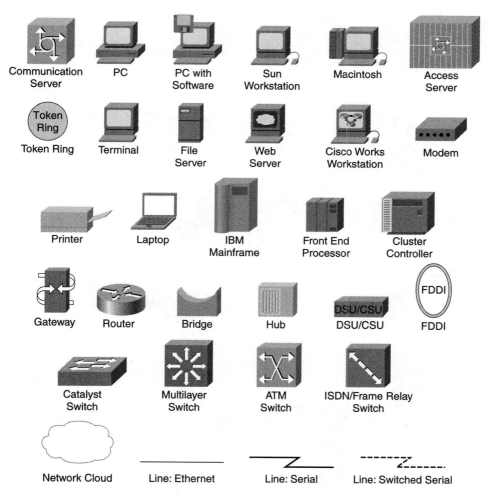

Communication Server

PC

PC with Software

Sun Workstation

Macintosh

Access Server

Token Ring

Terminal

File Server

Web Server

Cisco Works Workstation

Modem

Printer

Laptop

IBM Mainframe

Front End Processor

Cluster Controller

Gateway

Router

Bridge

Hub

DSU/CSU

FDDI

Catalyst Switch

Multilayer Switch

ATM Switch

ISDN/Frame Relay Switch

Network Cloud

Line: Ethernet

Line: Serial

Line: Switched Serial

PART I

Introduction and Architecture

What You Will Learn

After reading this chapter, you should be able to answer the following questions:

- ✔ What is TCP/IP?

- ✔ How are TCP/IP and the Internet related?

- ✔ What are five critical communications functions that TCP/IP can perform?

- ✔ How do you know when you are using TCP/IP?

- ✔ What can't TCP/IP do? (In other words, what communications functions must it rely on other mechanisms to do?)

Answers to these basic questions demystify TCP/IP and create the foundation of knowledge that you build upon throughout this book. After finishing this book, you will have a solid appreciation for TCP/IP, how it works, and why it's important.

CHAPTER 1

TCP/IP: The Official Protocol of the Internet!

TCP/IP isn't just random characters left in the bottom of the bowl when you're finished with your alphabet soup; it just looks that way! *TCP/IP* is a mouthful of an acronym that stands for *Transmission Control Protocol/Internet Protocol*. One look at the full name and it's immediately obvious why you use the acronym instead. Neither its full name nor its acronym do TCP/IP any justice. Both are uninformative and even a bit misleading.

It's impossible to understate TCP/IP's value and significance. Without it, you literally wouldn't be able to access the Internet or anything connected to it. Think about it: no swapping MP3 or DivX files, no catching the latest news or stock quotes, no e-mail, no instant messages or online chat rooms…okay, so maybe you could live without chat rooms! The point remains: Everything you do via the Internet would be impossible without TCP/IP. A bunch of other private networks would be equally unusable, too!

TCP/IP is a set of data communications mechanisms, embodied in software, that let you use the Internet and countless other private networks. Each mechanism— also known as a *protocol*—is designed to perform a specific function. These protocols are divided into two categories based on their function:

- One focuses on processing and handling data from applications and is known as the Transmission Control Protocol (TCP) suite.

- The other is more network oriented and designed to accommodate the transmission and receipt of application data across a network. This second suite is called the Internet Protocol (IP) suite.

This extensive set of protocols forms the TCP/IP suite of protocols. TCP/IP enables different types of computers and other devices to use networks to contact each other and share information in a wide variety of ways including e-mail. Networks and networking protocols existed before TCP/IP came along; they just didn't allow a network as powerful and universal as the Internet to be built! That was the beauty of TCP/IP.

What Is TCP/IP?

TCP/IP is an open-standard communications protocol suite that is the standard for communicating on the Internet. That's the official line, but what exactly *is* it? That's a tougher question to answer! Part of the reason TCP/IP is a murky and mysterious topic—even to those people knowledgeable about data networks—is that it's so vast and complex. It contains all the fundamental mechanisms needed to support any and all types of networked communications.

A good way to make sense of this is to look at your computer's operating system. Today's operating systems can easily be several gigabytes in size. They include thousands of small files designed to do just one specific task. Separately, they are almost worthless. Together, they form a powerful and comprehensive system that enables your computer to support a seemingly infinite variety of applications. TCP/IP is just like that: lots of little functions designed to do one specific task. Together, they enable your computer to support any type of networked communications activity you'd care to do.

Virtually every network-capable application in existence today relies on TCP/IP to function properly. That's no small accomplishment when you stop to think that today just about every software application is network capable. E-mail and web browsing are applications that obviously require a network to function. The World Wide Web has permeated computing so completely that it is difficult to say where the browser ends and the operating system begins. Consequently, even applications such as word-processing software now have features that require network connectivity—and TCP/IP—to work properly. To further complicate matters,

TCP/IP also contains a number of useful applications that enable you to do things like transfer files or log on to remote computers. These are native to TCP/IP and are what's left of the earliest TCP/IP software utilities.

Today, TCP/IP is maintained in an open forum. The forum consists of representatives from various companies that have a vested interest in the Internet and its technology base. Each representative participates in developing proposed changes, analyzing the impact of each proposal, and voting on whether to actually incorporate each change into the TCP/IP suite.

Changes to the protocol suite requires consensus among all the participants in that forum. This consensus-based approach enables computers made by different companies to communicate and share data despite their differences. The result is a set of communications mechanisms that does not belong to any one company. Instead, it is a public, or *open*, technology that can be implemented by anybody. Chapter 3, "The Quest for Freedom of Choice," more closely looks at this open forum and its consensus-based approach to building standards.

The combination of TCP/IP's sheer size and the unconventional way in which it is maintained make for a rather steep learning curve for anyone trying to figure it out. To best understand this arcane subject, look at where it came from and trace its evolution.

Finding TCP/IP's Roots

Given the enormous success of the Internet and TCP/IP, it is ironic that TCP/IP was intended for use in a small environment. Even more irony lies in the fact that TCP/IP wasn't even designed! It emerged slowly over time, first appearing as shareware created by computer engineers, scientists, and researchers at different organizations as a way to communicate and collaborate on defense projects. Despite such humble origins, TCP/IP is now actually used more broadly than the Internet.

The Birth of TCP/IP

The roots of TCP/IP are difficult to pin down due to the nature of its piecemeal development, but one recognized milestone (sometimes called its "birth") occurred on January 1, 1983. On this date, approximately 400 computers connected to a network called ARPAnet all started communicating with each other with a collection of mechanisms known informally as TCP/IP. *ARPAnet* was a network sponsored by the U.S. Department of Defense (DoD) in support of its *Advanced Research Projects Agency (ARPA)* to facilitate the research and development of military and defense technologies. This network interconnected computers that were owned and operated by different companies, government agencies, research bodies, and other institutions, which all contributed to the ARPA's research and development efforts.

These 400 computers also consisted of a wide variety of different brands and models in a time when each hardware manufacturer went out of its way to make sure that its products were incompatible with anybody else's products. This approach, known as *closed* or *proprietary architecture*, was based on the belief that it forced brand loyalty. In a closed architecture, if you bought Brand X for your mainframe computer (this was before the client/server revolution), you had to also buy Brand X's printers, workstations, disk and tape drives, and even wires! After you purchased those products you had to purchase ongoing maintenance or product support from that manufacturer. Products made by different vendors quite simply weren't designed to be interoperable.

TCP/IP became a unifying element that enabled collaboration and interoperability across incompatible systems. The benefits of this approach proved so compelling as to literally revolutionize networked computing and transform the DoD's little internetwork into the Internet!

The Early Days of Networking

ARPAnet existed (in fact, it dated back to the 1960s) prior to January 1, 1983, but lacked a single official mechanism for communications. Thus, the proprietary architectures of that era's computer systems posed significant barriers to networked communications. The result was that some computers could communicate with others, but that ability was far from ubiquitous. Some of the systems administrators who operated these disparate computers talked to each other and developed special-purpose programs. One person might have, for example, developed a small program that transferred data files. Another might have developed a program that enabled you to log into a remote computer. Somebody else might have developed a utility that helped track how many machines your data was passing through before reaching its destination. These files might have been developed informally, but they were enormously useful. Consequently, the programs were shared throughout ARPAnet.

This informal and sometimes collaborative process of developing utility software slowly built up the set of shared mechanisms that ARPAnet used. It actually took a couple of decades of piecemeal, consensus-based development for TCP/IP to reach a critical mass in terms of features and functionality. After ARPAnet declared TCP/IP its official communications protocol, there was no turning back!

Enabling the Internet's Success

TCP/IP soldiered on through the 1980s, laboring in the shadows of other, more popular and successful commercial network protocols. ARPAnet continued growing and eventually became known as the *Internet*. TCP/IP remained dedicated to supporting this network, but saw widespread acceptance. This occurred when the U.S. federal government converted Internet from a private military-oriented research facility into a public facility to which anyone could connect from around the world.

Commercialization of the Internet brought forth a frenzy of activity, both technical and economic. The first knee-jerk reaction was akin to a 20th century gold rush. Companies rushed to establish connectivity and a website presence on the Internet. Often, this rush was done with undue haste and without thought of what said companies would do with that connectivity or website.

When the Internet fever subsided, rational thought once again was possible. Individual people learned how to use the Internet, and commercial enterprises learned what those individual consumers wanted. One stark fact became obvious: TCP/IP had just experienced a dramatic increase in its user base. Not only was it now the de facto standard communications protocol for all connected residential users, but enterprises and organizations also had to support it. That meant many businesses were using one protocol suite for communicating across their internal network and another (TCP/IP) to connect to the Internet.

It didn't take long for businesses to realize that TCP/IP could be used throughout their internal networks and could free them from the burden of supporting two different protocols. In this manner, TCP/IP literally became more popular than the Internet.

One of TCP/IP's most basic yet critical functions is its preparation of application data for transmission across a network. TCP/IP accepts data of virtually any size from applications (typically in the form of a file) and chops it up into smaller, more manageable chunks. These chunks are known as *segments* and the process of splitting files is known as *segmentation*. Segments of data are then wrapped in a data structure known as a *packet*. A packet contains all the information a network needs to deliver it to its destination and then to acknowledge delivery.

Packetization is the communication by two or more computers by sending and receiving individual packets of data. It was first demonstrated on September 2, 1969, when two computers at the University of California-Los Angeles were linked together with a 15-foot cable. This cable functioned as a primitive internetwork, and the test validated the theory that computers could send and receive packetized data. Until then, data was sent one bit at a time without the benefit of having first been segmented for transmission. This simple test paved the way for radical changes in technology and society that no one could have predicted.

The Abilities and Limitations of TCP/IP

TCP/IP is a communications protocol that fits in the middle of a larger set of mechanisms. TCP/IP provides the linkage between communicating software applications and a physical network that carries messages sent by computers to other computers or devices. In this regard, TCP/IP complements and extends the capability of a physical network, but can't work without that network. Although TCP/IP does blur across some boundaries, it actually fits between the application software, operating system, and network or communications device such as a cable modem or local-area network (LAN). To visualize this, see Figure 1-1.

Figure 1-1   TCP/IP Fits Between the Network and Your Software

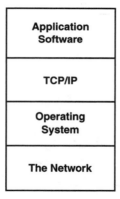

Figure 1-1 shows a logical model. Logical models can be confusing due to their nature, but the best way to understand is to think of them as a necessary sequence of events. In this particular model, if you want to communicate across the Internet, you start with your application. Say you are sending a file directly to a friend across the Internet. The first thing you do is pick an application that lets you do that.

Fortunately, TCP/IP contains just such an application: It's called the *File Transfer Protocol (FTP)*. You supply FTP with the necessary information, which is basically your friend's computer address and the file you want to send. FTP needs to engage the operating system to access your computer's physical resources including memory, CPU, and the peripheral device that connects your computer to the physical network.

The preceding example shows how TCP/IP can blur the traditional distinctions between types of software. Even though TCP/IP is just a communications protocol, it also contains numerous utilities or applications, such as FTP. It's part communications protocol and part application software.

On the receiving end, your friend's computer performs the same process, only in reverse. The file comes through the network, where your operating system uses whatever physical resources it must and ensures that TCP/IP gets the file via its own copy of FTP. Figure 1-2 illustrates this process.

Figure 1-2   A Logical Perspective of Using TCP/IP to Transfer a File to a Friend

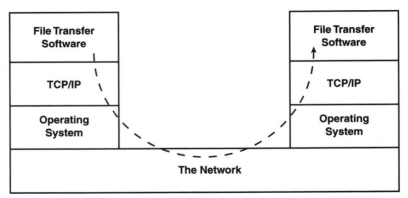

In its role as intermediary between software and the physical network, TCP/IP provides the rules and mechanisms that enable two or more different machines — even if they are very different machines—to communicate and share information with each other.

TCP/IP's mechanisms are designed to enable communications between any two or more machines connected to a network regardless of the device type, who made them, or their physical proximity to each other. Bridging the gap between dissimilar devices is a phenomenally powerful concept: You have created a mechanism that brings everybody together regardless of where they are or what technologies they use.

As shown in the preceding FTP example, the boundaries between operating system, application software, and communications protocols are blurred quite a bit by TCP/IP. When installed, TCP/IP functions as an extension of the operating system. So seamless is this integration that many people aren't even aware that they are using TCP/IP to communicate!

Even more confusion is added when you remember that TCP/IP contains quite a few simple applications that enable a user to directly do simple tasks like push files through a network or log on to remote computers. Part IV, "User Services— Making the Most Use of Your Network," looks more closely at those utilities. Users who are familiar with such utilities might think of TCP/IP as an application. They'd have justification for thinking that way! However, these utilities are just one small piece of the comprehensive set of protocols that you know and love and call TCP/IP.

Economically, too, TCP/IP has been a boon. The concept of an open mechanism that is not owned or controlled by any one commercial organization has opened doors few people could have imagined possible. For example, TCP/IP has become widely accepted around the world simply because it becomes the means by which different manufacturers' products can interoperate with each other. More importantly, TCP/IP broke new ground by pioneering a new method for developing new technologies that anyone could manufacture. Now, entities trying to develop a new communications-based product or technology can simply start with TCP/IP's openly published specifications and focus on adding value based on that preexisting set of capabilities. More importantly, developing products around TCP/IP brings a tremendous base of users who could easily integrate any new products based on that protocol suite.

TCP/IP's Top Five Critical Functions

By now you're probably anxious to get into what TCP/IP can do for you. Some of the applications that rely on TCP/IP (such as web surfing and e-mail) have been discussed, but you have seen how one set of mechanisms can so successfully support a rich and diverse array of applications.

The answer lies in determining the basic underlying capabilities any application requires to communicate. At the risk of sounding like a late-night talk show host, TCP/IP's top five critical functions follow:

1. **Globally Unique Addresses**—An addressing system that permits you to uniquely identify any given machine connected to the Internet. This system affords the ability to create literally billions of unique addresses.

2. **Packet**—Merely having an address for a networked machine isn't enough to permit communication. You also need a mechanism that allows you to send data to, and receive data from, the machine with that address. That mechanism is called a *packet*. Packets contain all the address information that a TCP/IP network needs to enable two or more devices to talk across a network.

3. **Segmentation and Reassembly**—The ability to chop up application data into manageable pieces called *segments* is crucial to communicating across a network. These segments are then placed inside a packet for transmission across a network. The machine receiving this stream of packets can extract the segments of data and restore the data to its original form.

4. **Resequencing**—TCP/IP also enables computers that receive a series of related packets to put them back into the correct order. This ability is important because you can't guarantee that packets will be received in the order they were sent. Networks are made of intelligent and autonomous devices known as *routers*, which decide where to send each packet. Their decisions can vary based on congestion and failures discovered within the network. The result is that packets are commonly received out of sequence!

5. **Data Integrity**—Lastly, you can't always assume that what you put on a network will get to its destination intact. For that matter, you can't assume that it will get there at all! Lots of things can go wrong when data is traveling through a network. The result can be garbled data or even packets that get lost or dropped. TCP/IP is smart enough to detect data that was damaged or lost as it traveled through the network. Data that was damaged is discarded and TCP/IP's mechanisms ensure that—when appropriate—the damaged or lost block is retransmitted until it is successfully received.

TCP/IP can, of course, do many other things. Thus, this list is not comprehensive. Instead, these five things form the basis for communicating. Other features, including those that are part of TCP/IP and those commercially developed around TCP/IP, build upon this foundation.

What It Can't Do

TCP/IP is not a proverbial silver bullet. It offers tremendous capabilities, but it does have its limitations. Those limitations have more to do with the intended scope of the protocol suite than weaknesses. Please consider all the "can't dos" in this section as being by design rather than indicative of a flawed implementation.

First of all, TCP/IP is not an *operating system (OS)*. An OS is the software that runs on a computer and creates the environment in which other applications can run. The various Windows platforms are examples of operating systems. When installed, TCP/IP becomes an important extension of your computer's operating system, but it does not replace it.

There was a time when some software vendors billed their operating system software as a *Network Operating System (NOS)*, but that term is misleading. It indicates a computer OS that supports a robust ability to communicate. One critical component of that ability was the inclusion of communications protocols, such as TCP/IP. However, bundling a set of communications protocols with an operating system doesn't make those protocols the operating system! As networking ability has become a more integral part of both operating systems and application software, this distinction has fallen by the wayside; consumers began expecting their operating systems to offer a rich networking capability.

TCP/IP also isn't a network! Installing and configuring TCP/IP on your workstation or home computer does not, in and of itself, mean you can use that computer to communicate with other computers or devices. TCP/IP, by itself, is incapable of transmitting or carrying data. Those functions remain in the purview of a physical network such as an Ethernet or a wide-area network (WAN). TCP/IP prepares data received from applications for transmission and provides all the logical mechanisms needed to send and receive data between two devices connected via a physical network.

Chapter Summary

TCP/IP is a large set—sometimes called a *suite*—of communications protocols that fit in the middle of a larger set of mechanisms. These protocols provide the linkage between applications that can communicate and a physical network that carries the communicated data. Thus, TCP/IP complements and extends the capability of a physical network, but can't work without it.

However, the best thing about TCP/IP isn't what it can do, but what it has enabled! TCP/IP has literally and truly enabled people and organizations around the world to get past the artificial boundaries of technology choices and vendor preferences. The protocol enables the global quest for freedom of choice and rewards those who have implemented TCP/IP with an unprecedented bounty of online information and services.

Enough of the history and the hype: You're ready for some more concrete information that solidifies your grasp of what TCP/IP is and how you use it every time you communicate via a network. The next chapter looks more closely at what TCP/IP means to you.

Chapter Review Questions

The following questions reinforce the key concepts in this chapter.

1. What is TCP/IP?

2. How are TCP/IP and the Internet related?

3. What five critical communications functions can TCP/IP perform?

4. How do you know when you are using TCP/IP?

5. What can't TCP/IP do? In other words, what communications functions must it rely on other mechanisms to do?

What You Will Learn

After reading this chapter, you should be able to answer the following questions:

- ✔ How can TCP/IP satisfy the network performance requirements of an unlimited number of software applications?

- ✔ What are the two basic network performance requirements imposed by software applications?

- ✔ Is TCP/IP a tool designed for business or pleasure?

- ✔ For what is TCP/IP used?

- ✔ What does the term *reliable delivery* mean?

- ✔ What does the term *best-effort delivery* mean?

CHAPTER 2

What Has TCP/IP Done for Me Lately?

What has TCP/IP done for you lately? Plenty! If you are an Internet user, you are also a TCP/IP user. Even if you never use the Internet, chances are excellent that you are still a TCP/IP user. The fact is that TCP/IP has become bigger than the Internet! It's true. Although massive in size and scope, the Internet is not the only computer network in the world. Probably hundreds of thousands of smaller networks are in homes, schools, companies, stores, and everywhere two or more computers need to communicate. The vast majority of these private networks use TCP/IP.

The technological advances in desktop computing and software applications have enabled network users to start thinking about networks solely in terms of applications—not in terms of the underlying wires and switches and communications protocols.

This chapter looks at some of the various types of applications that TCP/IP supports, as well as how TCP/IP is able to support as many applications as it does. By the end of this chapter you know exactly what TCP/IP has done for you lately!

Business and Pleasure?

In today's fast-paced world, as you chase tomorrow, it's easy to forget the achievements of the past. No part of the world moves quite as fast—or is as unforgiving—as the Internet. Obsolescence is always just a technical innovation away! TCP/IP has soldiered on in this merciless environment for more than

20 years. During that time it has successfully kept up with technological change by constantly adding features and capabilities.

Ironically, for all its successes, TCP/IP has remained just out of sight for most people. Most people don't even realize how dependent they have become upon it (or even when they are using it). That's a tribute to the seamless manner with which it supports the Internet and all its content and applications.

TCP/IP supports you in ways you can't even imagine. TCP/IP, quite literally, supports any software that communicates across the Internet. More precisely, it supports any software that has the ability to communicate across the Internet regardless of whether it actually uses the Internet. That might sound like splitting hairs, but it is a distinction that needs to be made.

TCP/IP might have been designed to support communications across the Internet, but it has far transcended that initially limited role. Today, TCP/IP has become the de facto standard communications protocol in networks around the world, regardless of whether those networks were designed to help you work or play.

At Play

Some of the things TCP/IP lets you do include literally anything that connect to the Internet. When you aimlessly surf the Internet looking for its end, you are using TCP/IP. It doesn't matter whether you're checking your auctions on eBay, searching for your own name, or checking real-time stock quotes: You are still using TCP/IP. When you download digital tunes for your iPod, guess what? You are using TCP/IP! Are you using an Internet phone? Those rely upon TCP/IP, too. Sending the latest joke via e-mail to your friends and family? E-mail uses TCP/IP, too! Defending the universe against an infinite hoard of malicious invaders? Online games use TCP/IP as well. The same goes for chat rooms, instant messaging, and webcams.

At Work

TCP/IP has a practical side, too. Chances are, when sending a print request to the *local-area network (LAN)* printer at work, you are using TCP/IP. When accessing your file server to compose your letter of resignation, well, you're still using TCP/IP. When checking the latest benefits e-mail from Human Resources, chances again are really good that you are using TCP/IP.

What's the Secret?

Now there's a question! What's the secret behind the great mystery? How can TCP/IP work so ubiquitously? How can it possibly support every application—literally? Sure, some of the applications have similarities, but a world of difference lies between others! How can it possibly be equally useful in a business environment and in online interactive gaming? Surely, some secret enables TCP/IP to achieve feats of Herculean proportions.

The mystery deepens when you stop to consider the fact that not only does it support an incredibly large array of applications, it does so globally! That means TCP/IP must span countries and support applications and computers that use a tremendous variety of languages.

A slightly more subtle aspect of TCP/IP's universality is that it binds together all kinds of different networks. Think about it; the Internet is a collection of networks. The owners of those networks are free to choose whatever products they want. Consequently, the Internet is composed of virtually every type of network gear you could possibly imagine. Different languages, different hardware manufacturers, even different network technologies are all bound together by TCP/IP.

Getting back to the original point: What's the secret? How can TCP/IP possibly do all it does? As so often happens in life, no single answer explains it all. However, a couple of points go a long way toward helping you understand how TCP/IP can work as universally as it does:

- Open standards
- Functional abstraction

Open Standards

The concept of *open standards* dominates information technologies. In essence, it means no secrets: Everyone agrees on the technical specifications for a technology and those specifications are made publicly available. Anyone can build products based on that technology. The good news in an open-standard industry is that consumers can be confident that products—made by different manufacturers—work well together.

The bad news is reserved for the manufacturers. The direct competition caused by the lack of trade secrets means difficultly proving that their products are worth a premium. Consequently, competition tends to be price-based and consumers are free to shop for the lowest prices, without worrying about how it affects their network's functionality.

Another open-standards benefit is the creation of a common framework for understanding any given technology as a series of sequenced events or functions. Some of those functions must be performed in a specific sequence, while others can be performed at various times in the overall process. An open standard carefully and publicly defines the sequence of events, the boundaries between functions, and how those functions interact with each other. That framework greatly simplifies the task of supporting applications. Software manufacturers know, by virtue of the openly published standards, how to work with physical networks and network protocols. Thus, there is no need to reinvent the wheel.

Applications that allow you to communicate with other users tend to focus on two things. First, they provide a specific function or group of related functions. Second, they either provide or enable communication through a network. For example, electronic mail (e-mail) software provides a vast array of related functions that allow you to send electronic messages to other people, organize those messages, manage your contacts, and on and on. In other words, everything a user needs to manage e-mail and e-mail addresses is bundled in, including a graphical user interface (GUI) that makes it easy to actually use the software.

As complete as the functionality might appear, e-mail software is not complete unto itself. For example, the software absolutely depends on other preexisting mechanisms for many network functions. Some of those functions include discovering other networks, figuring out the best way through the network to those machines, and keeping track of how well communications with those devices are going. Obviously, it needs the network, too! Without a collection of pipes and mechanisms to provide the physical connectivity, not much else is going to happen. You can see how it is preferable to use existing mechanisms for networking and communications rather than try to duplicate all that for each application software package.

Somewhere between the physical network and the e-mail software lies TCP/IP. TCP/IP is actually a family of protocols. Together, those protocols provide all the logical functions needed to link your application software with the physical network and to use that network. You need that network for several things, including finding the people you want to correspond with and figuring out how to get e-mails back and forth through the network. That's a long-winded way of saying that applications work with TCP/IP because it's easier than trying to develop their own secret way of communicating through networks.

Chapter 3, "The Quest for Freedom of Choice," takes a much closer look at open standards. For now, know that using open standards is the way TCP/IP overcomes the challenges of supporting communications over a network made up of different products and technologies made by different manufacturers. The other way TCP/IP works so universally, alluded to earlier, is found in the concept of functional abstraction.

Generalizing to See the Patterns

A wise old saying holds that sometimes you can't see the forest because all the trees are in the way! That's a humorous way of saying that when you look at details, all you can see are those details. The same is true with technologies. Perhaps the best way to think about this aspect of TCP/IP follows: divide first, then conquer!

It is impossible to figure out how to support each application individually. Too many exist. Instead, TCP/IP benefits by using open standards as a forum for communicating to software vendors. That way, software vendors design their products

so they work with TCP/IP. Although that simplifies things greatly, and certainly explains how things work today, it leaves one wondering if there wasn't a chicken-and-egg conundrum to resolve. In fact, there was!

This conundrum is relatively easy to explain, but remarkably difficult to solve in real life. Before a communications protocol such as TCP/IP can be successful, it has to support a lot of applications. After a while, it supports so many applications that you can safely assume it has been installed on a majority of computers. When it reaches that point, it becomes easy to convince software vendors to design their software for TCP/IP compatibility. The catch is figuring out how to support that initial batch of applications! Those applications, by virtue of having existed before TCP/IP was created, weren't designed for compatibility. Rather than falling into the trap of trying to design a communications protocol to work with each individual software application, it becomes necessary to divide…and then to conquer!

Generalization comes into play here. You can lump various applications into broad categories for a more manageable number. Instead of developing protocols that work with each specific application, the challenge is reduced to developing protocols that work with groups of related applications. You need to look past the details to see the trends—the commonalities—that make this possible.

Generalizing from TCP/IP's Perspective

TCP/IP benefits by generalizing the network performance requirements of various application types. When you look at network performance requirements for all application types, you quickly see that only two true general types exist:

- Those that require timely communications
- Those that require highly reliable communications

That might sound too simple, but it's true! Literally every single application you can think of fits into one of those two categories. It's just not obvious because those two categories lie one layer of abstraction beyond the obvious.

Categorizing is a useful approach to managing large amounts of anything. For example, when faced with a bewildering array of software, most people look at the individual software packages and then start categorizing them. Another approach is to categorize by function. It would, of course, be equally valid to categorize by manufacturer or even by the color of the box they came in. The actual categories are much less significant than the fact that you are categorizing.

A Closer Look at the Example

The example works only if you use function to categorize the software. Tens of thousands of software packages might be available, but they are easily reduced into a manageable number of categories such as word processing, web browsers, electronic mail, games, chat, videoconferencing, and so on. Figure 2-1 shows this: All software applications can be distilled into a finite and manageable number of categories. In other words, they are abstracted by some common trait. To keep the example simple, categories are limited to three.

Figure 2-1   Categorizing Applications by Function

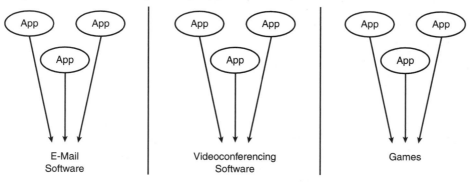

The next level of generalization isn't quite as intuitive as the one in Figure 2-1. Basically, you look at each generalized category and try to find another basis for further categorization. At this level, manufacturer and box color aren't options because you're not looking at individual software products—you're looking at functional categories. You could, for example, further generalize categories by minimum hardware requirements (such as the required amount of memory or disk space). Alternately, you could look at network performance requirements.

That second generalization enables you to further reduce categories. In this case, you go from an unlimited number of applications, to handfuls of functional categories, to two network performance requirements. TCP/IP looks at applications this way. From TCP/IP's perspective, just two types of applications exist: those requiring reliable delivery and those requiring timely delivery. Figure 2-2 illustrates this.

Figure 2-2   Generalizing the Network Performance Requirements

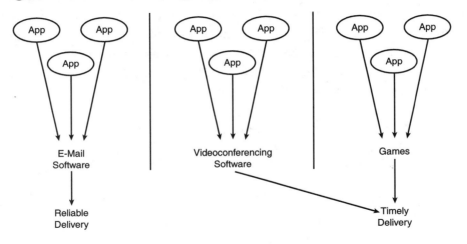

It really is that simple: TCP/IP doesn't try to work with every application (or with every application type). It does, however, bend over backward to satisfy two general types of network performance.

The Need for Reliable Communications

The first broad network performance requirement category is characterized by reliable data delivery needs. Perhaps the best example of a reliable delivery service is the U.S. Postal Service. Their legendary motto assures you that the mail will be delivered regardless of the prevailing regional meteorological conditions. Of course, the mail is delivered quicker on nice, sunny days than when there's a foot of snow accumulating, but that's okay! The guarantee is that the mail will get delivered. Nobody said anything about timeliness! You should be thrilled when the mail arrives in a timely fashion. Timeliness is just a pleasant bonus. The delivery itself is the only thing guaranteed by the U.S. Postal Service.

Take that analogy back to TCP/IP by discovering how that relates to the network performance requirements of application software. Many application types require reliable data delivery. Think about this: When you withdraw money from your ATM, you are conducting an electronic transaction through a computer network. Transaction processing is one of the timeless classics of networked computing. It's one of the oldest types of software around and it's impossible to imagine a world where you wouldn't need electronic transactions.

Although ATM transactions don't occur over the public Internet—that would be far too dangerous!—the network it uses is remarkably broad. You can conduct this transaction from almost anywhere and rest assured that your transaction is reliably processed (and the appropriate adjustment made to your account balance). Implicit in that description is that you are using a computer network—albeit a secure computer network—to send the details of your request to your bank for processing and recording.

 This is probably the only time you'll find ATM in a Cisco Press book defined as automatic teller machine. In the world of computer networks, ATM has another meaning: Asynchronous Transfer Mode, which is a specific type of network protocol.

If you were withdrawing cash you might argue that you don't care if the transaction record makes it to your bank. Life just doesn't work that way. Besides, that argument wouldn't hold for both sides of the equation (withdrawing and depositing). For the modern banking system to function properly, each transaction *must* be reliably returned to its origin and confirmation delivered to the ATM you are using. You might have to wait for your transaction to clear, but that's a function of the reliable communications between the ATM and the computer system managing your bank account. You won't get any cash from the ATM until after it is assured you have sufficient funds.

Reliable delivery, in retrospect, should be intuitive to understand and appreciate. In fact, it might be challenging to think of any application that wouldn't want its data delivered reliably! Fear not: Such applications do exist, and Chapter 9, "Best-Effort Deliver: It's Now or Never," introduces you to them. These applications require a timely delivery of data, but do not take any extra steps to ensure reliable delivery.

The Need for Timely Communications

Several types of applications have such strong timeliness requirements that data delivered late—or early—is worthless. Consequently, it is simply discarded! That might sound absurd, but it's true. An example of such an application is talking live over the Internet. Known as *voice over IP (VoIP)*, this technology is a classic example of an application that requires timeliness instead of reliability when it comes to data delivery.

VoIP doesn't always match the quality of a good, old-fashioned telephone connection. In fairness, it was never intended to match it. VoIP was designed to be cheaper, not better, than the traditional telephone system. If you have a solid, fast, and problem-free network, VoIP's connection quality is surprisingly good. If, however, you are using VoIP to communicate across long distances and using a network prone to congestion, you will notice that speech gets clipped, garbled, and even dropped! That's by design. While those symptoms might be bad, trying to correct them might be even worse.

Here's how it works: When you talk, the sounds of your voice get chopped into tiny pieces. Each piece is carefully wrapped up and shipped off to the person with whom you are conversing. For that person to understand you, each of those pieces must be put back together in the right order. Putting them together out of sequence creates a small but noticeable interruption in the sounds.

The Internet is a dangerous and unpredictable place and sometimes bad things happen to good data. In the case of the VoIP session, say that 1 in every 1000 pieces sent gets lost, damaged, or just arrives late. Although that's not a horrendous error rate, it can be made worse, particularly with late arrivals.

For the sake of simplicity, assume you are calling your best friend using VoIP across the Internet. That communications session generates 500 pieces of data, each individually wrapped and sent on its merry way through the Internet. Each piece could, theoretically, take a different path through the Internet. Thus, you can't guarantee in which order you receive them. In a perfect world, they would arrive sequentially, but this is far from a perfect world. Plus, the conversation is real time, so your PC must process the data and send it on to you as quickly as it is received. Therein lies the requirement for timely delivery!

Continue the example: If you receive the first 100 pieces of data fine and in the proper sequence, all is well. However, you have a decision to make if you receive piece number 102 when you were expecting 101. You have no way of knowing if it's about to be delivered or if piece 101 was lost in transit.

It almost doesn't matter; because the conversation is real time, your computer is obligated to forward the data as it is received. You notice a minor disturbance in the flow of your friend's voice as you hear the contents of data piece 100 and then 102, skipping 101. Although losing that piece of data might make for a slight annoyance, it's better than the alternative! What if, for example, that missing piece showed up just as you were listening to piece 102? What if your computer sent it on you? You would actually hear a second glitch in the conversation. You would have heard 100, 102, and then 101. In this particular case, guaranteed delivery creates a bigger problem. Data that's late gets thrown away, thereby creating a disturbance. That's better than trying to jam it where it doesn't belong. Doing so creates a second disturbance.

Like applications requiring reliable data delivery, applications requiring timely delivery regard the reliable delivery as a pleasant bonus. It's not a bonus that they

are willing to wait for, though. If the data arrives, it arrives. If it doesn't...on to the next packet!

Timely delivery is better known as ***best-effort delivery***. Best-effort delivery suggests that the communications protocol makes one attempt—its best effort—to get the data delivered. If it isn't delivered, it isn't delivered. Your communications protocol has already given its best shot and does not try again.

Chapter Summary

TCP/IP is something you use every day, for business and for pleasure. It works universally and helps overcome disparities in network technology, application software type, language barriers, and geographic distance. Perhaps the most amazing thing is that you don't even know when you are using it! This seamless ubiquity is made possible by the use of open standards, and by abstracting the network performance requirements of application software into two categories: timely, or best-effort delivery, and reliable delivery of data.

Chapter 3 explores the concept of open standards in much more detail, so you can appreciate exactly how TCP/IP accomplishes all it does.

Chapter Review Questions

The following questions reinforce the key concepts in this chapter.

1. How can TCP/IP satisfy the network performance requirements of an unlimited number of software applications?

2. What are the two basic network performance requirements imposed by software applications?

3. Is TCP/IP a tool designed for business or pleasure?

4. For what do you use TCP/IP?

5. What does the term *reliable delivery* mean?

6. What does the term *best-effort delivery* mean?

What You Will Learn

After reading this chapter, you should be able to answer the following questions:

- ✔ What is the IETF?

- ✔ What is the difference between open standards and closed, or proprietary, technologies?

- ✔ What is interoperability?

- ✔ What is the benefit of interoperability?

- ✔ How do you create and maintain the technical standards that enable the Internet and its technologies to be interoperable?

- ✔ What is a reference model and why is it needed?

- ✔ What is logical adjacency?

CHAPTER 3

The Quest for Freedom of Choice

The freedom of choice: It seems like such a basic right that people almost take it for granted. That's especially true when it comes to choosing whose hardware and software products to buy for your home or office networks. You're obviously free to spend your money on technology products in any way you please. Customers have grown accustomed to buying computers from one company, printers from another, and network equipment from yet another. More to the point, buyers expect all these different brands to work together perfectly. That capability is known as *interoperability*. For example, customers expect to buy a PC from one manufacturer, a network interface card (NIC) from another manufacturer, and local-area network (LAN) equipment from a third company and still expect all to work together seamlessly.

Things didn't always work that way. In fact, it wasn't so many years ago when technology manufacturers couldn't imagine sharing their technical secrets with anyone and took great pains to ensure that if you purchased their brand, that you also had to purchase their peripherals. They made certain nothing else would work with their computer!

This chapter introduces the concept of vendor interoperability, including how it became possible, how new technologies are designed for interoperability right from the start, and how the standards permitting interoperability are created and maintained. These important concepts, not coincidentally, also tell TCP/IP's story.

Open or Closed?

Which is better, open or closed? The question is simple to ask, but not necessarily easy to answer. For one thing, open and closed aren't physical states, such as an open door versus a closed door. In the context of information technologies, *open* or *closed* refers to the way a product or technology was developed. You can't determine that development just by looking at the product in question.

A *closed*, or **proprietary**, technology is developed in secret. Details about how it is made or how it works are kept a secret. Conversely, an **open** technology is developed publicly. Its technical details are shared freely with anyone who would like to know them. These two polar opposites represent the before and after perspectives of the information technology industry.

Emotionally, the notion of working hard, developing something special, and then keeping it a secret so nobody else can profit is appealing. In some industries, collaborating with a competitor is self defeating. Consequently, the benefits of collaborating publicly with competitors on a new technology are not readily apparent.

Take a closer look at the benefits and limitations of both open and closed approaches to technology development. Then you can better understand them and appreciate why TCP/IP might be the ultimate open technology.

The Case for Closed Technologies

The time-honored approach to creating an advantage over competitors was to secretly develop something and then jealously guard that secret. You created something special—your competitors don't know how and buyers can only buy it from you. This approach is logical and intuitive. You invested your time and effort to develop something, so why give it away? Why let someone else profits from your efforts? When you look at closed or proprietary technology from that perspective, it seems quite logical and even fair. The business world is full of trade secrets, from McDonald's secret sauce to the Colonel's blend of secret seasonings.

It's an accepted business practice, and keeping trade secrets provides real and tangible benefits.

In fact, the first few generations of information technologies were created and sold under this mindset. One great distinction lies between secret recipes and proprietary computer technologies. Those proprietary technologies won't work with other products and other products won't work with them: They were designed to not interoperate with other vendors' products!

The Consumer's Benefits

The benefits of proprietary computing are few and easy to enumerate. This approach greatly simplifies the following things for consumers:

- **Purchasing decisions.** If you pick Brand X, you pick Brand X for everything! Only Brand X has the cables that work with its computers. In a proprietary computer market, deciding to purchase a particular brand is a de facto decision to buy all peripheral parts, products, and supplies from the same company for as long as you continue to own and operate that computer system.

- **Vendor management.** In an attempt to find something positive to say about such an approach to buying technology, it's that vendor-management duties are greatly simplified. You only have one vendor to worry about! Instead of trying to keep track of multiple vendors with different products and prices, you can deal with only one vendor that handles all your needs. Make one single call to a single vendor when you need new items.

- **Trouble escalation.** Troubleshooting is greatly simplified in this instance. You still need to identify potential causes, isolate them, and test them one at a time until you found the problem's source. However, you never have to worry about your network vendor pointing the finger at your computer vendor and vice versa: All parts come from the same vendor! You can rest assured it all works together because it was all designed to work together.

Aside from this paltry list of consumer benefits, the benefits of a closed approach to information technologies accrue to the manufacturers.

The Manufacturer's Benefits

From the manufacturer's perspective, the consumer benefits listed in the previous section are nothing more than reflections of their own significant benefits.

The total investment is so great that customers find it nearly impossible to change vendors. They have to scrap their entire investment to do so! Consequently, the customer becomes more a hostage than a customer.

Think about it: A proprietary approach to a computer system is an all-or-nothing proposition. The customer loses all leverage over the vendor as soon as she commits to purchasing that vendor's products. Needless to say, this works in the vendor's favor with respect to negotiating prices. Thus, manufacturer efforts to create and maintain proprietary products are rewarded with healthy profit margins.

Of course, anyone can buy one a product (a cable, for instance) and take it apart to figure out how it was made. That person could then manufacture his own version of those proprietary cables and sell them at a discount relative to the manufacturer's prices. Such practices, though not necessarily illegal, run contrary to manufacturers' goals of keeping their products tightly integrated and proprietary. Manufacturers fought this practice by declaring their warranties and maintenance agreements null and void if anything other than their own products were used.

A proprietary approach to computer systems afforded manufacturers tremendous profit potential and long-term customers. They stubbornly fought and resisted efforts to circumvent their secretive approach. Yet, we know that this approach has faded into oblivion…at least within the world of information technologies! In its place is a radically different paradigm—an industry in which customers expect the products of different companies to work together perfectly.

The Case for Open Technologies

A technology intentionally developed to permit multivendor interoperability is known as an *open* technology. In the vast majority of industries, giving away your secrets can be fatal to your business. In addition, you just looked at the how the computer industry started out following that business philosophy.

However, information technologies are a different story! You almost have to give away your secrets if you want any chance at all of making money from your newly developed product. That might sound like a paradox, and it is in some ways. It's an approach that works so well, however, that it became an almost sub-conscious expectation amongst the world's computer users.

The Benefits of Open Computing

The benefits of open computing platforms should be fairly obvious:

- **Multivendor interoperability**—The most obvious benefit of open comput-ing has been this chapter's focus thus far: the ability to build a networked computing infrastructure from pieces mixed and matched from any brand you like. This allows you to pick the best of breed in each technology cate-gory, such as servers, printers, network switches, and so on.

- **Price-based competition between manufacturers and vendors**—The sin-gle biggest benefit of choosing technology suppliers is getting to shop around for the best product and the best prices. Unlike the days when you picked one manufacturer and became its hostage, today the consumer is in the driver's seat.

- **Communications between different end systems**—A subtle implication of multivendor interoperability is that with the right set of open standards, you can share data between computers that aren't connected to the same net-work. All you need is for some connection (however slight or indirect) to exist between the two networks and to agree on which protocol to use.

TCP/IP: The Ultimate Open Technology

By now you're probably wondering why so much ink was spent talking about open versus closed technical architectures. Rest assured this reason is good! You see, TCP/IP is an open technology. If it weren't an open technology, you might have an awful time trying to access your favorite websites.

For example, when you access www.cisco.com, you don't care about the computing platform or operating system, nor do you care who developed the TCP/IP protocol

stack that runs that website. Instead, you trust that you can access that website and all its contents thanks to the open standards that underlie the Internet's technologies—including TCP/IP.

These days, you might tend not to think much about buying a TCP/IP protocol stack; it's just not a piece of software that gets purchased. There was a time, back at the dawn of personal computing's time, when you had to shop around, purchase TCP/IP, and then figure out how to install it. Today, TCP/IP is bundled into every computer operating system that gets sold. Thus, deciding where to buy your copy of TCP/IP is moot. Instead, you have to decide only which operating system and computing platform you like.

How Do You Not Keep a Secret?

Having explored the ins and outs of open versus proprietary architectures, it should be fairly obvious why the benefits of openness have proven so compelling.

The next logical question is this: How do you develop a technology without keeping it secret? That sounds funny—usually keeping a secret is difficult. As you see in this section, keeping a secret can be child's play in comparison to the complex process by which new open technologies are hammered out in political committees.

Open Architectures Equals Open Standards

Every open technology is based on an open standard. An *open standard* is simply one not kept secret. That open standard might have been developed privately and then introduced publicly, but the result is the same: It is a public technology.

Alternately, it might have started out as a committee initiative to explore a vexing problem. Regardless of its actual origin, every open technology conforms to a set of technical specifications that are laid out in a public document. Typically, a neutral organization maintains the open standard. Such organizations are known as *standards bodies*.

Today, everything has open standards, from the size and shape of credit cards to what dictates how the Internet works. The more complicated the function, the more likely it is to have multiple open standards working together to perform that function. That last point is worth further investigation. Though it's quite a neat trick to get a political committee to agree on the technical specifications for one technology, creating a framework within which multiple open technologies can interoperate can quickly get out of control.

Fortunately, a rather handy mechanism keeps things organized in both the short and long term. That mechanism is known as a *reference model*.

Reference Models: Keeping Things Organized

One of the simplest, yet most confusing, concepts to understand is a reference model. A *reference model* is a simple tool. In essence, this framework enables you to dissect a complicated function into a series of individual steps and keep those tasks organized relative to each other. A common framework enables different people or companies to collaborate even if they aren't working directly with each other. That's a powerful and valuable capability!

When you start dissecting a function into its individual components, one thing becomes remarkably clear: Those tasks usually have to occur in the same sequence for things to work right. Using a rather mundane and not necessarily technical example to illustrate this point, consider driving a car. The first step is gaining entry to the inside of the vehicle. Usually that's done by unlocking the door, but not always. Some people leave their doors unlocked, or it might be a top-down convertible whose driver can hop inside. (Alternatively, an entire profession is dedicated to gaining entrance to cars without having to rely on keys, but that's another issue altogether!) The point is that entering a vehicle—regardless of how you achieve that task—is necessarily the first step in the function of driving.

The next steps are sitting in the driver's seat, buckling up, and making sure your seat and mirrors are properly adjusted. The sequence of these events doesn't leave a lot of room for debate. You could, for example, adjust your mirrors before adjusting your seat, but then you'd probably have to readjust the mirrors after getting the seat in the right position.

Thus, these tasks have a natural or logical sequence. A more subtle point is that they can be lumped together and generally regarded as a set of related functions. Their relationship is that people do these things to prepare to drive. For the sake of example, call this set of related functions Personal Preparations. The next set of functions comes immediately after completing Personal Preparations.

Start visualizing your reference model for driving a car. Figure 3-1 shows the Personal Preparations in their logical order.

Figure 3-1   Organizing the Personal Preparations into a Simple
Reference Model

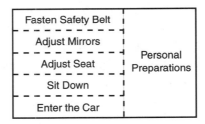

Despite completing Personal Preparations, you're still not quite ready to drive. Take your preparations a bit further and actually engage the mechanical systems that let you drive the car. Again, letting logic guide you, the next thing to do is start the car. Thus, inserting the key in the ignition and turning it should result in the engine starting. Release the parking brake and put the car into gear!

These steps should be separate and distinct from Physical Preparations because they represent a higher level of readiness: You are preparing the car's mechanical systems for operation. Call this group of functions Mechanical Preparations.

Figure 3-2 shows the reference model with Personal Preparations and Mechanical Preparations. At a glance, you should see how they relate to each other and why you want to complete all Personal Preparations before starting Mechanical Preparations.

Figure 3-2   Adding a Higher Layer of Functionality to the Reference Model

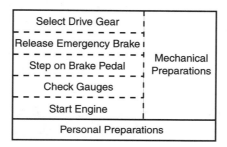

After making yourself comfortable behind the steering wheel and engaging (or disengaging) all the necessary mechanical systems, you are finally ready to drive! Rather than try to deconstruct the act of driving into discrete tasks, take one last look at your fictitious reference model. It shows how driving is yet another higher level of functionality and how that functionality relates to other functions.

Driving can be thought of as the application and the reason you're bothering with both Personal and Mechanical Preparations. The relationship between these tiers of functions is depicted in Figure 3-3.

Figure 3-3   The Act of Driving Becomes the Highest Layer of Functionality in the Reference Model

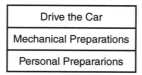

Note that the logic works in two directions. This model is based on the logical steps needed to start and drive a car. It works in reverse, too. The model shows the logical sequence of events in which you would stop driving a car. You might not need all the same steps, but the sequencing of steps you do need remains valid, as does the grouping around layers of functions.

For example, you stop driving (which means stop the car), disengage the mechanical systems (first the transmission, then the engine), and deal with Personal Preparations (unbuckle your seatbelt and get out of the car). This important concept takes on greater meaning when you look at reference models for data communications later in this chapter.

Although this rather simple example demonstrates the concept of a dividing a complex function into a logically arranged sequence of individual tasks, it's important to recognize that no standards body governs this function! The layered sequence of tasks might be a de facto standard, but that's logic and common sense at work, not a political committee.

The next section looks at some real reference models that are indispensable when it comes to understanding open standard networking technologies and the standards bodies that developed them.

Speaking of Political Committees...

Interoperable products requires companies to agree on the technical specifications for those products. In other words, a consensus must be reached on important design criteria, such as what the product will do, how it will do it, what it won't do, and so on. Developing such a consensus amongst competing companies isn't easy and, more often than not, requires a neutral third-party to mediate or judge during the consensus-building process.

The world, it seems, is full of neutral third-party organizations whose business is to standardize all kinds of things. Rather than bore you to tears with an exhaustive review of all the standards bodies, the discussion is limited to just three that set standards for data networking and communications technologies. You look at three organizations:

- Electronics Industry Association and the Telecommunications Industry Association (EIA/TIA)

- Institute of Electrical and Electronic Engineers (IEEE)

- Internet Engineering Task Force (IETF)

Many other organizations are chartered to set and maintain technical standards, some of which focus on networking technologies. This chapter focuses on these three.

EIA/TIA

One common set of technical standards is attributed to the EIA/TIA. These important standards focus on the physical wires that build networks and carry data between machines connected to networks. The acronym EIA/TIA actually stands for two different standards organizations: the *Electronics Industry Alliance (EIA)* and *Telecommunications Industry Association (TIA)*. Thus, standards from the EIA/TIA are endorsed by both organizations.

This is not uncommon. Quite frequently, two or more standards organizations see a technology as being their responsibility. Such overlap usually results in cooperation, rather than competition, for the development of that standard. Sometimes that cooperation means working together to actively develop a standard; other times it means one group does the work and the other endorses its output.

The EIA/TIA standards for network cabling are interesting in that they do *not* specify physical standards! Instead, they standardize a set of performance levels that cables must meet or exceed. Most technology standards spell out, in minute detail, everything about how a technology should be built, how it will work, and all its specific attributes and capabilities. However, this is just a piece of wire; there's not much to it! You shouldn't care about what it looks like, or what kind of metal it is, or even how thick that metal might be. All you need to know is that it meets your needs. Consequently, the EIA/TIA settled on standardizing performance levels as opposed to more complex physical standards that define the wires' physical properties.

The EIA/TIA performance levels, known more properly as *categories of performance*, are numbered 1 through 6. The higher the category number, the higher the performance capability. Performance capabilities are defined in terms of how fast can data be transmitted and for what distance. The most commonly used cable these days is known as *Cat-5*, which is an abbreviation of Category 5. Cables that comply with the EIA/TIA performance Category 5 support transmissions of up to 100 megabits per second for up to 100 meters. Cables must meet this minimum capability set before they can be advertised and sold as Cat-5 cables.

 For more information on the EIA, please visit its website at http://www.eia.org. Additional information about the TIA and its standards activities can be found at http://www.tiaonline.org.

IEEE

The *Institute of Electrical and Electronic Engineers* (*IEEE* or *I Triple E*, as it is more commonly pronounced) is an independent, nonprofit organization that sponsors research and establishes the technical standards for a wide variety of electrical and electronic technologies. The IEEE's contributions to the data networking industry are numerous, but the single most significant was the research project it launched in February of 1980. That project, known formally as *Project 802* in deference to the year and month it launched, defined the technical standards for *local-area networks (LANs)*. That research initiative resulted in the standardization of numerous LAN technologies, including Ethernet and Token Ring (among other, less recognizable ones).

Ethernet was a particular standardization priority. This LAN technology was developed by scientists at Xerox Corporation's Palo Alto Research Center (PARC) as a way of sharing an expensive new laser printer. Over time, the value of the LAN they created became apparent, and steps were taken to market it commercially. These steps resulted in a couple of Ethernet variations.

Though each variation could legitimately claim to be Ethernet, they were not necessarily compatible. Consequently, the IEEE set out to create an open standard version of Ethernet, as well as an open standard version of Token Ring. The bonus of using a layered model to organize their efforts: Interoperability between Ethernet and Token Ring also became possible.

To create technical standards for all the LANs popular at that time, the IEEE launched several engineer teams, each asked to develop the standards for a specific task. Recognizing that certain functions were common to any LAN, the IEEE sought to avoid duplicating the wheel. The first thing they did was identify all those logical steps—and their sequence—necessary in any LAN. This became the foundation for the IEEE's 802 LAN reference model.

Some of these basic steps and functions included a system for end-point addressing and tools for monitoring and managing the LAN. With the foundation built, all that was left was chartering different teams to develop the rest of the LANs that needed standardization.

To help correlate activities between the various engineering teams, the IEEE developed a reference model. This model helped everyone understand the boundaries of certain functions and kept everything organized. Figure 3.4 shows the IEEE's reference model.

Figure 3-4   The IEEE's Reference Model for Local-Area Networks

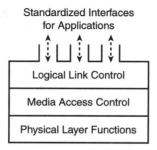

The Project 802 reference model and the steps it organized became the foundation for all the IEEE's LAN standards within Project 802. Each of the LANs standardized within that initiative, including Ethernet (known as IEEE 802.3) and Token Ring (IEEE 802.5), shared this common foundation.

It is important to note that although the IEEE developed protocol standards for sending data out over several types of physical wires, it did not develop standards for those wires. That distinction is subtle, but important. Ethernet and Token Ring needed to support transmission over wires, so they relied on the work of other standards bodies, such as the EIA and TIA.

For more information on the IEEE, you can visit its website: http://www.ieee.org.

IETF

The *Internet Engineering Task Force (IETF)* is responsible for developing and maintaining the Internet's technologies, as well as for guiding its growth and development. A short list of their achievements include the definition of TCP/IP, IP version 6, *Simple Mail Transfer Protocol (SMTP)*—which is the foundation for literally exchanging e-mail between open systems—and many other equally significant technologies.

The IETF is composed of engineers who volunteer their time to the various development efforts constantly underway at the IETF. Typically, a working group is chartered to perform a specific task. Numerous working groups might be launched to tackle related tasks. In that manner, a large and complex project can be completed more quickly, because of parallel work on smaller pieces.

Literally everything the IETF does is in the open; every participant in each working group has an equal vote in the proceedings and recommendations. Consensus is the mechanism by which standards are developed and accepted. Plus, consensus and request for input aren't limited to select members of any given working group. You see, all work is documented in a publicly accessible document. These documents, known collectively as *Requests For Comments (RFCs)*, are available without charge to anyone via the Internet.

The phrase *Request For Comments* is a bit misleading. Not all RFCs are requests for comments in the literal sense. Some are little more than wild ideas an individual created and then posted for the world to see. In the spirit of openness, anyone can write and publish an RFC for the Internet community's consideration. Most RFCs are created by a working group that the IETF sponsored to solve a specific problem. Such RFCs probably carry the weight of a technical standard someday, although it might take a while for them to be accepted.

Some RFCs are jokes. It has become tradition for an outrageous technical proposal to be published on April 1 each year. To the uninitiated, these might at first appear serious, but the date should be a clear indication that someone is trying to have fun on April Fool's Day.

To learn more about the IETF, please visit its website at http://www.ietf.org. To see the many RFCs that spell out the rules for virtually every aspect of TCP/IP and the Internet, please visit the RFC page on the IETF website.

Each RFC is serially numbered in the order it was published. E-mail, for example, came to life through RFC 821 in 1980. That document has long since been made obsolete by much more complicated and feature-rich versions of e-mail. Yet, you can see it at http://www.ietf.org/rfc/rfc0821.txt. Substituting any four-digit number for the 0821 in the preceding URL lets you browse that RFC.

RFCs are, quite literally, the source documents in which all the Internet's technical details are published. The vast majority aren't fun to read, but they are available. That's just how open the IETF is when it comes to enabling interoperability via the Internet!

Layers of Layered Standards

Having just seen a small sample of the standards bodies that organize data networking and communications technologies, you might have noticed that they focus on different aspects of network-based communications. The EIA and TIA standards are limited to the wires carrying electronic signals. The IEEE is best known for its work in standardizing Ethernet and other LAN technologies. Lastly, the IETF focuses on the Internet and all the technologies that let you communicate between LANs. Communicating from one LAN to another LAN is known as *internetworking*, and TCP/IP has become the world's preferred internetworking protocol.

The work of these three different standards bodies do not overlap; each focuses on a distinct area. However, their work is highly complementary! All three sets of standards are necessary to all network functions, including Internet functions. Assume you use at least three sets of open standards when you are online and that those standards always work well. The standards' creators logically, then, can keep things coordinated between themselves.

You saw the IEEE reference model for Ethernet and took a look at the IETF reference model for TCP/IP. The two models bear little, if any, resemblance to each other. Yet the two work so well together that IP over Ethernet has become the de facto standard for LANs around the world, including large enterprise networks and home networks.

How do you make sure two technologies, developed separately, continue to interoperate well over time? The answer is simple: by using a neutral, third reference model! The reference model most frequently used in this capacity is the OSI reference model.

OSI Reference Model

Sometimes, the alphabet soup-like atmosphere of the information technology industry gets carried to a ridiculous extreme. This section's reference model and the standards body that developed it form a marvelous example of that extreme.

The *International Organization for Standardization (ISO)* was chartered by the United Nations and founded in 1946. Its mission is to set global standards for virtually everything. Everything, that is, except for anything electrical or electronic. ISO developed a generic model for the interconnection of open systems. That model is known as the ***Open Systems Interconnection (OSI) reference model***. This model contains seven layers that encompass every aspect of communication between networked computers.

Although it doesn't describe a particular product or technology, the OSI reference model has become the de facto standard means of correlating other, technology-specific reference models and for ensuring interoperability between open computer systems. For this reason, it has become the single most frequently encountered reference model. The problem is that though it is overused, it is seldom adequately explained. Consequently, most people who encounter it for the first time usually walk away, scratching their heads and wondering what it is all about!

ISO's OSI (how's that for alphabet soup?) reference model is shown in Figure 3-5.

ISO's official name is the *International Organization for Standardization*. Conventional wisdom holds that it should be identified by its abbreviation: IOS. That Anglocentric abbreviation is for a global organization. To transcend language barriers, ISO was chosen. In Greek, which forms the foundation of many languages, *iso* means equal or standard. That seems much more fitting for an international organization.

You might be wondering how a reference model for connecting computer systems isn't a violation of the ISO charter. Remember: Things electrical or electronic are not within their domain. (Yet connecting computer systems seems to require electricity!) The answer is that the model describes a standardized *process*, but not any particular electronic or electrical *product*. Table 3-1 describes the layered functions from the top up.

Figure 3-5   OSI Reference Model

OSI Reference Model Layer Description	Layer Number
Application	7
Presentation	6
Session	5
Transport	4
Network	3
Data Link	2
Physical	1

Table 3-1   OSI Reference Model

Layer #	Layer Name	Description of Functions
7	Application layer	This layer is the top of the stack, or the highest level of functionality. In the driving example, the application drove the car. In the OSI model, the application layer is your computer program. It could be your browser, e-mail, or instant messaging software.
6	Presentation layer	The presentation layer is responsible for directly accepting data from the application, as well as preparing data that was received from another computer for the application. This could include things like encrypting or decrypting data and a lot of other, less familiar, functions.
5	Session layer	The flow of communications between two computer systems is known as a *session*. The session layer describes all the mechanisms and processes needed to manage a session.

Table 3-1   OSI Reference Model (continued)

Layer #	Layer Name	Description of Functions
4	Transport layer	The next set of necessary functions manages the data sent and received in a session. When sending data, this includes breaking received data into smaller pieces for transmission and uniquely numbering each piece so the recipient knows how reassemble them. When receiving data, this set of steps includes making sure the data arrives intact (not damaged) and then putting everything together in its original order before handing the data off to the session layer.
3	Network layer	A communications session doesn't necessarily always occur between two computers on the same network. Sometimes, those computers are literally half a world away from each other. In such cases, the network layer contains the mechanisms that map out the best route for that session.
2	Data link layer	The data link layer is where the rules, processes, and mechanisms for sending and receiving data over a LAN are defined.
1	Physical layer	This layer includes all the procedures and mechanism you need to both place data onto the network's wire for transmission and to receive data sent to you on that same wire.

Note that, like your model for driving a car, these function layers work in both directions. In this case, those two directions are sending and receiving data.

Using the OSI Reference Model

The best way to understand the OSI reference model is to remember that it is a framework that establishes the sequence of events that interconnect two open computer systems. No single product or technology fulfills the requirements of all seven layers! Instead, you tend to find that communications between open systems is more a patchwork between at least four different sets of open-standard technologies.

Consequently, the OSI reference model serves marvelously as a neutral frame of reference for correlating two or more dissimilar technologies.

Take a look at Figure 3-6, which shows the OSI model correlating the functions of the EIA/TIA, IEEE, and IETF open standards.

Figure 3-6   Using the OSI Reference Model to Correlate Functions on Other, Technology-Specific Reference Models

Applications	OSI Reference Model Layer Description	Layer Number
Online Games, Instant Messaging, Internet Chat, E-Mail, Web Browsing	Application	7
	Presentation	6
TCP/IP	Session	5
	Transport	4
	Network	3
Ethernet	Data Link	2
	Physical	1

In Figure 3-6, you can see that any good piece of software, such as e-mail, takes care of the functions laid out in Layers 5, 6, and 7. The IETF standards for TCP/IP typically take care of Layers 3 and 4. Layer 4—the transport layer—provides the logic for accepting data from applications (a higher level of functionality) and preparing that data for transport across a network. Layer 3, the network layer, provides the mechanisms for finding and accessing a remote computer system across a network.

TCP goes beyond just being a Layer 4 technology: It encompasses many small utilities that span up through Layer 6. A visual representation of this can be misleading—truthful, but misleading. TCP/IP focuses on Layers 3 and 4 of the OSI model. You use it to support other products that span Layers 5–7. Such products are known generically as application software, and they can include anything from e-mail and browsers to chat or instant messaging. All need TCP/IP for their Layer 3 and 4 mechanisms.

Figure 3-6 also shows how the IEEE's Ethernet standard occupies Layers 1 and 2 (physical and data link layers, respectively). This illustration does not make clear why the EIA/TIA standards are not considered part of the physical layer. The answer lies hidden in the fact that this is a logical model only—it does not describe a physical product or technology. Thus, what is described in the physical layer isn't the actual wire. Instead, the physical layer is limited to the processes and mechanisms required to place data on that wire and to receive data on that wire. This includes the wire's required performance category, the physical connector at its ends (such as the modular jack at the end of your telephone cord), but does *not* include a physical description of the wire.

Put Layers 1 and 2 together with the physical wire and you have a complete system capable of reliably providing communications between open computer systems. This is possible only because the clearly defined steps create a logical and well-understood sequence.

What It Looks Like

One of the neat things about having a reference model so well defined is that hardware and software manufacturers can focus on what they are good at, entrusting the remaining functions to someone else. The net effect is that a software developer that makes e-mail software for PC users can focus on e-mail features and functions, without worrying much about the other steps necessary for two users to communicate using e-mail.

From that software developer's perspective, as well as from the user's perspective, the two e-mail software packages appear to communicate directly with each other. This concept is known as *logical adjacency*. Figure 3-7 shows how logical adjacency works. For the sake of example, assume your application software (Layer 7 on the model) is a PC e-mail software package such as Microsoft Outlook.

Figure 3-7   Using the OSI Reference Model to Show Logically Adjacent E-mail

Layer Number	OSI Reference Model Layer Description		OSI Reference Model Layer Description	Layer Number
7	Application	◄- - - Logical Flow - - -►	Application	7
6	Presentation		Presentation	6
5	Session		Session	5
4	Transport		Transport	4
3	Network		Network	3
2	Data Link		Data Link	2
1	Physical		Physical	1

In this illustration, John is sending an e-mail to Jane. Each enjoys the perception that the e-mail is sent directly from the e-mail software on his PC to the e-mail software on her PC. You know that many other steps lie between sending and receiving the e-mail. However, that perception feels real. The two e-mail packages appear to be communicating directly with each other.

What It Really Does

What happens when John sends Jane an e-mail? A whole series of lower-level mechanisms in TCP/IP and Ethernet actually send the e-mail. Jane's PC performs all the same steps as John's PC, only in reverse. This is shown for you in Figure 3-8.

Each layer of functions occurs in the order necessary for everything to work. Anyone who has ever sent an e-mail over the Internet knows just how smoothly it goes! You quite literally take the underlying mechanisms for granted because they work so reliably and consistently.

Figure 3-8   Using the OSI Reference Model to Show What Happens
When John Sends Jane an E-mail

Layer Number	OSI Reference Model Layer Description
7	Application
6	Presentation
5	Session
4	Transport
3	Network
2	Data Link
1	Physical

OSI Reference Model Layer Description	Layer Number
Application	7
Presentation	6
Session	5
Transport	4
Network	3
Data Link	2
Physical	1

Actual Flow

Gotcha!

Now that the case for interoperable technologies is built and you have looked at how committees develop technologies standards, you might be wondering if this is real. The standards bodies do create and maintain open technical standards and they do rely on volunteers from for-profit companies in the industry to do so. That much is true. However, those volunteers—and their employers—are not necessarily as altruistic as they might appear.

Interoperable products are also, by their nature, interchangeable. Thus, a LAN *switch*, a device similar to a router that performs packet filtering before forwarding, from Nortel Networks can be replaced by a switch from Cisco Systems without any functionality change impacting users. The switch is literally a commodity—it is functionality in a box that doesn't vary appreciably, regardless of who made it or where you bought it.

What would compel you to buy one manufacturer's product instead of someone else's? Marketing and brand loyalty are two easy answers, but the open-standard technology development process is more subtly exploited to create an advantage.

Two common exploits follow:

- Releasing products in advance of a completed open standard

- Creating products that embrace an open standard, but also include proprietary features outside that standard

These hidden "gotchas" apply to both hardware and software, and can even be found amongst advances made within the TCP/IP protocol suite.

Getting a Jump on Emerging Standards

One way companies can use an open standard to their own advantage is by jump-starting the development of a new open-standard technology. Think about it: You don't want a system that stifles creativity or innovation, but you do want interoperability. The information technology industry has evolved so that most people who volunteer for work within the various standards-settings bodies are contributing on direct behalf of their employer. Thus, they tend to lobby and argue in favor of things that benefit their employer. Often, they argue in favor of things their employer has already developed.

This technique rewards proprietary forays into new technologies, or advances of existing technologies, by creating a small window of opportunity in which that company is the only game in town. Everyone else who agrees to the proposal has to play catch-up!

People who buy products before that product's standard is completed must realize they are buying a nonstandard product. That product anticipates what the standard will be and might be close to the standard when it gets finished—but you can't be sure!

Using Open Standards to Create Proprietary Products

Another approach is to create proprietary technologies through open-standards–setting processes. That sounds like a contradiction, but is a fairly common practice. Companies embrace an open standard, but then add special features that weren't a part of the original standard. Consequently, those features are only a part of that particular manufacturer's product set.

The net effect is that interoperability is okay within the confines of the open standard. Interoperability breaks down when you attempt to use a proprietary feature. Because most consumers don't know where the standard ends and the proprietary extensions begin, symptoms of the mismatch are often viewed as a problem with standards-compliant products, as opposed to a problem with products that go beyond the standard.

Making Sense of the Chaos

The world of open technology standards is far from perfect. In fact, its strength—collaborative development—also creates the potential for some serious traps that can ensnare the unwary buyer! Despite the seemingly altruistic goal of openly collaborating for the greater good, companies are tempted by the profits had by offering proprietary technologies. The net result: Let the buyer beware!

Take time to research when you need to buy any piece of network or computing gear. The newer the technology, the more critical it is to research each manufacturer's products. More importantly, you need to figure out the current state of any open standard that guides the development of those products and see how closely they conform to that standard.

You can tell if what you are buying meets your expectation of interoperability by understanding the standards and asking questions before you buy.

Chapter Summary

Interoperability across vendor platforms is something users take for granted. It's been a long, hard struggle to get to this point! You could argue that it's still not over. The information technology industry has well-defined public standards for virtually everything. These standards, and their ready availability (openness), are what enable products from different companies to interoperate with each other.

These standards, in turn, are built upon a well-understood and necessary sequence of functions. Those functions are kept organized through the use of layered reference models. Different reference models might draw the boundaries between the layers a little differently, but the sequence of steps within those layers remains constant.

Traps await the unwary; some companies do try to recapture some of the lost bounty of proprietary hardware by embellishing open standards. Yet, the era of open computing has begun and shows no signs of ending.

Having seen how open communications works, as well as where TCP/IP fits in the grander scheme of things, focus a little more on this book's subject. TCP/IP, like driving a car, can be thought of as a complicated function that consists of a tremendous array of simple, individual tasks. These tasks are embodied in individual, single-purpose software programs known as *protocols*. Together, protocols enable open communications between dissimilar computers across networks that span both large and small distances. The next chapter takes a much closer look at TCP/IP—the networking protocol that changed the world!

Chapter Review Questions

The following questions reinforce the key concepts in this chapter.

1. What is the IETF?

2. What is the difference between open standards and closed, or proprietary, technologies?

3. What is interoperability?

4. What is the benefit of interoperability?

5. How do you create and maintain the technical standards that enable the Internet and its technologies to be interoperable?

6. What is a reference model and why is it needed?

7. Explain the concept of logical adjacency.

What You Will Learn

After reading this chapter, you should be able to answer the following questions:

- ✔ What are TCP/IP's major architectural components?

- ✔ Which architectural components occupy the host-to-host layer of the TCP/IP reference model?

- ✔ How does IP relate to the other protocol components in the TCP/IP architecture?

- ✔ What five most important network-oriented functions does IP provide?

- ✔ What seven most important network-oriented functions does TCP provide?

- ✔ Which TCP/IP component is considered an unreliable, or best-effort, protocol?

- ✔ What's the difference between reliable and best-effort delivery?

- ✔ Under what circumstances would you prefer a best-effort delivery instead of a guaranteed, or reliable, delivery?

CHAPTER 4

TCP/IP: The Networking Protocol That Changed the World

TCP/IP has changed the world. Okay…so the earth is still round and mostly covered with water; a good communications protocol can't change some things. TCP/IP *has* revolutionized the way people around the world communicate, share information, and transact business. The Internet gets all the publicity, but the TCP/IP suite of protocols labors quietly, behind the scenes, to make it all possible!

This chapter introduces you to TCP/IP's major structural components, their roles in the communication process, and their relation to each other. You see how they work together to support other applications that need to communicate. TCP/IP does this so well that you almost don't know it is there!

The Official Protocol of the Internet

TCP/IP was born approximately 20 years ago. Its precise genesis is hard to pin down because of the way it emerged. Unlike Kazaa or Doom or even Windows 2000, a date when it was first made available to the public just can't be nailed down. For that matter, it isn't possible to identify TCP/IP's creator. It simply wasn't developed by a software development company. Instead, it emerged piecemeal, over time, thanks to the individual efforts and contributions of people who weren't trying to revolutionize the way the world communicated. Their intent was far more humble: They were merely trying to make their own jobs better.

That might sound a little strange. Today, everyone is so spoiled by sophisticated and powerful software that it is difficult imagining what it was like to try and use a computer 20 years ago. Around that same time, 20 years ago, is when TCP/IP and the Internet began their symbiotic lives. Over time, they would jointly revolution-ize the way the world communicates. That revolution can be summed up in just one word: interoperability.

There was a time when you could shop around and pick your favorite brand of TCP/IP software. You could then install this software on your computer so that any applications you installed could communicate using TCP/IP. That was back when the Internet hadn't yet become so widely used. The Internet's success forced the manufacturers of operating sys-tems, such as Windows and Linux, to make TCP/IP a built-in part of their operating systems.

Today, interoperability is achieved by interconnecting all the private networks via the same network and then using TCP/IP to communicate. Back in internetwork-ing's early days, the engineers who maintained these different networks for their organizations often created their own software utilities—things that made their lives easier or provided some user-requested functionality that was not yet com-mercially available. Those engineers collectively decided to share their utilities amongst each other. In this manner, different approaches to solving the same problem were aired, and the best ideas prevailed through consensus. If someone didn't like a particular utility or protocol, that was okay—there was no mandate to use it. It was all consensual and voluntary.

Before they knew it, a remarkably sophisticated and feature-rich communications protocol emerged. With each additional contribution, this communications proto-col began looking more like today's TCP/IP.

Originally, the collection of communication utilities that emerged from the Department of Defense's (DoD) internetwork was known as the *Network Control Protocol (NCP)*. NCP continued to grow and evolve over time. Today, this collection of protocols and utilities is known as TCP/IP.

Groups of Functions

After learning a little about how TCP/IP emerged, you might be wondering just how schizophrenic and ill behaved a piece of software it is. It's well behaved, but it does look a bit like a Swiss army knife—an attachment for everything. Its internal pieces do everything from taking data from applications to preparing it for the network, managing to act like a whole bunch of applications that make networks useful.

The net effect is a powerful suite of communications protocols that work so well and seamlessly, that it's easy to forget that TCP/IP is there at all. It achieves this remarkable feat by playing sort of a zone defense. It organizes related or similar functions into layers and carefully delineates each layer's role and responsibilities. The passing of data between layers also is carefully orchestrated.

The key to TCP/IP's success, as well as the key to understanding how it works, is the layered functions. At the risk of oversimplifying, three main groups of functions are embedded in TCP/IP. These groups can be thought of as separate layers, much like the driving reference model in Chapter 3, "The Quest for Freedom of Choice."

The three main groups of functions can be categorized as follows:

- Tools for users

- Tools for applications

- Tools for the network

Figure 4-1 shows you these categories in a layered reference model. This isn't the real TCP/IP reference model, but it helps keep things in perspective as you walk through more of the details. Besides, these layer names make a lot more sense than the official names!

Figure 4-1   TCP/IP's Functional Layers

Tools for Users
Tools for Applications
Tools for the Network

Inside the Tool Box

Anybody who owns more than two screwdrivers and a hammer knows that organization is the key to finding and using tools with maximum efficiency. Part of that organization is organizing tools by function. Put all your screwdrivers in one drawer and the wrenches in another.

This same logic works for software and communications protocols. TCP/IP, for instance, can be overwhelming to anyone trying to learn it. The only way to avoid sensory overload is to organize it into subfunctions, and then tackle them one at a time. Divide and conquer works every time!

Again, TCP/IP can be broken into three main tool categories: tools for users, tools for applications, and tools for the network. The next three subsections walk you through each category, help you understand what they do, and explain why you need them.

Tools for Users

All those utilities that became part of the NCP are the first, and perhaps most obvious, group of functions supported by TCP/IP. These utilities are still quite useful, although they might seem primitive compared to more modern tools.

Many utilities are embedded in TCP/IP and are truly users' tools. Some of these tools enable you to do the following:

- Send or receive files across a network between two or more computers

- Log on to a remote computer

- Check to see if a remote computer is reachable through the network (which is useful if you are trying to connect to that machine and can't)

- Identify the specific path that you will take through a network to any given destination

At this stage in the book, understanding TCP/IP's organization is more important than understanding any specific tools or protocols. You go back to these tools later in this book. Chapter 14, "Taking the Next Step," introduces you to some of the more useful of these tools, shows you how to use them, and explains their remaining value.

This chapter focuses on TCP/IP's architecture. The preceding list is just a sample of the types of functions available in TCP/IP. The intention was to whet your appetite by showing the array of available tools. If someone were to build a reference model for TCP/IP, they would probably put all these tools into one category: They are all software tools for users.

Tools for Applications

User applications—including those native to TCP/IP and those you purchase separately—all have one thing in common: They are not completely autonomous. That is, they are not complete unto themselves. They must rely on the other layers of related functions within TCP/IP to deliver the capabilities they offer. Specifically, they rely directly on a set of tools designed to work with applications that need to communicate across a network.

These tools accept data from the application(s) and prepare it for its journey through a network to a destination. How near or far that computer might be is irrelevant; it just needs to be accessible via a network. The applications tools take care of finding that machine and getting data to it.

This set of functions must be thought of as separate and distinct from user applications. Applications can't communicate without them, but these tools are equally useless without applications to support. Unlike users' tools, application tools are designed specifically to work with software applications. Users can't access them directly, but these functions perform some critical tasks that applications need to coordinate their data-transmission activities.

This set of functions includes all the tasks needed for one host (or computer) to communicate with another host. That communication's purpose is coordinating their activities to permit applications on two different machines (a sending and a receiving machine). Thus, for someone to send an instant message requires that the computers talk to each other, agree on rules for sending and receiving messages, and then follow those rules! If it weren't for the application (and the user pushing that application's buttons), the computers would have no reason to communicate.

It's important to note that even though TCP/IP contains functions that look and act like applications, it can support far more than its own user tools. In fact, TCP/IP can and does support virtually any application that communicates. These applications don't have to be a native component of TCP/IP; they just have to know how to work with TCP/IP.

Within TCP/IP, these tools lie in the layer called tools for applications in this chapter. The specific architectural subcomponents in this layer are known more properly as the *Transmission Control Protocol (TCP)* and the *User Datagram Protocol (UDP)*. Each and every application that communicates using TCP/IP must use one of these two protocols—but only one!

Figure 4-2 shows how TCP and UDP fit into the stack of functions shown in Figure 4-1.

Figure 4-2   Adding TCP and UDP to the Stack

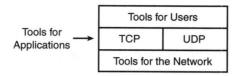

The following two subsections explain the similarities, differences, and uses of each of these protocol suites.

TCP

The *Transmission Control Protocol (TCP)* provides a high grade of service. It is capable of guaranteeing these things:

- Data is delivered to the correct destination machine and application.

- Any damage is fixed that occurs to data as it traverses the network.

- Any data lost in transit is replaced.

- Data that is received can be reassembled into a perfect copy of the sent application data.

That's a fairly tall order! As you might expect, TCP is a complex and feature-rich protocol suite. To achieve these lofty goals, TCP has some critical functions:

- Chopping up, or *segmenting*, application data for transmission across a network and wrap it in an envelope addressed to the destination machine and application. Each piece of data is known as a *segment*. This envelope also contains information that ensures the data arrives intact and can be reassembled correctly upon receipt by the destination machine.

- Assign a serial number, better known as a *sequence number*, to each segment of application data. This number comes in handy when the receiving machine tries to reassemble all the pieces.

- Assign a *port number* that functions as the address of the application that is sending/receiving data.

- Track the sequence of received data pieces.

- Ensure that data received was not damaged in transit by retransmitting that data as many times as needed.

- Acknowledge that something was received undamaged.

- Ensure that nothing was lost during transmission.

- Regulate the rate at which the source machine sends data. This helps prevent the network from melting completely when congestion begins.

These functions are typical of a communications session using TCP. The receiving machine performs some of these functions, and the sending machine performs the others. All are critical TCP functions.

As mentioned in Chapter 2, "What Has TCP/IP Done for Me Lately?" TCP is considered a reliable mechanism for delivering data. Its design makes sure that data arrives at its destination undamaged, requests a new copy of any damaged piece, reassembles the data to its original form, and passes the newly re-created piece of data to the correct application.

Just like the driving example in Chapter 3, preparing data for transmission across a network also requires a proper sequence of events. Take a closer look at that sequence. Figure 4-3 shows you this sequence of events from the source machine using the reference model that you have been building as a context. Remember: The *source machine* is the one transmitting and the *destination machine* is the one receiving.

The sequence of events, when you stop and think about it, is quite logical. The first thing TCP must do is accept data from an application. Only after it has accepted this data can it begin preparing the data for its journey. This preparation begins with segmenting it.

Figure 4-3   TCP's Sequence of Events When Transmitting

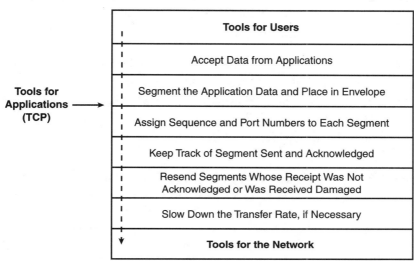

Segmentation is a useful function. You could argue that it is more efficient to send the data in its original form, but keep in mind that applications tend to reference data in nebulous terms such as records, files, and databases. Just how big is a file? Well, that depends! Networks, however, require a bit more precision with respect to the size of data they carry. Besides, the smaller the piece of data, the less risk of getting damaged in transit. Thus, you are spreading your risks by segmenting application data.

The next step after segmenting is wrapping the data in an envelope. This envelope, also known as a *segment*, gets its own sequence number. The sequence number helps the sending and receiving machines figure out which segments were received, which were received damaged and need to be re-sent, and which were never received. The segment also includes the ***port number***, which is the address of the destination machine's application. Without this information, the destination machine has no way of knowing which application is the intended recipient.

Keeping track of all this is a fairly complex process. For right now, recognize that the sequence number plays a critical role in TCP transmissions. Chapter 5, "Peeking Under the Covers," shows you a bit more of this process in detail.

The destination machine has a different set of tasks to perform. Some of these tasks are the mirror opposite of what the sending machine did, and others are unique to the receiving machine. Figure 4-4 shows what happens on the destination machine. Viewed side by side with Figure 4-3, you can see both sides of a TCP/IP communications session.

Figure 4-4   TCP's Sequence of Events When Receiving

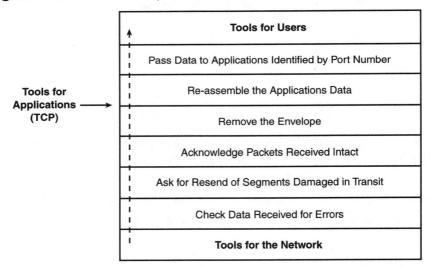

The onus is on the receiving machine to check everything it receives for errors. If errors are found, it must request a retransmission. TCP is to make sure that the data arrives intact. Errors are cause for retransmission. Segments sent but not received are cause for retransmission, too. Ultimately, TCP on the destination computer must put all the segments of data into their original form and then pass that data back to the application that's waiting for it.

UDP

User Datagram Protocol (UDP) runs a bit leaner and doesn't bother with many functions seen in TCP. It is designed to provide timely delivery, although the phrase most often describing it is ***best-effort delivery***. UDP literally makes one attempt to send the data. If it gets there, fine. If it doesn't, that's fine, too. If it gets there late or damaged, that's fine, too! The lost data is simply forgotten and the damaged data discarded.

Although UDP embraces a strictly minimalist approach to communications, it isn't a brain-dead tool. UDP's more critical functions include the following:

- Accepting data from applications for transmission through a network

- Wrapping an envelope around the data known as a ***datagram***

- Adding a port number so the recipient can figure out which application should receive it

- Figuring out whether the data arrived intact or was damaged in transit

Take a closer look at how UDP works from both the sending and receiving perspectives. Figure 4-5 shows the sequence of events within the context of a layered reference model.

Figure 4-5   UDP's Sequence of Events When Transmitting

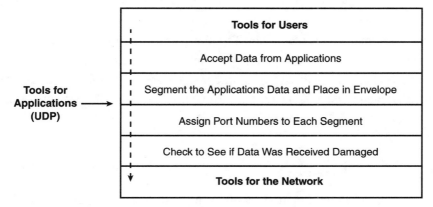

You might tell by looking at Figure 4-5 that UDP greatly simplifies things for the receiving machine. Quite frankly, there's not much to do other than receive the data, check for damage, strip off the envelope, and hand it back to the right application. This sequence is shown in Figure 4-6.

Figure 4-6   UDP's Sequence of Events When Receiving

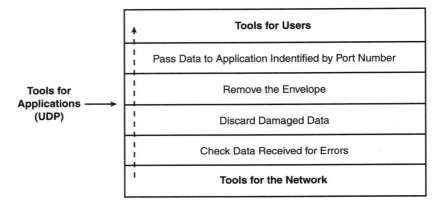

TCP is a *reliable* transport mechanism. That means it guarantees that transmitted data is a perfect copy of the original data. UDP is a *best-effort* transport mechanism that makes no guarantees about its abilities, other than it will make one good attempt to deliver that data.

TCP and UDP make a nice tag team. Together, they satisfy virtually any set of performance requirements an application might impose for its data's trip through a network. As capable as these two protocol suites are, their abilities are limited. Specifically, they are data-centric. They know nothing about the network! Consequently, both rely upon an underlying set of tools for the network.

Tools for the Network

The next layer of related functions contains tools for the network. This first layer of functions has nothing to do with either users or their applications. This layer focuses on how to use a network rather than helping users and their applications communicate. In the world of TCP/IP, the network tools are embodied in the *Internet Protocol (IP)* for short. Figure 4-7 shows how IP fits into the grander scheme of things.

Figure 4-7   Adding IP to the Stack

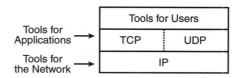

IP is a large, complex, and multifaceted protocol suite. It supports all network functions for both TCP and UDP, which is quite a trick given the differences of those protocols. A few of its most critical functions include the following:

- Providing a unique address for each device connected to the network.

- Permitting the network's routers to figure out how best to get from the source machine to the destination machine.

- Setting up rules for communicating between hosts regardless of how far apart they are located. This set of rules is comprehensive enough that the number of networks your data passes through is irrelevant.

- Issuing an envelope that carries data between two or more computers through a network.

- Imposing a maximum *Time-To-Live (TTL)* for each packet. Though it's important for a packet to reach its destination, you wouldn't want it to roam the network forever. Thus, IP gives it a finite amount of time to reach its destination before it destructs.

IP's job begins with a machine that wants to send data across a network. An application initiates the process by engaging the services of either TCP or UDP. That protocol performs all its steps (as you saw in the previous section) and then passes

the data onto IP. IP accepts the data and wraps it in its own type of envelope, known as a *packet*.

IP must first figure out the destination machine's address. IP provides an addressing system that enables each computer in the world to be uniquely identified. The question it must figure out quickly: Which one of the four billion or so possible addresses is the right one? When IP figures out which address to use, it adds it to the packet that envelops the segmented data. That becomes known as the *destination address*. IP also adds the address of its own host so replies and acknowledgments can be returned through the network. That address is known as the *source address*.

IP adds a bunch of other information to the packet, including how much data it contains and how long that packet can live in the network. When that's done, it's time to say *bon voyage* and hand off the packet to a physical network. Figure 4-8 shows this basic set of steps.

Figure 4-8   IP's Sequence of Events When Transmitting

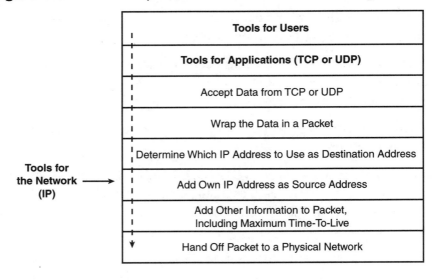

IP on the receiving machine has a much easier job. It does little more than accept the data that comes to it over the network, strip the segment from the packet, and hand it to either TCP or UDP.

IP supports many other functions, too. The functions presented in this section, however, are the most important from the perspective of sending data between two computers in a network.

Now that you've taken a quick tour of TCP/IP's major architectural components, step back and look once more at the big picture. This helps solidify each component's role and how they relate to each other.

The Big Picture

TCP/IP, as a suite of protocols, is divided into several large components, each of which focuses on a different set of related functions. Remember the example from Chapter 3, where you grouped the related car-driving tasks into layers for a reference model? That exercise was a nice way of providing a framework for understanding how TCP/IP is constructed.

Just like driving a car, those sets of related functions can be broken down into individual tasks. Preceding sections use the word *tools*, but the words *tools* and *tasks* are functionally equivalent. In TCP/IP, those tools or tasks are known as protocols. A ***protocol*** is a small piece of software designed to perform one small, specific task.

As you might have guessed, those original small utilities created by the Internet's first group of engineers became the protocols that now comprise TCP/IP! Of course, a lot of other protocols representing new features and functions have been added over time. The result is a comprehensive and complicated suite of communications rules and tools.

Dissecting TCP/IP

A good way to understand how something works is to take it apart. OK, so that's my personal rationalization for all of those things I've disassembled in my life and reassembled—with varying degrees of success. Without getting into too much detail, the electric toy trains proved unsalvageable, but I hear the GTO did eventually run again! But, I learned a LOT by taking them apart, so dissecting things is good way to learn…if you are prepared to lose the patient during the process.

Unlike cars or toy trains, you can't physically disassemble software. However, you can logically dissect TCP/IP. The TCP/IP protocol stack includes four functional layers. These four layers follow, from the highest level of functionality to the lowest:

- **Process/application**—Provides tools for users

- **Host-to-host**—Provides tools for users' applications

- **Internet**—Provides tools for the network

- **Network access**—Is the network itself and not a native part of TCP/IP

Figure 4-9 contains the TCP/IP reference model, including how these four layers stack up.

Figure 4-9   TCP/IP Reference Model

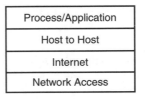

If you look closely at the layers in Figure 4-9, you see that the functional layers referred to in this chapter correlate nicely to the actual layers of the TCP/IP reference model. The one noticeable difference is that this chapter has mentioned three layers of related functions; the TCP/IP reference model contains four! Don't worry—I can explain that discrepancy! You see, even though the TCP/IP reference model identifies all the functional layers required to support open communications through a network, TCP/IP itself doesn't directly provide tools for all those layers. The layers of tools that TCP/IP does provide are the following:

- **Process/application layer**—The process/application layer is equivalent to tools for users. When you stop and think about it, that's exactly what an application is.

- **Host-to-host layer**—The host-to-host layer is where tools for applications reside. This layer contains all the mechanisms applications need to talk to each other on different computers.

- **Internet layer**—The internet (lowercase *i* intentional) layer is equivalent to tools for the network.

A simple process of elimination reveals that network access is the difference between the TCP/IP reference model and the functional layers that were introduced to you. The reason for this disparity is simple: Even though TCP/IP's reference model includes a layer for physical network access, it is not a native component of the TCP/IP protocol suite! That protocol suite assumes you already have a physical network.

Now that you've seen the big picture—TCP/IP's architecture and its major components—take a slightly closer look at each of its four functional layers. As you walk through these layers, you probably notice the strong similarities between these layers and the groups of functions explained earlier in this chapter. That was not an accident!

Process/Application Layer

The process/application layer contains just what you might expect—processes and applications! As mentioned earlier, TCP/IP contains some basic applications. These applications live in this functional layer. However, as the name *process/application layer* indicates, some processes live there, too! The difference between a process and an application lies in their functionality. An application lets

you do something using a native component of TCP/IP. A process allows you to use other applications that aren't native components of TCP/IP and have those applications communicate using TCP/IP.

Some utilities examples in this layer include those mentioned earlier in this chapter—simple, but useful tools that let you send and receive files, check on the reachability of a remote computer, log on to a remote computer, and check the communications path through a network.

Later, you are introduced to these tools and shown how to use them. For now, continue looking at the architecture and how the groups of functions are related.

Host-to-Host Layer

The IP host-to-host layer is where *Transmission Control Protocol (TCP)* and *User Datagram Protocol (UDP)* live. Why do you need two different host-to-host layer protocol groups? The answer lies hidden because applications' needs can vary widely. So widely, in fact, that the two main approaches to conveying data through a network are almost exact opposites.

To better explain that point, here's a business maxim that holds you can have two of the following: fast, cheap, or good. You can pick your pair of criteria, but you can't have all three! For example, you can have fast and cheap but not good, or fast and good but not cheap, or cheap and good but not fast. When it comes to TCP/IP, cost is not a relevant factor, so you have to choose between fast and good. You can't have both!

As Chapter 2, explains, applications tend to be one of two types: those needing reliable data delivery ("good") and those needing timely ("fast") data delivery. You can't have reliable and timely, so pick the one that's best for your application's needs. Applications that require reliable delivery for their data must use TCP. Applications that require fast or timely delivery use UDP.

Internet Layer

Continuing with the dissection of TCP/IP's layers, the internet layer is next. This layer consists of all the protocols and procedures necessary to allow data communications between computers (regardless of how near or far apart those two machines might actually be)!

Classifying this group of tools for the network stops short of actually including the network. The network is yet another set of completely separate functions that lies outside TCP/IP boundaries. This distinction is subtle but critical: TCP/IP is *not* a network. It is a communications protocol. As such, it absolutely needs a network before it is useful. Because it doesn't include a physical network, it is imperative that TCP/IP spell out clearly all the rules for communicating across a network. All networks that use TCP/IP for communications must follow the same set of rules. The *Internet Protocol (IP)* spells out these rules.

The heart and soul of IP is its address system. The IP addressing system enables each machine in the world to have a unique address. More importantly, it enables networks to find different paths between source and destination machines, compare them mathematically, and pick the best path. That science is known as *routing*. Entire books are dedicated to routing; one paragraph of one chapter in a TCP/IP book cannot do that topic justice. Suffice it to say that IP offers invaluable capabilities that transcend the limited host-based interactions described here.

Network Access Layer

Different types of networks exist, including *local-area networks (LANs)* and *wide-area networks (WANs)*. These networks are self contained in that they hold all the logic and tools needed to operate. They stop there! None contain the facilities for working with an application to get data to or from the network. That's why you need TCP/IP.

The network access layer is included in the TCP/IP reference model because it contains some critical functions. This layer describes the physical and logical mechanisms you need to actually send data across a LAN or a WAN. Just because TCP/IP needs this set of functions, however, doesn't mean it has to re-create them.

Many standards and technologies provide this capability. TCP/IP merely has to acknowledge they exist and develop a way to work with them.

This layer winds up being a placeholder as far as TCP/IP is concerned. TCP/IP contains no tools or mechanisms that correlate to the network access layer. However, TCP/IP does expect that some other technology (such as an Ethernet LAN) will provide these functions.

Chapter Summary

TCP/IP is part application software and part communications utility. It contains many useful tools that help you use a network. Also, it provides the underlying functionality required for any application to communicate over a network. TCP/IP is the de facto standard communications protocol in the world thanks to its co-evolution with the Internet. The fact that users rely upon it without knowing it is a tribute to how well it works.

Chapter Review Questions

The following questions reinforce the key concepts in this chapter:

1. Name TCP/IP's major architectural components.

2. Which architectural components occupy the host-to-host layer of the TCP/IP reference model?

3. How does IP relate to the other protocol components in the TCP/IP architecture?

4. What are the five most important network-oriented functions IP provides?

5. What are the seven most important network-oriented functions TCP provides?

6. Which TCP/IP component is considered a reliable protocol?

7. Which TCP/IP component is considered an unreliable, or best-effort, protocol?

8. What's the difference between reliable and best-effort delivery?

9. Under what circumstances would you prefer a best-effort delivery instead of a guaranteed, or reliable, delivery?

PART II

Protocols:
The Building Blocks of TCP/IP

What You Will Learn

After reading this chapter, you should be able to answer the following questions:

- ✔ What is a header and why is it significant to TCP/IP?

- ✔ What function does a port address serve?

- ✔ What's the difference between a source port address and a destination port address?

- ✔ What's the difference between a well-known port address, a registered port address, and a dynamic port address?

- ✔ What are the four most important network-oriented functions provided by IP?

- ✔ What are the two most important network-oriented functions provided by UDP?

- ✔ What are the six most important network-oriented functions provided by TCP?

CHAPTER 5

Peeking Under the Covers

Having walked you through some of the basic capabilities of TCP, UDP, and IP in previous chapters, you might be wondering how on earth these protocols can do all the things that they do! The answer is quite simple: All their capabilities are made possible by adding a little bit of information to each piece of segmented data. You can't see this information, but by peeling back the cover, you will understand how TCP/IP actually works.

As the covers are peeled back, you'll notice that each protocol (TCP, UDP, and IP) works in a different manner from the others. That's a direct reflection of each protocol's purpose and demonstrates that each one requires different pieces of information. This chapter explains what information each protocol needs to work properly. That sets the stage for the next chapter, when I walk you through how these components work together using this information to support you and your application's needs.

Tools of the Trade

To do all of the work necessary for communications to work predictably (notice I didn't say "reliably") across the Internet or other networks, TCP/IP must have a bunch of tools in its bag. Those tools aren't quite what you might expect; there are no hammers or screwdrivers or other recognizable implements. Instead, these tools are much more subtle and soft. They are little more than bits of data that get pasted onto the front of an application's data. This information is *prepended*, or added in front of the data, in a mechanism called a *header*. Generically speaking, the data in the header is called *header information*.

What makes these pieces of data useful and usable is that they adhere to conventions set forth by the Internet Engineering Task Force (IETF) and all TCP/IP protocol suites follow these conventions. Any two or more computers that speak TCP/IP follow these conventions and, therefore, can communicate with each other. The end result? It works!

Figuring out how it works requires looking at the headers that TCP, UDP, and IP use. The header structure that each different protocol uses consists of specific fields that enable different functions. To put things into perspective, please remember that most people don't even know when they are using TCP/IP. Consequently, taking a look at the various fields and mechanisms that enable TCP, UDP, and IP to work is really peeking deeply under the covers! This isn't stuff you'll need every day, but knowing how TCP/IP works will enable you to better appreciate it and may even help you become more adept at using networked communications.

TCP's Functional Requirements

As explained in Chapter 3, "The Quest for Freedom of Choice," TCP provides a reliable delivery mechanism. *Reliable delivery* means that your application's data will arrive safely at its intended destination. It might take a while to get there, but it will get there! TCP does a whole lot more than that, too.

Revisiting TCP's Functions

Just as a quick refresher, TCP (Transmission Control Protocol) occupies Layer 4—the transport layer—of the OSI reference model, as shown in Figure 5-1.

Figure 5-1   TCP Is a Transport, or Layer 4, Protocol Suite

OSI Reference Model Layer Description	Layer Number
Application	7
Presentation	6
Session	5
Transport	4
Network	3
Data Link	2
Physical	1

TCP ⟶ (Transport)

TCP manages the flow of information between two applications, each of which resides on a different computer. Managing that flow of information—known as a *communications session*—requires TCP to continuously track certain critical pieces of information. This is where the header information comes into play.

Before digging into the actual structure and composition of TCP's header, it's worthwhile to revisit its specific functions. TCP's top six functions include the following:

- Accepting data from an application and chopping it into bite-sized chunks (known as *segments)* that will fit within an IP packet

- Managing the communications session

- Guaranteeing that data get delivered to the correct destination machine and application

- Finding and fixing any damage that occurs to data when it traversed the network

- Ensuring that any data lost in transit is replaced

- Reassembling data received into a perfect copy of the application data that was sent

A subtle but important distinction lies hidden in this short list of TCP's core functions: Only the first item, segmenting the application data, does *not* require interaction between the source and destination computers. The remaining five functions absolutely require the TCP/IP protocols on both the source and destination machines to be communicating and interacting with each other. The only mechanism for this communication and interaction is the information stored in the header of each TCP segment. Now take a closer look at that header.

TCP's Header

The TCP protocol header is at least 20 octets in length. When you look at it in terms of the number of characters, the amount of information stored in TCP's header is remarkably small—only about 20 characters. However, as I'll show you, TCP doesn't use these octets to carry readable words or characters. Trying to encapsulate words or phrases would be way too verbose and inefficient. Sometimes, all you really need is a pattern of 1s and 0s to get your point across.

 If you're not familiar, an *octet* is 8 bits. A *bit* is the smallest unit of data. The word is actually a compression of two different words: binary digit. Typically, 8 bits equals 1 byte. *Byte* is another compression of terms; it really means binary term. One byte can be thought of as one character or keystroke.

Looking at each bit—instead of each byte—you can have 160 pieces of information at your disposal. That's 8 bits multiplied by a minimum of 20 bytes per TCP header. As an introduction to each piece of data in the various protocol headers, notice that their size is identified in terms of bits, not bytes. This is consistent with how TCP/IP uses the fields in its headers.

As you read through the sections that describe the details of the TCP, UDP, and IP headers, please remember that the computer that initiates a conversation is known as the *source machine*. The computer that receives that conversation is known as the *destination machine*. Taking that another step, the specific application on the source machine is known as the *source application*. Its counterpart on the destination machine is known as the *destination application*.

This chapter's goal is to lay the foundation for better appreciation of the conversation that occurs between the source and destination machines. In Chapter 6, "Pushing the Envelope," you experience a typical TCP/IP communications session step by step.

The TCP header contains the following fields:

- **TCP Source Port**—The first 16 bits (or 2 bytes, if you prefer that term) of a TCP header contain the *source port field*. This field is where TCP stores the address of the application that is making the call. An application's address is more properly called a *port* or *port number*. All by itself, a source port number is almost useless. However, when you use it in conjunction with a source IP address, you have all that you need for a return address! The source IP address gets replies and acknowledgments back to the source computer and the source port number gets those replies in the hands of the right application on that computer.

- **TCP Destination Port**—The 16-bit destination port field is the address of the called (destination) port. The IP address is used to forward the packet to the correct destination machine. The TCP destination port is used to forward any received data to the correct application on that machine.

- **TCP Sequence Number**—The receiving computer uses the 32-bit sequence number to reconstruct the fragmented data back into its original form. In a dynamic network like the Internet, it is quite possible for some of the packets to take different paths and, consequently, arrive out of order. Similarly, if a piece of data were lost or damaged in transit, you can guarantee that upon retransmission that piece of data will arrive much later than the piece sent before it. A sequencing field enables the destination machine to overcome this potential inconsistency and ensures that the data gets reconstructed into their original form.

- **TCP Acknowledgment Number**—TCP uses a 32-bit acknowledgment of packets successfully received. If you look back at the TCP sequence number, you will notice that it, too, is a 32-bit number. That's not a coincidence! TCP uses that sequence number as the basis for its acknowledgments. That lets the source machine know which packet(s) have been received and acknowledged.

- **Data Offset**—This 4-bit field contains the TCP header size measured in 32-bit "words." By knowing exactly how large the header is, the recipient knows how to find where the header ends and where the data actually begins.

- **Reserved**—This 6-bit field is always set to 0. More precisely, each of those 6 bits is set to 0. It's not quite enough to equal a full character, so please don't misconstrue this as the binary value of the 0 character. It is actually quite common for standards bodies and technology manufacturers to leave room for future growth or feature enhancements. Having a 6-bit reserved field creates the possibility that TCP/IP can support new or different features in the future. We just don't know what they might be yet!

- **Flags**—The 6-bit flag field contains six 1-bit *flags* that enable specific control functions. For example, if the last of these 6 bits is set to 1 (instead of its normal value of 0), the receiving machine understands that the sender has finished sending data. Some of the other flags enable the two machines to do esoteric functions like reset the connection between them or resynchronize sequence numbers.

- **Window Size**—The destination machine uses this 16-bit field to tell the source host how much data it is willing to accept. The best way to think about this feature is as a traffic cop that regulates traffic flow between the source and destination machines. TCP guarantees data delivery. The only way it can do so is if it knows that any given piece of data made it safely to its destination. To do that, TCP must receive an acknowledgment from the recipient for each piece of data sent. Sending one acknowledgment for each piece of data can get onerous and inefficient. It, therefore, makes sense to batch them and send one acknowledgment for a bunch of packets that have been received. It is much more efficient to wait for 10, 20, or even 100 packets to be received satisfactorily before sending an acknowledgment.

Window size is the number of packets that a sending machine can send without an acknowledgment. There's a trade-off here: If the network is busy or having other problems, there is a strong probability that packets will get lost or damaged on their way to the destination. When that happens, a large window size will work against you! For that reason, the people who developed TCP/IP permitted a *sliding window*. TCP can sense when network conditions are deteriorating and can respond by telling the sender to reduce its window size. Similarly, when conditions are improving, TCP can signal the sender to increase its window size. In this manner, the window's size slides back and forth as TCP tries to find the optimal size at any given time.

- **Checksum**—The TCP header contains a 16-bit error-checking field known as a *checksum*. The source host calculates a mathematical value based upon the segment's contents. This value gets stored in the header's checksum field, where the destination machine can examine it. The destination host performs the same calculation using the data it just received. If the packet's contents remained intact during its journey through the network, the result of the two calculations will be identical, thereby proving the validity of the data.

 It is theoretically possible for data to be damaged such that the checksum operation would return the same value as expected if the data weren't damaged. However, the odds of this happening are so remote as to be utterly improbable. Thus, calculating a checksum is a marvelous way to determine whether a piece of data was damaged in transit, but it is not a perfect tool.

- **Padding**—Padding implies fluff, or extraneous material, that's not needed. However, in the world of data communications, padding is useful for maintaining the timing and/or sizing requirements of a communications protocol. In the case of TCP, extra 0s are added in this field at the end of the TCP header to ensure that the TCP header is always some multiple of 32 bits. Remember, the data offset field tells the destination machine's TCP how many groups of 32-bits there were in the header. If, for some odd reason, the header ends up being something other than a multiple of 32 bits, 0s must be added at the end to make up the difference. These 0s are called *padding*.

■ **Payload**—Okay, so the next field isn't really part of the TCP header. It's the *payload* (data). This is where the application data is stored. Together, the header and payload comprise the *TCP segment*.

You might be wondering why the TCP header includes only the port addresses and not the computers' IP addresses. The answer is simple: TCP is application oriented while IP is network oriented. Consequently, TCP concerns itself with identifying applications' source and destination addresses, whereas IP focuses on the other half of that equation—the computers' source and destination IP addresses. Together, the port and IP addresses enable each piece of data to find its way through a network and let the replies find their own way back to the source machine and application. This ensures that communications are truly bidirectional.

UDP

UDP is the other Transport Layer Protocol suite in TCP/IP. That means that like TCP, UDP also occupies Layer 4 of the OSI reference model, as shown in Figure 5-2.

Figure 5-2   UDP Is a Transport, or Layer 4, Protocol Suite

OSI Reference Model Layer Description	Layer Number
Application	7
Presentation	6
Session	5
Transport	4
Network	3
Data Link	2
Physical	1

UDP ⟶ (Transport)

However, UDP differs substantially from TCP in the way it works and the types of network performance it is designed to support. Its structure, too, is radically different and directly reflects its role in the TCP/IP protocol suite.

Revisiting UDP's Functions

If TCP and UDP were cars instead of communications protocols, TCP would be a Rolls Royce—heavy and loaded with features but durable and highly reliable. The *User Datagram Protocol* (UDP), on the other hand, would be a stripped-down racing car that was built for just one purpose: speed! UDP makes no effort to do anything but process data as quickly as possible.

 Great debate and misinformation surround the terms *packet*, *datagram*, and *segment*. Generally speaking, a *packet* is an IP structure, a *datagram* is a UDP structure, and a *segment* is a TCP structure.

Before we dig into the actual structure and composition of UDP's header, it's worthwhile to revisit UDP's specific top two functions:

- Accepting data from an application and encapsulating it within a UDP header. The combined structure of data and header is known as a *datagram*. The datagram is handed to IP for further processing.

- Checking to see whether data is received undamaged before it gets handed to its intended destination application.

That's it! No attempts are made to manage the communications session or negotiate for the retransmission of packets lost or damaged in transit. One fundamental difference between TCP and UDP is that applications that use TCP tend to transmit large quantities of data. UDP, on the other hand, typically receives small quantities of data. The data is usually in pieces small enough to make chopping it up or segmenting it unnecessary. Consequently, there is no need to put a sequence number in the header or worry about reassembly at the destination machine. The fact that UDP does *not* chop up application data into smaller pieces means that it is technically incorrect to identify UDP datagrams as segments. TCP segments data; UDP does not.

UDP's Header

One look at UDP's header composition shows you what I meant when I said this was a stripped-down racer built for speed. For example, the UDP header contains just 4 fields and is a mere 64 bits in total length. That's just 8 octets or bytes! In comparison, TCP's header contains 10 different fields and is a minimum of 20 octets or bytes long. That's quite a difference and it directly reflects UDP's streamlined architecture.

The UDP protocol header has the following structure:

- **UDP Source Port Number** — The first field in a UDP header contains the source application's 16-bit port number (or address, if you prefer that term). The *source application* is the one that started the conversation. It is imperative that UDP be able to uniquely identify the source application because UDP still must support a two-way conversation with the destination machine.

- **UDP Destination Port Number** — The next field in the UDP header is another 16-bit application address. This address identifies the application on the destination computer to which the packet is addressed.

- **UDP Message Length** — The 16-bit message length field informs the destination computer of the size of the message (payload) attached to the header. This field provides a useful way for the destination computer to see if the sent data was damaged during its journey through the network. If, for example, the message size is different than indicated in this field, the recipient can assume that it was damaged in transit. In the event that happens, UDP simply discards the data and moves on to the next packet without trying to negotiate a retransmission.

- **UDP Checksum** — Just like TCP, UDP provides a mathematical mechanism for validating the data it is delivering. That mechanism is the checksum and it works in exactly the same way as TCP's checksum. Remember: UDP is designed for best-effort delivery of data. Its goal is the timely delivery of accurate data. Accurate data delivered late is discarded. The flip side of that is that inaccurate data delivered on time is equally worthless! For that reason, the destination computer performs the same mathematical function as the originating host. If there is a discrepancy in the two calculated values (that is, the value calculated by the destination machine and the value stored in this 16-bit field), it is safe to assume that an error has occurred during the transmission of the packet.

- **UDP Payload** — For the sake of consistency, I'm including the UDP payload here even though it isn't really part of UDP's header. The payload is just the application data and the header is built to ensure that the data gets delivered appropriately through a network. The combination of UDP's header and its payload make up a single packet. UDP packets are also sometimes called *datagrams*.

Comparing TCP and UDP

The similarities and differences between TCP and UDP's header fields should be readily apparent. TCP is much more feature rich and the fields in its header directly support those features. UDP, on the other hand, is built for speed. UDP's header is the paragon of minimalism. It contains nothing that isn't absolutely essential to a timely delivery of data.

It is interesting to note that TCP's header contains almost all of the same fields that UDP's header includes. The fields that both have — source and destination ports and checksum — should be regarded as absolutely essential. Additionally, both have a mechanism for telling the recipient how large the packet should be (although TCP and UDP implement this capability in slightly different ways).

The differences between TCP and UDP are also readily apparent: TCP includes a lot more information in its header to support its various features, including flow control, sequencing, acknowledgments, and retransmission capabilities. These features enable TCP to provide a guaranteed delivery instead of just taking one hack at getting the data delivered. The penalty, of course, is lowered speed. That just reinforces what I've been telling you about UDP being a radically stripped-down protocol that's expressly built for speed!

IP

IP is one of those things that you use without really knowing that you are using it. Given that, it shouldn't be too much of a surprise to find that it does a whole lot of things that you probably have never even thought about. Peeling back the covers, though, helps you develop a much keener appreciation for exactly what IP does, why it does it, and how it gets the job done.

Simply stated, IP is responsible for carrying data through a network to its intended destination. Before peeling those covers back, you need to understand the most critical functions of the Internet Protocol. IP stands in stark contrast to TCP and UDP in that it occupies Layer 3—the network layer—of the OSI reference model, as shown in Figure 5-3.

Figure 5-3   IP Is a Network, or Layer 3, Protocol Suite

OSI Reference Model Layer Description	Layer Number
Application	7
Presentation	6
Session	5
Transport	4
Network	3
Data Link	2
Physical	1

IP ⟶ (Network)

Revisiting IP's Functions

At the risk of oversimplifying an already underappreciated protocol suite, IP performs four critical functions:

- Creating an envelope for carrying data through a network or internetwork.

- Providing a numeric addressing system that lets you uniquely identify virtually every machine on the Internet around the world.

- Enabling each envelope, or packet of data, to be specifically addressed to its intended destination. This is the packet's destination IP address.

- Enabling each envelope, or packet of data, to also tell the recipient machine who sent it. This return address is the source IP address.

IP provides other functions, too. These will be quite evident when I show you the IP header's various fields. However, these are the functions I consider most critical. As you might have noticed from this short list, IP has a much different purpose than either TCP or UDP. In fact, it must support the network requirements of both. As such, it is not at all interested in information about applications. Instead, it fixates on information about the network.

IP's Header

To better explain what I mean about IP being focused on the network, take a quick look at its header. The IP header has the following size and structure:

- **Version**—The first 4 bits of the IP header identify the specific version of IP that is being used. Only two versions—4 and 6—are worth talking about. IP version 4 (IPv4) is the current standard throughout the world today. IP version 6 (IPv6) is the next generation of IP. Although it is being used today, it has seen limited acceptance. Chances are extremely high that you are using an IPv4 network wherever and whenever you connect to an IP network.

- **Internet Header Length**—The next 4 bits of the header contain the header's length. That length is expressed in multiples of 32, so a header that is 128 bits in length would be identified here with a value of 4 ($4 \times 32 = 128$).

- **Type of Service**—The next 8 bits contain 1-bit flags that can specify various attributes that can support a preferential treatment of specific packets. For example, a packet with a high time value could be given a priority through the use of the flags in this field. Each device in the network would look at this field and treat the packet accordingly.

- **Total Length**—This 16-bit field contains the total length of the IP packet measured in octets, or groups of 8 bits.

- **Identifier**—Each IP packet is given a unique, 16-bit identifier. This is much akin to a serial number and does not affect the operation of an IP packet as it travels through the network.

- **Flags**—The next field contains another set of 1-bit flags. This set contains only three flags. These flags indicate whether it is possible to take the payload and chop it up into smaller pieces and whether that has already been done. This process is known as *fragmentation*. Either TCP or UDP usually handles the process of fragmenting your application's data into bite-sized pieces. However, IP also has this capability, as it may sometimes become necessary to further chop up a packet en route. This would be almost transparent to you as a user, although you might notice a little extra delay in getting things done through the network.

- **Fragment Offset**—This 13-bit field measures the *offset* of the fragmented contents relative to the beginning of the entire datagram. This value is measured in 64-bit increments.

- **Time-To-Live (TTL)**—The Internet is a busy place that supports millions of people and their communications needs. These aren't necessarily patient people, either! How long would you wait for a web page to download before hitting Stop? Five minutes? One hour? The point is that IP packets cannot be allowed to roam the network forever. You don't want to wait forever and it's not good for the network, either. Sooner or later you have to acknowledge that you can't reach a destination or complete a transaction. Rather than leave this decision solely at each user's discretion, IP contains a mathematical means of deciding when it's time to call it quits. That's this field: Time-to-Live. This 8-bit field keeps track of the number of network devices through which the IP packet passes. When a certain threshold is hit, the packet is discarded.

- **Protocol**—This 8-bit field identifies the protocol that follows the IP header. Usually, this field identifies either TCP or UDP; however, IP can transport other protocols.

- **Checksum**—The IP checksum field is 16 bits in length. By now you should be fairly familiar with the purpose of a checksum field. So familiar, in fact, that you're probably wondering why you would bother having two checksums on the same data! Because both TCP and UDP already perform this function on the application's data, what's the purpose of doing it all over again in IP? After all, the TCP and UDP packets are embedded inside the IP packet; you should be all set. The point is that the network is constructed of devices that speak IP but not necessarily TCP or UDP. Having a checksum embedded in the IP header enables these network devices to see if the packet is worth passing on or if it has become damaged.

- **Source IP Address**—You have seen how both TCP and UDP headers contain application addresses. The IP address is 32 bits in length and responsible for keeping track of the machine's network address. This address is better known as the *IP address*. When a computer brands each IP packet with its own IP address, it is providing a way for the recipient, or destination machine, to send it replies.

- **Destination IP Address**—The destination IP address field is also 32 bits in length and, as you can guess by now, contains the IP address of the computer to which this packet is being sent.

- **Padding**—As was the case with the TCP header, IP can pad its header with extra 0s. The IP header must always be a multiple of 32 bits and IP can pad as necessary to meet that requirement.

- **Payload**—Just like TCP and UDP, IP packets have a payload. The interesting twist is that an IP packet's payload is the complete TCP or UDP datagram. That is, the structures I showed you in the preceding sections (header and payload) would be treated as a payload by IP.

At first glance you might note some of similarities between TCP and IP. Both are, in fact, fairly heavy and feature-rich protocols. Some stark differences exist, however, the most significant of which is function. TCP is focused on applications, whereas IP is aimed squarely at the network. Looking a bit closer you'll notice that even though IP is geared toward the network, it contains nothing that would guide the packet through a network toward its destination except for the destination address. That implies the network is responsible for figuring out how to deliver each packet. A more subtle point is that this process is performed for each packet. That creates the possibility that each packet can take a slightly different route.

Now that you're quite familiar with TCP, UDP, and IP headers and packet structure, regress and take a closer look at application port addresses.

A Closer Look at Port Numbers

You have seen how both TCP and UDP use port numbers as a form of application address. You learned how this information is explicitly embedded in the header of each packet that those two protocols create. The concept of port numbers or why they are so critical to the health and well-being of the Internet and other TCP/IP networks.

In order for people and/or machines to communicate, it is essential that they agree on each other's addresses. This correlation between popular applications and their TCP/IP port numbers is maintained by Internet Assigned Numbers Authority (IANA) as a courtesy to maintain the Internet's operating integrity. Otherwise, absolute chaos would set in! If we didn't have such a list, one of two things would have to happen:

- Each application on a computer would have to listen to every port to figure out which, if any, inbound calls were destined to it.

- Computer operating systems would have to become much more sophisticated and adept at figuring out how to forward packets of data received from the network.

Either way, your computer's workload would spike up and the performance of communicating applications would hit the floor.

A *socket* is the concatenation of the source machine's IP address, source port address, the destination machine's IP, and port addresses. Together these components uniquely identify a specific communications session between the source computer and destination application.

TCP and UDP both utilize port numbers to uniquely identify an application. In fact, the concatenation of the source machine's IP address and port number with the destination machine's IP and port number form a *socket*. By virtue of how it is formed, a socket can uniquely describe a specific communications session. These numbers, particularly destination port addresses, are not just randomly picked. In fact, to avoid confusion many applications use the same port number all the time. That's not always the case! When you research port numbers you'll find four categories:

- Well-known port numbers

- Registered port numbers

- Dynamic port numbers

- Private port numbers

Although they work the same from TCP/IP's perspective, they differ in a few significant ways, including their numeric range, how they get assigned to a specific application, and whether any given port number is assigned to the same host for both TCP and UDP.

That last point is a subtle but critical one. Remember: Port numbers are application addresses. Applications tend to be developed to use either TCP or UDP depending upon their network performance requirements (timely versus guaranteed delivery, for instance). Thus, it makes sense to keep two lists of port assignments: one for TCP and one for UDP. That is, in fact, the way it is done. However, to avoid confusion it has become common practice for an application to be assigned the port number it needs in both the TCP and UDP lists of assigned ports.

When you stop to think about keeping lists of port assignments per application, one question might pop into your head: Who is responsible for creating and maintaining that list? Fair question! The answer is *Internet Assigned Numbers Authority (IANA)*. IANA is part of the *Internet Engineering Task Force (IETF)*, the guardians of the Internet's technology.

Let me take a few minutes to walk you through some of the other critical differences between port number types. Table 5-1 shows you a bit more detail at a glance about the various types of port numbers.

Table 5-1   Types of Port Numbers

Type	Numeric Range of Addresses	Regulated by IANA?	Same for TCP and UDP?
Well known	0 through 1023	Yes	Usually
Registered	1023 through 49151	Yes	Usually
Private	49152 through 65535	No	No
Dynamic	49152 through 65535	No	No

If that range sounds weird to you, please take a moment to calculate out 2 to the 16th power. The number 16 is significant because the port number is a 16-bit binary number. In binary, you only have two symbols to work with: 0 and 1. Calculating 2 (for example, the number of symbols) to the 16th (for example, the number of digits in the address) power gives you the total number of unique addresses possible with a number of that size. You find that 2 to the 16th power works out to be 65,536. Because you start counting at 0 instead of 1, you have a range of 65,536 valid addresses that ends at 65,535.

Well-Known Port Numbers

The well-known port numbers represent some of the oldest—but not necessarily the most widely used—applications on the Internet. To be fair, some of the well-known port numbers are assigned to truly indispensable applications such as e-mail (port 25) or the World Wide Web (port 80). Others are so esoteric—including the Quote of the Day in port 17—as to have faded into obscurity.

IANA regulates membership in this exclusive club. Software developers or standards bodies must have IANA review and approve their application and/or technology before it can receive one of the precious few well-known port numbers still unassigned. A couple of criteria must be met before any application or proposed technology qualifies for a well-known port number. Perhaps the most stringent requirement is that it must be a *system-level process*! That means that it's not something you will ever find yourself consciously running or using. Instead, it will be a process kicked off by an application that you use.

One way to better appreciate the complexity of port numbers is to look at the WWW. Although that application uses well-known port 80, you don't run it directly. Instead, you launch your browser and your browser runs WWW. Perhaps a better example is Doom. You can play the game Doom against the computer or against someone else across a network. In either case, you are launching the same application. When you play against the computer, you have no need to communicate. Consequently, you are not using TCP/IP. However, when you choose to play against an opponent elsewhere on the network, you are using TCP/IP. In that case, Doom launches a background task to handle the communications between you and your opponent. That background task meets the criteria for a well-known port number. Perhaps in an effort to prove that even standards bodies have a sense of humor, Doom was assigned the well-known port number 666.

Upon approval by IANA, a well-known port number is assigned to that piece of software from both the TCP and UDP lists of assigned numbers. Thus, port 80 is assigned to the WWW on both lists even though it may not be used by both protocols. That's just to avoid confusion.

If your curiosity has been piqued, you can find a complete list of all well-known and registered port numbers in an online database at http://www.iana.org/assignments/port-numbers.

Registered Port Numbers

The next category that IANA maintains is known as the list of *registered port numbers*. As with well-known port numbers, applications that receive registered port numbers usually receive that number from both the TCP and UDP lists. Again, that's just to avoid confusion and does not indicate that an application needs both to function properly.

The key distinction between a well-known and registered port number is that registered port numbers are assigned to applications that can be run directly by people. If you'll recall, well-known port numbers are only assigned to system-level processes that users can't directly run. Registered port numbers span from number 1024 to 49151.

Private and Dynamic Port Numbers

The last two categories of port numbers are private and dynamic. Although these different tools serve different purposes, a couple of similarities make it logical to look at them together. For example, both share the range from port address number 49152 through 65535. IANA doesn't regulate this range of port addresses. That's not necessarily either a good thing or a bad thing; it just creates yet another option for software manufacturers.

Instead of going through the potentially arduous process of getting approval for either a well-known or registered port number, it may be quicker and easier to just develop your application software to use the next available port number from a pool of available numbers. Thus, your software would monitor a range of addresses and coordinate with the application to determine which free port to use. That coordination is a dynamic process and you can't reliably predict which port number will get assigned to your communications session. This coordination would have to occur each time you run that application.

Private port addresses are a close cousin to dynamic port addresses. Rather than develop your software to select the next available port number, you can further simplify your workload by picking an oddball port number from this range. This is sort of a luck-of-the-draw approach to developing applications: There are no guarantees! In theory, by picking a port number from this range of addresses you won't have any conflicts from the applications that dynamically choose ports because they will see that port in use and select a different one.

The other worry is that two or more applications will have been written to use the same port number. That's a risk, but is mitigated by the sheer number of addresses available in this range. What are the odds that you will need two applications that were both designed to use the same application? Pretty remote! Generally speaking, this high range of port addresses is used by applications that either don't have extensive communications requirements or are relatively unsophisticated and inexpensive. That's a polite way of saying quick-and-dirty applications.

Chapter Summary

In this chapter, I lifted the covers off TCP/IP so that you could peek at what lies underneath. Specifically, I showed you the size and structure of the headers used by TCP, UDP, and IP. Each serves a different purpose, yet they all work together to support you and your networked applications' needs.

In Chapter 6, I put all these pieces into a more coherent order by showing you how they work together in the typical communications session.

Chapter Review Questions

The following questions reinforce the key concepts in this chapter.

1. What is a header and why is it significant to TCP/IP?

2. What function is served by a port address?

3. What's the difference between a source port address and a destination port address?

4. What's the difference between a well-known, registered, and dynamic port address?

5. What are the four most important network-oriented functions provided by IP?

6. What are the two most important network-oriented functions provided by UDP?

7. What are the six most important critical network-oriented functions provided by TCP?

What You Will Learn

After reading this chapter, you should be able to answer the following questions:

- ✔ What does an IP packet do?

- ✔ How many stages are there in an IP packet's life?

- ✔ Can an IP packet roam the network forever in search of its destination?

- ✔ What is an IP address?

- ✔ Why do you need IP addresses?

- ✔ Do you need the periods between numbers in an IP address?

- ✔ How do you use IP addresses?

- ✔ How does a network use IP addresses?

- ✔ What's the difference between a host address and a network address?

CHAPTER 6

Pushing the Envelope

Chapter 4, "TCP/IP: The Networking Protocol That Changed the World," introduces you to both the Transmission Control Protocol (TCP) and the User Datagram Protocol (UDP). They are the Layer 4 protocols geared toward applications. Everything they do involves either accepting data from or passing data to software applications. IP, on the other hand, is distinctly network oriented.

IP is the functional area of TCP/IP that focuses on the logistics of sending and receiving data across a network. It provides the envelope that carries your data across networks. It contains all the information needed to make sure the data gets to its destination and for that destination to know how to respond to the source machine. The key lies in IP's capability to package application data for its journey through a network. No small part of that capability is IP's addressing system. Without both an envelope and an address, getting anything delivered is impossible.

This chapter takes a closer look at IP, its addressing system, and how it stuffs your data into an envelope and pushes it through the network.

The Life of a Packet

Don't get your hopes up—a packet doesn't live a glorious, long, or even interesting life. However, it does serve a vital function for the brief time it exists.

Simplified, an IP packet's life has three stages:

1. **Wrap it up.** A packet's life begins when a host wraps user data (already encapsulated by either TCP or UDP) inside an IP packet.

2. **Pass it on.** The second stage in an IP packet's life begins when it leaves the nest. Only one machine can create an IP packet, but lots of other machines might handle it, open it, and examine its contents. These machines are the network devices, such as switches and routers, that lie between the source and destination machines.

   Their job is to make two decisions. The first is to check the packet's Time-To-Live (TTL) and see if it has expired. If it has, the device drops that packet, notifies the sender that it has expired, and grabs the next one. If the packet is alive and well, the device must figure out how best to pass the packet through a network so it reaches its intended destination.

3. **Take it away.** The last stage in an IP packet's life occurs when it finally reaches its destination. The machine that receives the IP packet must make sure the packet wasn't damaged in transit. It accomplishes this by running the same mathematical algorithm as the sending machine and comparing the results stored in the IP packet's Checksum field.

The following sections take you through each of these stages in an IP packet's life. Before you dig into these functions, it's important to reflect on the car-driving example in Chapter 3, "The Quest for Freedom of Choice." The reference model in that example shows how a necessary sequence of events works in two directions. In that example, starting and stopping a car were the directions.

In the case of TCP/IP, those two directions are *sending* and *receiving*. Those terms are relative and their meanings can vary with your perspective. As you go through the three stages of an IP packet's life, you see just how relative those terms can be!

The potential for ambiguity between the sender and receiver is real. The terms *source* and *destination* are used to help avoid confusion. The source machine is the one that starts the conversation; the destination is the recipient of that conversation. During a conversation, both machines actively create and send IP packets, thereby functioning as both a sender and a receiver.

Stage 1: Wrap It Up

The IP envelope isn't an envelope in the traditional sense of the word. It isn't made of paper, nor can you lick a gummed surface to seal its contents inside. Remember: An *envelope* in this context is a mechanism for moving data through a network. That data exists only in the most tenuous and fleeting of forms; it is literally flashes of light in a fiber-optic network or pulses of energy in an electrical network. For your envelope to carry data through either type of network, it must be physically compatible with that network. Thus, the envelope takes the same form as the data it is intended to carry. Just like regular mail, an envelope won't get far unless it has a destination address. That address enables everyone who touches the mail during its journey to see where it must go.

The envelope is more properly identified as a *packet*. Chapter 5, "Peeking Under the Covers," shows you the structure of TCP, UDP, and IP headers. A packet is nothing more than an IP header with data attached. The data, as explained in Chapter 5, is a TCP header and a segment of application data. IP does not differentiate between the TCP header and application data. Both are data from IP's perspective.

Figure 6-1 shows an IP packet being created by wrapping a new envelope around the TCP segment. In reality, no envelope is used in the physical sense. Instead, wrapping an IP header around a TCP segment creates a packet.

Figure 6-1   A Packet Gets Created

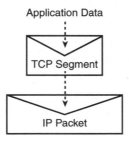

After a source machine creates an IP packet, the next logical step is to pass it on!

Stage 2: Pass It On

Generally speaking, two types of networks exist: local-area networks (LANs) and wide-area networks (WANs). *LANs* are the mechanisms to which you connect your PCs, servers, printers, and other devices. LANs are typically made up of either hubs or switches, and they are capable of great speeds. However, their ability to span distances is distinctly limited. Consequently, LANs are typically kept to a single building or a small area within a building. Examples of LANs include Ethernet, Fast Ethernet, Gigabit Ethernet, Token Ring, and *Fiber Distributed Data Interface (FDDI)*.

Even though LANs can't span great distances, other devices more than make up for the distance limitation by interconnecting two or more LANs. These devices are known as routers. A *router* is the network device that enables WANs. WANs are made up of long-distance telecommunications lines interconnected by routers. Routers can be used in two ways: as the backbone of a WAN or as the boundary between LANs and the WAN. The router's role is to figure out what to do with IP packets that it receives. One thing routers can't generally do is function as a LAN. They can interconnect LANs, but they are not LANs in and of themselves.

How does an IP packet traverse these types of networks?

The second stage of an IP packet's life begins when the source machine (the machine that created the IP packet) places that packet onto the network. However, you can't place an IP packet on a network. Recall the OSI reference model's layers. Physical networks consist only of Layer 1 and 2 mechanisms. IP is a Layer-3 mechanism. Therefore, the IP packet can't travel through a physical network. It must be wrapped inside something that a physical network can recognize and use. That something is known as a *frame*. Figure 6-2 shows an IP packet being wrapped inside an Ethernet frame for the start of its journey.

Figure 6-2   A Packet Is Wrapped and Sent

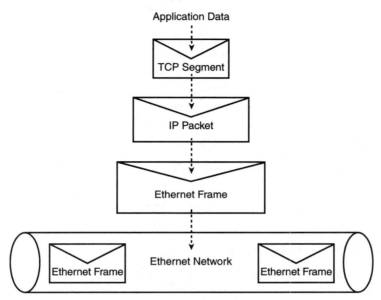

A frame is just like a packet except that it is specific to a physical network. Frames can't go too far, either. Typically, a frame is good only within one network, whereas an IP packet can travel through many networks en route to its destination. Consequently, the IP packet shown in Figure 6-2 will likely be subjected to more iterations of wrap-and-unwrap along the way.

Thus, frames come and go with each network but the IP packet remains untouched (aside, of course, from constantly being wrapped and unwrapped in physical network frames en route to its destination). Each time an IP packet is unwrapped, the network device that's unwrapping it peeks at the IP destination address and quickly decides whether it is past its TTL and, if not, where to send it.

Figures 6-3 and 6-4 show just what an IP packet endures during its brief journey through a network.

Figure 6-3   A Packet Is Unwrapped and Examined

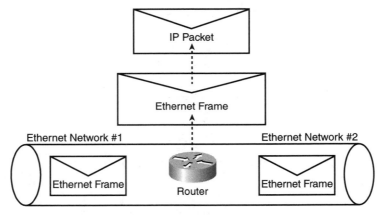

Figure 6-4   A Packet Is Rewrapped

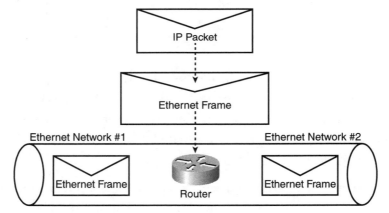

Stage 3: Take It Away

When a packet reaches its destination, it gets unwrapped for the last time.
Remember that the packet arrives embedded within an Ethernet or other physical
network frame. Before any of the fields in the IP header can be examined, the
packet must first be stripped of that frame. Figure 6-5 illustrates this.

Figure 6-5   The Packet Is Unwrapped for the Last Time

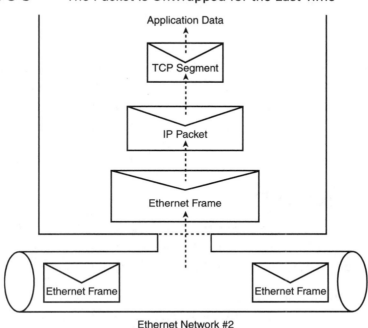

Ethernet Network #2

After the recipient machine unwraps the packet, it has some serious work to do! This work represents the last stage in the short, uncelebrated life of an IP packet. That destination machine must first assess whether the data inside the IP packet has been damaged during its trip through the network. As mentioned previously, it does so by running the Checksum algorithm against the packet's payload. That algorithm's results must be compared with the sender's results, which were stored in the IP header's Checksum field. If it's a match, the contents are still good and can be processed further.

The segment (which can be either TCP or UDP) can then be stripped of the IP packet. If the contents were sent using TCP, their receipt must be acknowledged. The acknowledgment can be for a single packet or for a batch. This acknowledgment is required to support reliable data delivery. If the sender doesn't get a positive confirmation that packets sent were actually received, then it can't meet its

obligations for reliable delivery. Only undamaged packets can be acknowledged. Packets with damaged contents are not acknowledged, nor are packets that were not received!

You see how this works for both TCP/IP in Chapter 8, "Guaranteed Delivery: Your Package Will Get Delivered...Eventually!" and UDP/IP in Chapter 9, "Best-Effort Delivery: It's Now or Never." For now, concentrate on the mechanism that allows packets to be pushed through a network: the IP address.

The Numbers Game

Like so many things in life, numbers are more complicated than initially meets the eye. IP addresses, in particular, are much more complicated than they appear. To truly appreciate them, you need to understand not one, but two number systems!

What's a number system, you ask? A number system is an organized approach to identifying mathematical values. A number system includes such features as a set of symbols and a standard means of correlating each symbol with a specific value. In the case of IP addresses, the address is an easy way to represent a much larger and harder to remember binary number. Done right, a number system with any symbols can represent literally every possible number from negative infinity to 0 to positive infinity, and every number in between. That might sound like a tall order, but number systems are remarkably simple. After you establish the symbols and their corresponding values, the rest builds on that basic foundation.

To understand IP addresses, you need a solid grasp of both the Base10 and Base2 number systems. Those names are just fancy ways of telling you how many symbols form the basis of each system. The Base10 system has 10 symbols, whereas the Base2 system has just 2. Yet, each is equally capable of symbolizing any given mathematical value. The only difference is one of efficiency. After reading the following sections you have all the tools you need to better understand IP addresses.

Before you get too far into the numbers game, it might not be a bad idea to become familiar with IP addresses. How do you find yours?

Finding Your IP Address

Figuring out which IP address your computer uses is remarkably easy to do. Despite how easily you can accomplish this, few people other than network or system administrators ever do so. The reason is simple: TCP/IP works so well and seamlessly that you don't have to worry about minute details.

If curiosity ever gets the best of you, you can run a command called **ipconfig** from within an MS-DOS window. It tells you which IP address your computer uses. Open an MS-DOS window to run this utility. From most modern Windows operating systems, you can open a DOS window by clicking the Start button in the lower left of your screen, scrolling your mouse pointer upward until you highlight Programs, and then selecting MS-DOS Prompt. This is illustrated in Figure 6-6, which shows a Windows 98 operating system.

Figure 6-6   Opening an MS-DOS Window

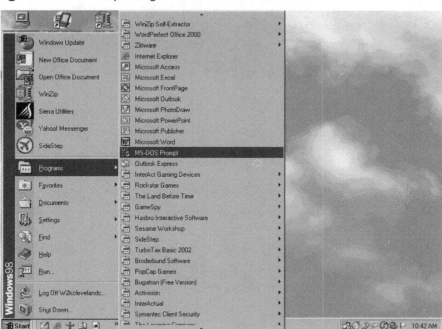

When you open the window, you see a blinking cursor; characters appear when you type them. Type the command **ipconfig** and press the Enter key. You see your computer's IP configuration. My computer's IP configuration is shown in Figure 6-7. Yours differs slightly, although the numbers adhere to the same format.

Figure 6-7   Running the **ipconfig** Command

```
MS-DOS Prompt                                                           _ 8 x
Auto          ☐☐☐☐ ☒☒ ☐☐ A

Microsoft(R) Windows 98
   (C)Copyright Microsoft Corp 1981-1999.

C:\WINDOWS>ipconfig

Windows 98 IP Configuration

0 Ethernet adapter :

        IP Address. . . . . . . . . : 0.0.0.0
        Subnet Mask . . . . . . . . : 0.0.0.0
        Default Gateway . . . . . . :

1 Ethernet adapter :

        IP Address. . . . . . . . . : 192.168.1.101
        Subnet Mask . . . . . . . . : 255.255.255.0
        Default Gateway . . . . . . : 192.168.1.1

C:\WINDOWS>
```

This command gives you three critical pieces of information about your computer:

- IP address

- Default gateway

- Subnet mask

All three pieces of information have a similar format: four decimal numbers separated by dots. This format is known as *dotted quad*. However, only two of these octets are IP addresses. The first is your computer's IP address. This is the address it uses when communicating over a network. The **ipconfig** report's other valid IP address is the third one. That's the IP address of your computer's default gateway. A *default gateway* is a network device that your computer relies upon to figure out how to find any and all other computers in the network. So, it's extremely important for your computer to know the address of this machine!

The other piece of information is your computer's subnet mask. Subnet masks follow the format of an IP address, but are not IP addresses. Instead, they help a network find your computer. Subnet masks are explained at the end of this chapter and again in Chapter 7, "More Fun with IP Addresses."

Decimal Numbers

If you are like most people, you think naturally in the *Base10*, or *decimal number system*. Most humans have 10 fingers and 10 toes, so it seems natural to seldom think about other number systems. Base10 is easy to understand; only 10 symbols identify all numeric values.

These symbols are used in the decimal number system: 0, 1, 2, 3, 4, 5, 6, 7, 8, and 9. Virtually every possible number can be represented using just these symbols. You might need them in different combinations, and you might need a lot of them, but you can identify every possible mathematical value using only these symbols.

The key to making this small set of symbols so scalable lies in the architecture of the decimal number system. The actual value represented by each symbol can only be determined by its position. For example, the number 2 can be 2 or it can be 2 groups of 10 (depending on where in the number each symbol is positioned).

Table 6-1 better explains how a symbol's value can vary based on its position in a number. The number dissected in this example is 123. That's actually shorthand notation for 1 group of 10 raised to the second power (which equals 100), 2 groups of 10 raised to the first power (which equals 10), and 3 groups of 10 raised to the zero power (which equals 1). Say it another way: You have 1 group of 100, plus 2 groups of 10, plus 3 groups of 1 for a grand total of 123.

Table 6-1   Values Increase by Powers of 10

Powers of 10	10^2	10^1	10^0
Column Value	100	10	1
Symbol	1	2	3

Although the elementary review of the decimal number system might seem a bit out of place in this book, the intention is to familiarize you with the basic elements of a number system. By introducing these concepts using a familiar number system, you can enjoy a much better frame of reference for understanding an unfamiliar number system.

Binary Numbers

As natural as it is to think using Base10 numbers, it is every bit as logical for computers to "think" in the *Base2*, or *binary number system*. Computers are electrical devices. Literally everything they do is done with 1s and 0s. More specifically, each 1 is a momentary electrical current and each 0 is the absence of such a current. A 1 and 0 are the only symbols available in the Base2 number system. How on earth could you count to infinity using just two symbols? That's not as tough as you might think. The only problem is that with so few symbols you need more of them to symbolize any given number!

To better show this, take a look at converting the decimal number 123 into binary. Instead of using columns that identify powers of 10, Base2 uses columns that identify powers of 2. Table 6-2 shows the powers of 2 up to 2 to the eighth power using the decimal number 123 as an example.

Table 6-2   Values Increase by Powers of 2

Powers of 2	8th	7th	6th	5th	4th	3rd	2^2	2^1	2^0
Decimal Value	256	128	64	32	16	8	4	2	1
Binary Symbol	0	0	1	1	1	1	0	1	1

In Table 6-2, you can see that a whole string of symbols identifies the binary equivalent of the decimal number 123. In fact, the binary number representing that value is 1111011.

The key to understanding binary numbers is to recognize that each column where a 1 is present represents a power of 2. Just like Base10, where it is necessary to add 1 group of 100, 2 groups of 10, and 3 groups of 1 to get 123, Base2 requires you to do the same addition. Thus, the Base10 number 123 is expressed in Base2 as 1 group of 64, 1 group of 32, 1 group of 16, 1 group of 8, 0 groups of 4, 1 group of 2, and 1 group of 1. Adding 64 + 32 + 16 + 8 + 2 + 1 equals 123.

 It's customary in mathematics to omit any leading 0s, because they have literally no value. A 0 in the middle of a number has great significance; omitting it shifts all the other numbers into different columns! The practice of omitting leading 0s is known as *zero suppression*. As you see later in this chapter, zero suppression doesn't always apply in the world of IP addresses.

What does any of this have to do with IP addresses? Plenty! These two number systems, and the ability to translate back and forth between them, are critical to appreciating IP addresses. Check out an IP address's architecture.

The Architecture of an IP Address

IP addresses, as you notice when checking your computer's IP configuration, use a dotted quad format. That is, they consist of four decimal numbers separated by

dots. Therefore, 10.28.118.225 is a valid IP address expressed in dotted quad format. That's nice, but those are decimal numbers. Remember: People think in Base10, but computers are designed to work with Base2. Using decimal numbers to identify computers seems a bit contradictory.

The truth is, those decimal numbers aren't your computer's IP address! They're a façade for the real IP address. That façade, more properly known as a *mask*, hides your real IP address because the real address would be utterly impossible to work with.

The Real Deal

The real deal on IP addresses is that they are deceptive. They're not made with decimal numbers, nor do they consist of four parts. The fact is that the dotted quad format was developed to make it easier for human beings to use IP addresses. The real IP address is a binary number. In fact, it is a 32-bit binary number. The term *32-bit* warrants closer examination. A *bit* is a computer term. Certainly you've heard of *bits* and *bytes*, but take a moment to ensure this book's use and your understanding are the same.

Although *bit* is a word with many different definitions, it is used here as an abbreviation. A *bit* is an abbreviation of *binary digit*. It is the smallest unit of data and can have a value of either 0 or 1. See the connection: binary digit—a value of either 0 or 1?

The potential for confusion here is tremendous: Bits can have a value of either 0 or 1, but please don't confuse them with the actual characters 0 and 1! You see, a single character is known in computer terms as a **byte** or a binary term. That byte is made up of usually 8 bits. You need all 8 bits to identify a specific character or byte. A binary digit, or bit, cannot be an entire character for the simple reason that there are only two of them: the 0 and the 1. When you see the term **bit**, think of it as the smallest unit of data—not a character unto itself. Bytes convey individual characters.

Given no design criteria other than a 32-bit binary number, an IP address could be this:

110000001010100000000101011101101

One look should tell you that such an address is not usable—at least not usable by humans! There are too many digits, and limiting your symbols to just two (0 and 1) means that the pattern will likely be highly repetitive. That repetitiveness makes it even harder to remember any given number. Clearly, if IP addresses were to be usable there had to be a better way.

User-Friendly IP Addresses

Although IP addresses are assigned to printers, servers, and even desktop computers that are attached to a network—and those devices are all quite comfortable with binary numbers—it is the user community that must use them. People tend to think more naturally in the Base10 or decimal number system. More importantly, people tend not to remember lots of long numbers.

Those simple facts raised a great challenge to the Internet Engineering Task Force (IETF): How do we make the Internet's addressing system efficient enough for the world's computers and friendly enough for people to use? There is no one correct answer. In fact, this quandary has three main solutions:

- Break the 32 bits into smaller pieces that are easier to remember.

- Use decimal numbers instead of binary.

- Support the use of user-friendly names that can be automatically translated to numeric addresses.

Of these three solutions, only the first two are architectural features of IP addresses. The last one is a critical function, but it's more an add-on than a native attribute. As such, you look at it much later in this book in Chapter 11, "How Do I Get There from Here?"

Decimal Numbers Are Easy to Remember

The absolute maximum number of unique addresses you can create with a 32-bit address is 2 to the 32nd power, or 4,294,967,296 addresses. Converting any given 32-bit string of binary numbers into decimal numbers would, at least in theory, make the number more human friendly.

Unfortunately, a 32-bit binary number can translate into a decimal number so large that it, too, is meaningless to human beings. Imagine trying to remember whether your computer's address is 4,217,824,125 or 4,217,842,125. Those numbers are much easier to remember than their binary equivalents (which are 11111011011001101110001101111101 and 11111011011001110010100111001101, respectively, in the Base2 number system). They are still far too cumbersome to be useful. You would have great difficulty remembering your own IP address, much less trying to remember the IP addresses of useful destination machines.

Clearly, converting binary numbers to decimal was a step in the right direction. However, large decimal numbers are only slightly easier to use than large binary numbers. If the Internet's address system was going to be accepted, it had to be even more user friendly.

Smaller Numbers Are Easier to Remember

One way to make a lengthy digit string easier to remember is to break it into smaller pieces. With an IP address, you start with a single binary number that is 32 bits long. Trying to subdivide that poses a couple of interesting challenges. For example, you first have to decide how finely you'd like to divide those 32 bits. The IETF has taken care of this by deciding that an IP address should be broken into four equal-sized pieces of 8 bits each. Then you need some way to identify the boundaries between those pieces. Such a device is known as a *delimiter* and can literally be any symbol. The IETF has decreed that a dot or period is the right delimiter for use in this case.

Thus, the convention was set: IP addresses would take the following format:

11000000.10101000.00001010.11101101

One interesting implication of arbitrarily sticking dots between the bits is that you must break away from the mathematical tradition of zero suppression. Did you notice the third group of bits in the preceding example starts with four 0s? If that were a number by itself, the value of the bit string would be the same with or without those leading 0s. However, it isn't a separate number. Instead, it's 8 binary digits in the middle of a larger sequence of binary digits. Suppressing those 0s wouldn't change the decimal translation of that group of bits, but it would change the entire address's decimal translation.

Smaller numbers are much easier to remember than larger numbers. However, this is still the highly repetitive binary number system and even these small numbers get confusing. Although this is another step in the right direction, it seems only slightly better than the full 32-bit string.

Small Decimal Numbers Are the Easiest to Remember

The best approach seems to be to use small decimal numbers, not unlike those you see when you check your computer's IP configuration settings.

When translated to decimal numbers, that bit string becomes 192.168.10.237. It isn't too difficult to see the advantages of using decimal numbers instead of raw binary numbers. That's still a mouthful of numbers and there aren't many people who memorize the numeric IP address of all the machines they access on the Internet. However, this dotted-decimal form of IP address is vastly better than raw binary numbers.

Learning to Count All Over Again

Understanding the IP address space requires a command of the binary mathematics on which it is founded. Although that might sound somewhat daunting, it is quite simple. You're just counting with just two numbers! Table 6-3 builds upon the format used in Table 6-2 and shows how to symbolize the decimal number 128 in binary digits.

One noteworthy difference between Tables 6-2 and 6-3 is that Table 6-3 only goes up to 2 to the 7th power. IP addresses consist of 4 groups of 8 bits each, so there is no need for numbers higher than 2 to the 7th power.

Table 6-3   128 Expressed in Base2

Powers of 2	7th	6th	5th	4th	3rd	2^2	2^1	2^0
Decimal Value	128	64	32	16	8	4	2	1
Binary Symbol	1	0	0	0	0	0	0	0

One practical implication of Table 6-3 is that an upper limit is imposed on the decimal value of each part of an IP address. Adding 128 + 64 + 32 + 16 + 8 + 4 + 2 + 1 equals 255. Thus, any of the 4 parts of an IP address can only range from 0 to 255. Table 6-4 presents the building blocks of this capability. If the Base10 equivalent does not appear intuitive, check the decimal value of the Base2 columns in Table 6-3.

Table 6-4   Value of Base2 Number Columns

Base2	Base10 Equivalent
00000001	1
00000010	2
00000100	4
00001000	8
00010000	16
00100000	32
01000000	64
10000000	128

Table 6-4 shows just the basics of counting in Base2. For simplicity's sake, you see how to count in the powers of 2: 1, 2, 4, 8, 16, 32, 64, and 128. You can tell they are powers of 2 because each is exactly a doubling of the number before it. Notice the binary number for each of these decimal numbers; it requires just 1 bit to be equal to 1. The others are 0s.

However, the same 8-bit binary string can be used to count from 0 to 255. Such values are calculated by summing the decimal values of each column populated with a 1. To actually count to numbers that aren't powers of 2 requires you to have more than 1 of the 8 bits set equal to 1. Table 6-5 shows more of how this works.

Table 6-5   Counting in Base2

Base2	Base10 Equivalent
00000000	0
00000001	1
00000010	2
00000011	3
00000100	4
00000101	5
00000110	6
00000111	7
00001000	8
00001001	9
00001010	10
00001011	11
00001100	12
00001101	13
00001110	14
00001111	15
00010000	16
...	...
11111111	255

Converting binary to decimal, therefore, requires you to sum the decimal equivalents of all columns in the binary string that have a 1 instead of a 0. This summation must be done separately for each group of 8 bits in the IP address.

Using IP Addresses

An IP address uniquely describes a single device connected to a network. That means you can use it to establish a connection to any specific machine connected to the network. In the case of the Internet, that means you can single out just one machine of the millions connected.

As you might have noticed, IP addresses aren't the friendliest things to use. More to the point, most people can spend a lifetime connected to the Internet and other IP-based networks and never even see an IP address. That might seem like a real paradox: IP addresses are what makes the Internet's vast resources accessible, and yet most people never even see them!

The answer to that paradox is quite simple. There's no reason the average person using an IP network has to use an IP address directly. Many other available tools enable resources networked via an IP network to be accessed using more familiar words or phrases. For example, you could use a browser to access the Cisco Systems website at www.cisco.com or you could point your browser to 198.133.219.25. Both bring up the same website. Given the choice between using an address that is intuitive, easy to remember, and based on language versus one that is just a bunch of numbers, it's easy to see why IP addresses aren't more widely used. At least, it's easy to see why people don't use them directly to access resources connected to the network.

Sometimes, an IP address changes. Although this is rare, particularly with established companies such as Cisco Systems, it is still possible. When that happens, attempts to contact a host using the old IP address will fail. However, attempts to contact that host using its name (such as www.cisco.com) work. That's because of the *Domain Name System (DNS)*. DNS tracks, correlates, and automatically translates user-friendly names into current and valid IP addresses.

IP addresses are used in at least four ways. First, as you might have surmised, they are used indirectly to access resources. Chapter 11 reveals more about this. For now, suffice it to say there is a mechanism that takes your words (such as www.cisco.com) and translates them into numeric IP addresses.

Network administrators—they are people, too—use IP addresses to organize the resources connected to their networks. Each IP address consists of two parts: a network address and a host address. This two-tiered hierarchy enables everything connected to the Internet to be better organized.

Third, networks you saw earlier in this chapter are made up of devices that peek inside each IP packet to see where it must be sent. This destination address forms the basis for a series of decisions that the network's routers must make with respect to where to send each packet.

Lastly, an IP addresses is used as a behind-the-scenes thing. *Routers*—network devices that interconnect LANs to form a WAN—use IP addresses as input to a mathematical process that enables them to pick the best path for your packets. You see, there can be a huge number of paths for your packets in a large and complicated network such as the Internet. Picking the best path is known as *routing*, and routers use IP addresses to share information with each other about known destinations and paths to those destinations.

The third and fourth uses of an IP address are highly interrelated and help you better understand exactly how IP addresses are used in a network.

How Can You Tell a Host Address from a Network Address?

Various types of devices make up a network. The role of these devices is to accept packets sent by other network devices, by computers, or by other machines that inhabit a network, and then decide what to do with them. That decision is based on each packet's destination IP address.

There is no magic here—just applied mathematics. Essentially, every computer, every printer, every anything that connects to an IP network gets an IP address. The network devices (such as routers and switches) typically won't care about application information, so they won't benefit by looking at TCP or UDP headers. However, the IP header contains all the information needed to figure out where each packet is going. After identifying each packet's destination, network devices figure out where to send it so that it reaches its destination. That implies that every network device knows how to reach every device connected to the network. In the case of the Internet, that's a tall order!

Although memory and computing power have both gotten inexpensive over the last few years, it is still beyond a router to remember how to get to every device on the Internet. This is where the two-level hierarchy of an IP address makes things much easier.

One Address, Two Parts

To this point, the chapter has treated IP addresses as a whole. Truth be told, each IP address contains at least two main parts: a *network address* and a *host address*. This two-part construction makes it possible to organize the chaos and makes the Internet feasible. The Internet is just too big for any one device to track all the other attached devices. That's significant because, despite technological advances made in computing, it's impractical and impossible for any one computer to keep track of every other computer, printer, and server in the world. There are just too many of them.

By deconstructing an IP address into a host and a network address, you can reduce the router's workload and figure out how to reach every device connected to the Internet. Each router only has to remember the path to a network address, rather than to every host's address. Each network consists of many different hosts, each of which shares the same network address. Figure 6-8 shows how this works.

Figure 6-8   All Hosts Share a Network Address

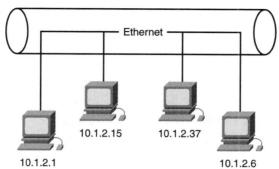

10.1.2.15   10.1.2.37

10.1.2.1   10.1.2.6

In Figure 6-8, all the hosts' addresses start with the same first three numbers: 10.1.2. It might be safe to assume that these numbers form the network address. After all, they remain the same for all hosts in the example network. That would be a guess; sometimes that guess would be right and sometimes it wouldn't. For accuracy's sake, check your computer's IP configuration. Earlier, this chapter shows you how to run **ipconfig**. One of those addresses is the subnet mask.

The subnet mask looks a little funny because, even though it is expressed in decimal numbers like the other IP addresses, it is made up of just two numbers: 255 and 0. The mask indicated in Figure 6-7 is 255.255.255.0. Having walked through the binary mathematics that are the foundation on which the IP address is built, you can probably quickly surmise that the first three numbers when translated to binary represent a string of 24 consecutive 1s.

Remember: An IP address is actually a 32-bit binary number, and each of the 4 decimal numbers is 8 binary digits. Thus, this particular 32-bit string is 11111111111111111111111100000000. This might seem like a strange address, but not coincidentally the 1s and 0s appear in a consistent, unbroken series. That's the mask! The 1s signify all the bits in the real IP address and identify the network address within the IP address. All the 0s are the bits that identify the bits used for the host address.

Getting back to the example, all the hosts in Figure 6-8 start with 10.1.2. Given a mask of 255.255.255.0, you can avoid guessing and know that the network's address is 10.1.2.0. Sometimes you see it identified as 10.1.2 or even 10.1.2.x. Either way, it means the same thing.

Although **ipconfig** is a useful tool, it wasn't designed to reveal your network's address. You saw how to use it for that purpose, but also it identifies the bits that identify the subnetwork to which your computer connects. It doesn't identify the network. That's a subtle distinction, and in some cases there's no difference at all. As the word *subnetwork* implies, a network can contain numerous subnetworks. A subnetwork's address is an extension of a network address. That extension is made possible by borrowing some of the bits from the host address.

This creates a bit of a dilemma: How can you tell how many of the bits indicated by 1s in a subnet mask constitute the network address, and how many are used for the subnetwork address? The answer lies in understanding the architecture of IP network addresses. Fortunately, there are only two different architectures and one is obsolete. These two approaches are known as *classical* (or *classful*) and *classless addressing*.

Classical IP: The Way It Was

As you start investigating the world of IP addressing, you might come across the words *class* and *classical*. When the IPv4 address system was first deployed, the engineers at the IETF recognized that a few large organizations might need Internet connectivity. Their logic continued that there would be a moderate quantity of medium-sized organizations and a lot of little organizations. Consequently, they carved the address space into mathematical zones known as *classes*. Each class was identified with an alphabetic character from A to D.

A *Class A* network address contains more than 16,000,000 host addresses, but there are only about 128 of them. There are thousands of *Class B* network addresses (each of which contain more than 65,000 host addresses) and even more *Class C* network addresses, which contain just 255 host addresses each. *Class D* addresses serve a different purpose, and do not identify network or host addresses. This approach to class-based allocation of the IPv4 address space has come to be known as *classical IP.*

Under the rules of classical IP, routers quickly figure out how much of an IP address identified the network's address. They do so by examining the address's first few bits. The classes form rigid numeric boundaries, and it is easy to tell whether an address is a Class A, B, or C network just by looking at the value of the first decimal number. If the number is between 0 and 127, it is Class A. If the number is greater than 128 but less than 191, it is Class B. If it is greater than 191 but less than 223, it is Class C.

The Class A address uses the first group of 8 bits for the network address and the remaining 24 bits for host addresses within that network. The Class B network address splits the 32-bit address right down the middle: 16 bits for the network address and 16 for the host addresses inside that network address. The Class C network, as you might predict, uses 24 bits for the network address and just 8 bits for the host addresses within each network address. Obviously, the more bits in any address field, the more addresses mathematically possible. These three classes represent different tradeoffs between the number of network addresses you can make and the number of hosts that can be created within each network address.

Over time, the underlying assumptions about the sizes proved incorrect. The small size network address (i.e., Class C) was too small, and the jump to the medium network address was too big. Organizations that needed more than 255 addresses typically were given a chunk of 65,000 addresses. Needless to say, that wasted a lot of addresses; in the mid-1990s, an address shortage threatened to disrupt the Internet's growth. This crisis led to an amazing burst of creativity within the IETF as they sought to prevent the Internet's impending collapse. One such effort was to apply the technique that creates subnetworks to networks. In other words, classes would be abolished in favor of the ability to create network addresses of varying sizes. This approach became known as *classless IP.*

Classless IP: The Way It Is

That's probably the wrong way to word it. Even though today the Internet has moved away from class-based network addresses, don't misconstrue the current system as having no class. It's not the Rodney Dangerfield of the Internet. In fact, it's quite elegant, flexible, and efficient. This new system is known as *Classless Interdomain Routing* or *CIDR* (pronounced just like the warm holiday drink made from squished apples).

CIDR allows you to create a network address with almost any number of bits. The largest network is a 5-bit network address (which is actually 8 times bigger than the old 8-bit Class A network address). The viable range extends all the way to a 32-bit address. A 32-bit address uniquely identifies a single host rather than identifies a network address and then a host within a network. The important point is that you can create a CIDR network address using between 5 and 32 bits. That's quite a contrast from the old classical addressing system, where you worked in multiples of 8 bits.

Chapter 7 goes into more detail on how subnetworks work. For right now, accept that CIDR was based directly on subnetwork addressing. The only real difference between subnetwork addresses and CIDR network addresses is that CIDR doesn't borrow any bits from the host address bits.

Perhaps the most significant implication of that difference is that the entire CIDR network address is *routable*, whereas only the network portion of a subnetworked IP address is routable. Routable identifies the part of an IP address that routers use when they share information about networks that each knows about, as well as possible paths to those networks. The subnetwork bits and the host bits remain unused by routers and, consequently, are regarded as unroutable pieces of information.

With CIDR, a new form of shorthand emerged. Rather than use the familiar old mask such as the 255.255.255.0, a new notation hides this mask from you. The new notation is much simpler and doesn't saddle you with any mathematics exercises. Instead, the number of bits used for the network (or subnetwork) is explicitly identified using decimal numbers. To make this a bit more real, the mask of 255.255.255.0 contains 24 consecutive 1s indicating the network portion of the IP address.

A more concise way of expressing that same fact relative to the IP address is 10.1.2.0/24. Notice the slash and the 24? That's the mask or 255.255.255.0. The expression reads like this: The network address begins at 10.1.2.0, uses 24 bits to identify the network, and uses 8 bits to identify hosts within that network address.

Chapter Summary

TCP/IP is an amazing but enigmatic communications protocol. It allows two machines separated by as much as half the world and who-knows-how-many-networks to communicate as easily as if they were sitting next to each other. Two keys that enable that type of communication are the IP packet and the IP address system. This chapter shows you the various stages of an IP packet's life and how it gets pushed through a network (or multiple networks) en route to its destination.

You also saw some of the mathematics on which the IP address system is based. Understanding the mathematics of the IP address system helps you become a much more astute TCP/IP user. The next chapter takes you another layer deeper into IP addressing, showing you how to create subnetworks within an IP network. You also discover why you would want to do that.

Chapter Review Questions

The following questions reinforce the key concepts in this chapter:

1. What does an IP packet do?

2. How many stages are there in the life of an IP packet?

3. Can an IP packet roam the network forever in search of its destination?

4. What is an IP address?

5. Why do you need IP addresses?

6. Do you need those dots between the numbers in an IP address?

7. How do people use IP addresses?

8. How does a network use IP addresses?

What You Will Learn

After reading this chapter, you should be able to answer the following questions:

- ✔ What is subnetting?

- ✔ How many addressing levels are possible in an IP address?

- ✔ What are some of the benefits of subnetting?

- ✔ What are two main drawbacks of subnetting?

- ✔ Can you see a subnetwork address in a dotted-decimal IP address?

- ✔ What is a base address?

- ✔ What is an extended network prefix and what does it do?

- ✔ What are three types of masks encountered in an IP network? What does each do?

CHAPTER 7

More Fun with IP Addresses

Just when you thought you learned all there is to know about IP addresses, you turned to the next chapter and realized you were wrong! There's a whole lot more to those little strings of dotted decimal numbers than meets the eye. The preceding chapter shows you how an IP address can be cut into two components: the network address and the host address. This chapter shows you a third dimension to IP addressing known as subnetting. **Subnetting** is a process by which you take a network address and chop it up into smaller pieces. Each piece can then be used as a network address. Thus, you can use a single network address space for several networks...if you know what you're doing!

This chapter shows you how subnets get created, why they are useful, and how they are used. It even walks you through the mathematics of subnetting so you can better appreciate this fascinating aspect of TCP/IP.

Subdivision: It's Not Just for Real Estate

Subdividing a piece of land conjures up images of suburban sprawl and mass-produced houses. Although that's not necessarily the most positive of images, the concept of subdividing a piece of land enables you to appreciate the basic concept: The process allows you to take a single resource and chop it up into many smaller resources. In the case of a piece of land, you can have many home sites instead of just one. In the case of IP addresses, you can create multiple, smaller network addresses from a single larger one.

The Need to Subdivide

As you may have noticed in Chapter 6, "Pushing the Envelope," each IP address has two parts: a network address and a host address. They aren't really two different addresses, just two different parts of the same address. Looking at the IP address hierarchically, each network address can support multiple host addresses—but each host address can be used on one host only. Figure 7-1 shows you how one network address supports numerous computers and other networked devices.

Figure 7-1 The Network Address Is the Foundation for All Addresses

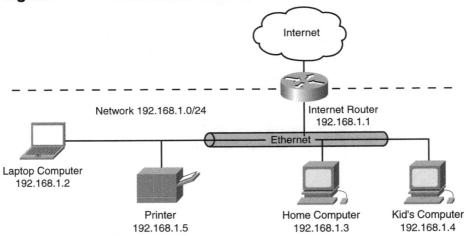

 Usually, you can't assign the same IP address to two or more computers in a network without causing some problems. You can, however, in some situations assign the same IP address to more than one computer. For example, some applications and services are so critical they can't ever be offline. Such applications are often built on a cluster of computers rather than just one. For example, you can have what's known as an *active/passive cluster* in which two computers function as one. In such a cluster, one computer is always active and the other waits for the active machine malfunction. In such clusters, you can safely assign the same address to both computers.

Figure 7-1 shows a small network; assume it's a home network. This network has three computers and a printer and the same family uses them. Although each computer has its own IP address, all the computers share a common foundation: the network's address. That means that each IP address has two parts: a network address and the individual host addresses within that network address. In other words, the address features a simple, two-level hierarchical structure. The network address portion of each IP address is indicated by underlining in Figure 7-1. In this scenario, a two-level address hierarchy is quite sufficient.

Consider a more complicated network—one in which four departments of a small company share a network environment. You might realize that a third hierarchical level of addressing would be quite beneficial. Figure 7-2 shows you a small enterprise network. The network enjoys just one connection to the Internet and all the users are contained in one location. Thus, there is no need for a wide-area network (WAN). This small network enjoys more addresses than it really needs. The IP address space supports the creation of 256 unique host addresses within that network address, yet this scenario has just a few more users than the home network illustrated in Figure 7-1.

Figure 7-2 depicts two critical implications of the network. The first is that anyone on the Internet can reach the network using the same network address: 192.168.1.0/24. That means that all the computers are connected to the same network and share the same network address. Although it isn't wise to make your company's entire network accessible to the Internet, that accessibility is a function of the network address. Restrictions can be imposed to protect your company's network through the use of things like access permissions on the router or even a firewall. For now, continue to focus on the implications of a single network address.

Figure 7-2   Multiple Departments in an Enterprise Share a Network

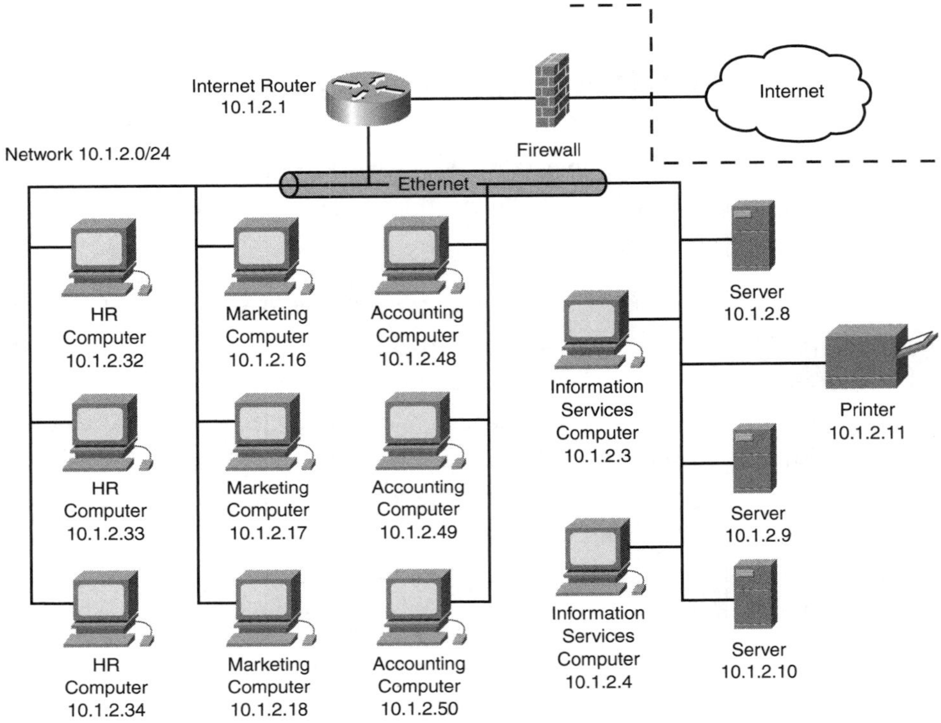

The second implication is that all four departments in this small enterprise—
Marketing, Human Resources, Accounting, and Information Services—share a
common network. Absent any other controls, such as IDs and passwords, anyone
in any of the departments can directly access any of the networked resources in
any other device. In essence, it is a single network and no security beyond a simple ID and password is required to gain entry to potentially sensitive information.
Can you imagine the consequences of payroll information being readily accessible to everyone in the company? How about performance review information?
That would certainly liven up discussions around the company's water cooler!

A basic tenet of computer security is to restrict sensitive information access to just those people who have a need to know. A *shared network* is the antithesis of that principle: Everybody has access to everything. One obvious solution is to cut the network into smaller pieces so there is a physical separation between departments. Splitting the network might not be as easy to do as you might first suspect!

Cut It Up!

Look again at Figure 7-2. It doesn't make sense to duplicate some of the fairly high-cost items in this network. For one thing, the Internet connection can be shared. The same goes for the *router* (the device that connects the local-area network [LAN] to the Internet). Another is the *firewall* (the device that protects the LAN from unwanted intrusions via the Internet). These are fairly expensive items that you don't need more than one of. What you need is a shared network backbone but physically separate LANs. Figure 7-3 shows how this can be achieved.

Physically separating the departmental networks is easy enough to do: You purchase some LAN switches, interconnect them with a router, and wire the departmental workstations and servers into the appropriate switch. Chapter 12, "Connecting to TCP/IP Networks," explains routers and routing in a lot more detail. For now, all you need to know about a router is that it is a highly specialized network device that interconnects LANs and WANs. It then acts as sort of a traffic cop and directs the network's traffic. It examines each received IP packet and figures out where to send it based on what the router knows about how the network is constructed.

The router, assuming it had enough cable ports to interconnect all the LANs, would perform the contradictory task of interconnecting yet separating the departmental LANs. That contradiction is easily explained by referring back to the OSI reference model. LANs operate at Layers 1 and 2 (physical and data link) of the OSI model. Routers and the process of routing operate at Layer 3—the network layer using IP. Thus, the router segregates the LANs by creating different Layer 1 and Layer 2 environments for each LAN, but interconnects them using IP.

Figure 7-3 Departmental Networks Are Created

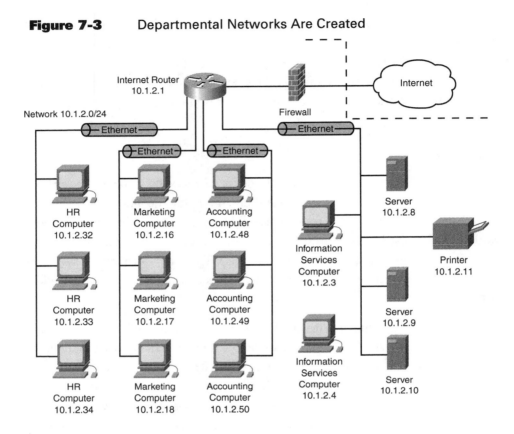

That's just the physical perspective. Logically, there's more work to do. For example, how does that physical separation affect the IP addresses? If the networks are physically separate, you need separate network addresses, too. You could just obtain more addresses, but you already have more than you can possibly use in the 10.1.2.0/24 network address. Besides, IP addresses are a finite resource and you might not be able to get more if you tried! The real problem is that the 256 addresses you have are in one big chunk. You really need four smaller chunks of addresses. This is where subnetting comes in handy.

Subnetting is a process by which a third level of addressing is created from IP's two-level address. A single network can create several subnetworks, each of which can support numerous hosts. In simple terms, *subnetworks* are just blocks of addresses reserved from within a network address. Each block of addresses can then function as a separate network-level address. When implemented in a network, each subnetwork address can function as a real network address.

Subnetting a Network

In Figure 7-4, you can see that the network that was segmented into departmental networks can share the original network address block. Each departmental network gets a small piece of that original address block. Figure 7-3 shows an abstraction of the network topology. Instead of individual devices, the department network appears as clouds. (That really is an accepted practice amongst network engineers.) Each cloud functions as its own network, even though it is really a subnetwork created from within the 10.1.2.0/24 network.

Figure 7-4   Ranges of IP Addresses Are Reserved for Each
Departmental Network

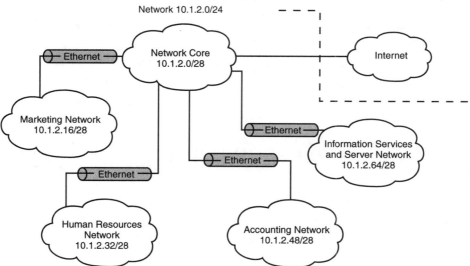

Figures 7-3 and 7-4 show the firewall as the device connecting the enterprise network to the Internet. This is not precisely accurate, but is a simplification for the sake of the example. In the real world, you would likely have two routers with the firewall sandwiched between them. That structure creates a semi-safe region of the network known as a *demilitarized zone* or *DMZ*.

Although Figure 7-4 isn't sufficiently detailed to show this, one cable port on the router must belong to each subnet. That way, the router forms a physical interconnection between each of the subnetworks, but treats them as separate networks. You *must* use IP addresses to get from one subnetwork to another.

Table 7-1 shows you how the original 10.1.2.0/24 network address is carved up to satisfy the four departmental networks. This table shows you the network address of each of the four subnets, the first valid host address in each subnetwork, and the last valid host in each subnet.

Table 7-1   Subnetting a /24 Network

Network Address	Use	Host Addresses
10.1.2.0/28	Router and core of network	10.1.2.0 to 10.1.2.15
10.1.2.16/28	Marketing	10.1.2.16 to 10.1.2.31
10.1.2.32/28	Human Resources	10.1.2.32 to 10.1.2.47
10.1.2.48/28	Accounting	10.1.2.48 to 10.1.2.63
10.1.2.64/28	Information Systems	10.1.2.64 to 10.1.2.79

As you can see from Table 7-1, each department enjoys its own range of IP addresses. The router is told how the original network address is carved so that it knows how to forward packets between the subnetworks.

Where's the Subnet Address?

Each subnetwork has been given a block of addresses of the same size: 28 bits (indicated by the /28) for the network and subnetwork addresses, which leaves 4 bits for the host addresses in each subnetwork. Table 7-2 shows you how this works for this particular example. The actual distribution of bits per field can vary widely, so please don't walk away thinking that a subnetwork address is always 4 bits in length.

Table 7-2   The Three Parts of a Subnetwork Address

Network Address	Subnetwork Address	Host Address
24 bits	4 bits	4 bits

The subnetwork address functions as an extension of the network address. The network and subnetwork addresses work together to form an extended network address. In fact, the network address and subnetwork address, when viewed together, are known as an *extended network prefix*. An extended network prefix enables IP packets to be routed directly to your network, but not to your specific workstation. You can think of this in terms of a mailing address. A mailing address precisely identifies where you live and how to get mail to you. Each mailing address also has at least three parts: a town, a street, and a house number. Notice the increased specificity? Town, street, house: Each level in the hierarchy is more specific than the preceding level. That town consists of many streets, and each street can have a differing amount of homes.

An IP address works the same way. The network address is analogous to the town you live in. The subnetwork address is more like a street in that it is not identifying a single, specific house; there are many contained inside the previous hierarchical address component (that is, the town). The network address and subnetwork address form the ***extended network prefix***. This term is usually only encountered when talking with real network geeks! The host address is directly comparable to your mailing address dwelling number. Although that's not a perfect analogy, it does get the point across.

If you look back at Table 7-1, it is not at all obvious that a two-level hierarchical address (network and host address) has been cut into a three-level hierarchical address by adding a subnet field. In fact, the subnet field is nowhere to be seen! You can see that the network address has been segmented into smaller pieces and that each piece has a range of IP host addresses, but that's it. The subnet address is absent. That's because you are just looking at a mask. You can't see the subnet address until you look at the IP address in its native binary form.

In this example, the subnet address is 4 bits in length. You already know that a binary address is 32 bits in length and that the decimal mask is created by segmenting that 32-bit address into four equal chunks of 8 bits each. Those 8 bits are separated visually by a dot. If the subnet address is only 4 bits in length, it wouldn't be represented by one of the four dotted-decimal numbers. Instead, it would be a piece of one of those decimal numbers.

The bits used to create a subnetwork address are always borrowed from the host address field. Remember, the original network address was 24 bits in length. The entire Internet knows about this address and uses it to send IP packets to this little enterprise. Consequently, you can't mess with the network address without causing sending and receiving problems via the Internet. That leaves little choice but to create subnetwork addresses from the host address field. Because the original network address was 24 bits in length, the host address has exactly 8 bits. Of those, 4 bits were borrowed to create the subnetwork addresses. That results in an extended network address of 28 bits long and just 4 bits for host addresses within each subnetwork.

Checking the Math

Now that you know how to create subnetworks from a network address block into subnetworks, the next step in mastering the arcane art of subnetting is doing the math. Table 7-1 shows you the different address ranges allocated to each of the five subnetworks. However, those ranges weren't chosen out of a hat! They were chosen because they made sense mathematically.

The problem is that the logic behind subnetting really only becomes apparent when you stop using decimal numbers. Remember, an IP address is a 32-bit *binary* number. It has become customary to use decimal numbers only because human beings can't remember long strings of highly repetitive binary numbers. The decimal numbers are nothing but a mask for the real address—the 32-bit binary number. That binary number, fortunately, usually remains hidden from view by a series of masks. You have to stare at the bits to appreciate subnetting.

Staring at the Bits

To see the subnet address, you have to look at the binary address itself. Table 7-3 takes the example from Table 7-1 and shows you the translation from decimal to binary numbers. To make the address's three parts more readily obvious in the binary column, the network address is shown in regular type, the subnet address bits in bold italics, and the host address bits in regular italics. To make things easier on your eyes, you see only the first host address (otherwise affectionately referred to as the *base address*) of each subnet in the Binary Host Addresses column.

Table 7-3   The Binary Side of Subnetting

Decimal Network Address	Use	Binary Host Addresses
10.1.2.0/28	Router and core of network	00001010.00000001.00000010.*00000000*
10.1.2.16/28	Marketing	00001010.00000001.00000010.*00010000*
10.1.2.32/28	Human Resources	00001010.00000001.00000010.*00100000*
10.1.2.48/28	Accounting	00001010.00000001.00000010.*00110000*
10.1.2.64/28	Information Systems	00001010.00000001.00000010.*01000000*

When viewed in dotted binary form, the subnet address really does leap out at you. Especially because bold italics are used! Even though the subnet address is really just 4 bits embedded within a string of 32 bits, you can see how you start counting at 0000 and increment that 4-bit field normally using binary addition.

The first subnet address is 0000, the second is 0001, then 0010, 0011, and finally 0100. Using this scheme, you could create 0101, 0110, 0111, 1000, 1001, 1010, 1011, 1100, 1101, 1110, and finally 1111 as additional subnet addresses. That makes sense, but you have to remember that each bit really represents a group of 16 as far as the decimal IP address is concerned.

Why 16? The reason is because even though 4 bits have been extracted from the 32-bit address to make the math more obvious, it really remains an integral component of that overall address. The least significant number (in mathematical terms) is always the rightmost number. In this subnetwork address, that rightmost number occupies the 16s column.

Remember, this isn't the Base10 number system with its all too familiar 1s, 10s, 100s, 1000s progression from right to left. You're working with Base2. The progression is in powers of 2, not 10. The rightmost bit of the subnetwork address is in the 2^4 column, which equals 16 in Base10. The result of this relative positioning of the subnetwork address's rightmost bit is that increments within the subnetwork address (such as from 0110 to 0111) are really increments in blocks of 16 when viewed in decimal numbers.

A total of 16 possible subnets could be created using a 4-bit subnet address. That makes perfect sense because 2^4 power is 16. You can create up to 16 host addresses inside each of those subnets because there are exactly 4 bits left for host addresses in each. In decimal terms, the base address of each subnet created would be a multiple of 16. They would start at 10.1.2.0 and progress as follows:

10.1.2.16

10.1.2.32

10.1.2.48

10.1.2.64

10.1.2.80

10.1.2.96

. . .

That pattern is obvious only when you know what to look for!

Leaving Room for the Network

One subtle but important point may have gotten lost in the details of Tables 7-1 and 7-3: An extra subnet was created. You were led down the primrose path by identifying the functional areas of the company that needed its own subnets, but then one more was created for the network itself. Why? Simply because it is a good way to design a network.

The router and network core must have its own range of addresses. In fact, the router and network core was the first subnet created in Table 7-1. This can be confusing because you know that one cable port on the router must belong to each of the subnetworks. Why can't the router just be a part of one of those subnetworks? Technically, it can. Actually, doing that is a bad idea! It limits your ability to secure the network and can cause performance problems for those users unlucky enough to share a network with what is likely the busiest device of all: the router!

By giving the *router* (which forms the core or center of the enterprise's network) its own subnetwork, you create the potential for improving network security and performance. As a general rule, the router (and maybe other devices) that will be shared by all the subnetworks should be at the center of your network. That is, all subnetworks should have equal access to it. For that reason, it is ideal to have the core of your network populated with essential shared resources such as a firewall and computers that run essential infrastructural services in their own subnetwork.

The Benefits and Drawbacks of Subnetting

Subnetting, like most things in life, is not perfect. In fact, it is really more of a mixture of ups and downs than anything else. Subnetting affords great flexibility and enhances your ability to manage and use a network, but all that comes at a price. In the end, the benefits far outweigh the drawbacks. Consequently, subnetting has become ubiquitous in IP networks. Quickly walk through the ups and downs.

The Benefits

Now that you know a little bit about subnetting, it's time to sit back and reflect on the benefits of this approach to managing IP addresses. There are, in my opinion, three main benefits of subnetting:

- **More efficient use of an IP network address**—By being able to cut up a single block of network addresses into smaller pieces, you avoid wasting IP addresses. This lets you avoid having to obtain multiple network address blocks. This was the original motivation that drove the Internet to accept subnetting. The supply of IP network addresses was being used up at an alarming rate, so the Internet Engineering Task Force (IETF) seized upon subnetting as a way of making the remaining supply last longer.

- **Resource organization**—You can create a subnet and fill it with just printers, or servers, or even computer programmers. One could argue that all three should be separated from the rest of the network's resources and users for the sake of optimizing network performance.

- **Security**—You can improve your network's security by compartmentalizing sensitive resources into their own subnetwork. Although that doesn't prevent other people from accessing them, it does make it a bit more difficult.

Drawbacks

One of the drawbacks to subnetting might seem a bit paradoxical. You just read that subnetting allows you to more efficiently use a block of network addresses, but subnetting can actually waste IP addresses. Each subnet requires you to reserve two addresses: one to identify the subnet itself and the other for broadcasting to all machines within that subnet. A /24 network contains 256 total addresses and you can use 254 of those addresses if you don't subnet it. For each subnet you create, you lose an additional two addresses. This is nitpicking; obviously subnetting has proven its worth over time. This just demonstrates that it is not perfect.

The other major drawback to subnetting is that it is not at all a simple science. Actually, it's quite complex! Even if you know what you are doing, you can make quite a mess of your network by improperly managing the address block. You don't get into details about how difficult it is to manage a subnetted IP network address block, but suffice it to say that not many people can think in Base2. You see how unintuitive the boundaries are between subnets when you look at the binary numbers back in Table 7-3. Now imagine that the address space you were managing contained dozens of subnets and thousands of endpoints. A larger address block just creates greater potential for a bigger mess.

Mystery Behind the Mask

A mask, generally speaking, is a device that conceals one's true identity. Although hiding one's true identity is despicable and cowardly, in the case of IP addresses that is actually a very good thing. Can you imagine having to remember an IP address consisting of just 32 1s and 0s? Neither can I!

Three different types of masks are used with IP addresses:

- Decimal mask (example: 1.1.1.1)

- Network mask (example: 255.0.0.0)

- Subnet mask (example: /24)

These masks are different tools intended for different purposes. I'll explain each of them to you before delving into the mathematics of subnetworking.

Decimal Masks

Whenever you encounter an IP address, it is most likely in a dotted-decimal form. That is, it consists of four decimal numbers separated by three dots. For example, 10.1.2.155 is a legitimate IP address. Repeatedly, this book says that an IP address is really a 32-bit binary number, and 10.1.2.155 sure doesn't look like a binary number. The reason is that it isn't. What you are looking at is the decimal mask of a binary address. Converted to binary, this address follows:

00001010.00000001.00000010.10011011

The dots, as mentioned in Chapter 6, are placed there just to make it easier to convert the long binary number into smaller decimal numbers. The true binary address, without any mask at all, follows:

00001010000000010000001010011011

If that address isn't enough of a reason to use masks, what is? The decimal mask conceals this utterly unusable raw address and makes the IP address a bit more human friendly. Each IP address you see expressed in dotted-decimal notation is really a *decimal mask* for the raw, 32-bit binary IP address.

Network Masks

A network mask is a bit more specialized. Much like a decimal mask, the network mask also uses the dotted-decimal format to conceal the ugly 32-bit binary number. The difference between a decimal and network mask is that the network mask has a more specific purpose. The *network mask* tells network devices (not necessarily a network's human users) how many bits of an IP address are used to identify the network address.

A network mask, all by itself, is almost useless. You won't encounter it in much technical literature nor find it in use on a daily basis. In practical terms, it does set the stage for a better understanding of subnet masks. Subnet masks are quite frequently encountered, so it makes sense to first look at network masks and then see how subnet masks build upon them.

Table 7-4 shows the dotted binary and decimal equivalents of network masks for some of the more commonly encountered IP network address sizes.

Table 7-4   Network Masks

Network Address Size	Network Mask in Dotted Decimal Form	Network Mask in Dotted Binary Form
/8	255.0.0.0	11111111.00000000.00000000.00000000
/16	255.255.0.0	11111111.11111111.00000000.00000000
/24	255.255.255.0	11111111.11111111.11111111.00000000

At quick glance, Table 7-4 probably doesn't make all that much sense. Each of the pieces is explained here so that it makes perfect sense. The *network mask* identifies just the portion of the IP address that constitutes the network address. The mask itself is actually a new number that takes the same form of an IP address but isn't an IP address. The decimal numbers by themselves don't make much sense, but the binary numbers do. The binary network mask indicates which bits are used to identify the network address by representing each such bit with a 1. The bits used to identify the host address are represented with 0s.

The binary numbers correlate perfectly with the network address size stipulated in the first column of Table 7-4. The first network address size is a /8. If you recall from Chapter 6, you know that means that the first 8 bits identify the network address. The remaining 24 bits can identify hosts within that 8-bit network address.

The dotted-binary form of the network mask simply shows you how to arrive at the network mask's decimal value. 2^8 is 256. Because IP starts counting at 0 instead of 1, the valid range is 0 through 255. Thus, a pattern of eight consecutive 1s yields a decimal mask value of 255.

The notion of consecutive 1s is a key point with subnetting. As you read through this chapter, you see that all subnet masks feature an unbroken string of 1s, starting with the leftmost bit and proceeding toward the right in the binary IP address. You can, in theory, create a subnet with a mask featuring nonconsecutive 1s, but you are surely asking for trouble! The result is that your network address block will be carved into a confusing and wasteful mess.

Subnet Masks

A *subnet mask* is a 32-bit binary number that can be expressed in either dotted-decimal or dotted-binary form. In this regard, a subnet mask is structurally similar to an IP address. There are, however, some important distinctions! For example, a mask is not a real address; you can't assign it to any device on the network. Nor

does it have to be unique. The best way to understand subnet masks is to think of them as just an extension of a network mask. Actually, they are directly based on the network mask.

Subnet masks tell *end systems* (including routers and hosts in the LAN) how many bits of the IP address' host field have been borrowed for subnet identification. The bits in the mask that identify the network address, as well as the subnet address, are set to 1s. The remaining bits, which are used for host addresses within each subnet, are set to 0s.

Table 7-5 shows you how many bits you need to borrow from the host field in a /24 network to create the following subnets. The bits that identify host addresses are shown in italics. The bits that were borrowed from the host field are indicated in bold italics.

Table 7-5   Subnet Masks

Borrowed Bits	Subnet Mask in Dotted Decimal Form	Subnet Mask in Dotted Binary Form
2	255.255.255.192	11111111.11111111.11111111.*__11__000000*
3	255.255.255.224	11111111.11111111.11111111.*__111__00000*
4	255.255.255.240	11111111.11111111.11111111.*__1111__0000*
5	255.255.255.248	11111111.11111111.11111111.*__11111__000*
6	255.255.255.252	11111111.11111111.11111111.*__111111__00*

In Table 7-5, the network mask is represented by the string of 1s in regular type. The subnet mask is the string of 1s in both regular type and bold italics. It is important to note that the borrowed bits are always the leftmost bits in the host field. Additionally, the number of bits you borrow from the host address field determines the tradeoff between the number of subnetwork addresses that you can create and the quantity of host addresses that each will contain. As is painfully apparent in Table 7-5, a subnet mask's dotted-decimal form is an efficient shorthand.

The binary makes sense visually and mathematically, but working with decimal numbers is much easier.

Table 7-6 shows you just a sample of how the number of bits you borrow to create a subnet dictates both the number of subnets you can create from a given network address as well as the number of host addresses that can be created within each subnetwork.

Table 7-6   Hosts Versus Subnets in a 24-Bit Network

Number of Bits in Network Prefix	Subnet Mask in Dotted-Decimal Form	Number of Possible Sub-net Addresses	Number of Possible Hosts Per Subnet
2	255.255.255.192	4	64
3	255.255.255.224	8	32
4	255.255.255.240	16	16
5	255.255.255.248	32	8
6	255.255.255.252	64	4

Please note that Table 7-6 shows the tradeoff between hosts and subnets that can be created in a 24-bit network address. Because a network address can be anything from 5 to 30 bits in length, a host address field can range from a maximum of 27 bits down to just 2 bits. That's quite a range!

On a practical level, it means that the possibility for splitting a host address field into different combinations of subnetwork and host addresses is quite large. To keep things simple, you see how this tradeoff works in a relatively commonly sized network address. The same principles would apply should you try to subnet any other size network address.

Two Types of Subnets

Throughout this chapter you might have noticed that segmenting a network address created subnets of equal size. That wasn't an accident. That shows you the simplest approach to subnetting. This approach has become known as *fixed-length subnet masking (FLSM)*.

FSLM offers all the benefits of subnetting, but tends to trade management ease for efficiency. It isn't realistic to expect all your subnets to be the same size. A one-size-fits-all approach probably wouldn't be the most efficient way to subdivide a network address block. The tradeoff for ease of management, however, is not a trivial trade!

The alternative to FLSM is *variable-length subnet masking (VLSM)*. VLSM, in theory, solves the problem of the inherent inefficiency of trying to use the same mask size for all your subnets. VLSM offers the ability to create subnet masks that are specifically designed for the number of devices you need to support in each subnet. That means that VLSM is much more efficient than FLSM when it comes to the efficiency with which an address block can be used.

However, VLSM has a dark side. Truth be told, variable-length subnet masking is so complicated and difficult that it makes managing a network address block almost impossible. Even if you know what you are doing, a pure VLSM approach can quickly degenerate into chaos.

If you want to learn more about either FLSM or VLSM, please refer to *IP Addressing Fundamentals*, published by the Cisco Press.

Imagine all your subnets being a different size. You couldn't predict the boundaries between any two subnets. Okay, so maybe that was a little difficult to imagine. Take a look at Table 7-7, which shows you exactly what such a subnet scheme looks like.

Table 7-7   Subnetting with VLSM in a 24-Bit Network

	Binary Network + Subnet Address	**Decimal Translation**
Base	11000000.10101000.01111101.00000000	192.168.125.0
Subnet 0	11000000.10101000.01111101.*00000000*	192.168.125.0
Subnet 1	11000000.10101000.01111101.***00100000***	192.168.125.32
Subnet 2	11000000.10101000.01111101.***00101000***	192.168.125.40
Subnet 3	11000000.10101000.01111101.***00110000***	192.168.125.48
Not used	11000000.10101000.01111101.*01000000*	192.168.125.64

Table 7-7 takes a 24-bit network address and carves it into four subnets of different sizes. It follows the previous convention of identifying the network address bits in regular type, the subnet address bits in bold italics, and the host bits in italics. Although this approach could work, it could also quickly spiral out of control! It just isn't as intuitive as fixed-length subnetting. Even looking at the Base2 numbers isn't much help relative to the Base10 numbers. Either way, it's confusing but potentially efficient.

VLSM can be so complicated that many talented professional IP address managers (known as *hostmasters*) prefer to base their subnetwork address schemes on FLSM rather than VLSM. That is, they first carve up their network address block into small subnetworks of fixed length and then add those fixed-length blocks together as needed to build subnets. Regardless of how you implement it, VLSM can be a tremendously powerful tool...if you can master it!

Chapter Summary

Subnetting is a way of segmenting a block of network addresses into two or more subnetworks. From the outside world's perspective, a subnetted address block looks just like a network address block—the subnetting is only visible and pertinent within the local network.

Subnetting works by borrowing bits from the host address field and using them to create subnetwork addresses. Although you rely extensively on decimal numbers and various masks to make IP addressing a bit more user friendly, it is only by seeing and understanding the underlying binary mathematics that you can really make sense of subnetting.

Although there are great benefits to subnetting, there is no free lunch. Implementing a subnetting scheme requires a long-term commitment to managing an IP address block carefully. Otherwise, the logic of the original design will quickly deteriorate and you will have a real mess on your hands.

Chapter Review Questions

The following questions reinforce the key concepts in this chapter.

1. What is subnetting?

2. How many levels of addressing are possible in an IP address?

3. What are some of the benefits of subnetting?

4. What are two main drawbacks of subnetting?

5. Can you see a subnetwork address in a dotted-decimal IP address?

6. What is a base address?

7. What is an extended network prefix and what does it do?

8. Name three types of masks encountered in an IP network. Explain what each does.

What You Will Learn

After reading this chapter, you should be able to answer the following questions:

- ✔ What are the various stages of a communications session?

- ✔ How does TCP regulate the flow of information between a source and destination machine?

- ✔ What is a three-way handshake and what is its purpose?

- ✔ What are the three uses for TCP sequence numbers?

- ✔ What is a session?

- ✔ How does a source computer tell a destination computer that the session is over?

- ✔ What are the four special types of TCP packets that do *not* carry any application data?

  - ✔ What is a datagram?

CHAPTER 8

Guaranteed Delivery: Your Package Will Get Delivered...Eventually!

At the risk of sounding like a commercial for a package delivery service, when it absolutely, positively, has to get there, use TCP/IP for your IP packet delivery needs. It is *the* mechanism for consistent and reliable information delivery. Although the technical community uses the term *TCP/IP* to generically describe the entire family of protocols, this chapter focuses on just the component known as TCP. The fact that TCP must use IP might lead to the confusing notion that TCP/IP can refer to both the entire family of protocols—specifically to the combination of TCP and IP working together to guarantee delivery of data.

This chapter helps you better understand the concept of reliability, as well as show you how TCP/IP delivers on that promise. You walk through the various stages of a communications session. You even see how TCP handles some unusual situations or error conditions during a communications session. Lastly, you see how TCP's various mechanisms work to guarantee delivery of data.

Reliability and Networking

Reliability is one of those words that one always uses in a positive way. You don't slander or insult someone by calling him or her reliable! Reliability is always an attribute that you can take pride in. In the world of networking, however, reliability takes on a different meaning—a meaning that is neither good nor bad. Reliability is simply a description of a specific approach to delivering data rather than being a point of personal pride.

164   Chapter 8: Guaranteed Delivery: Your Package Will Get Delivered...Eventually!

In a network, as explained throughout this book's earlier chapters, you must choose between timely or reliable delivery of data. Sometimes you are lucky and get both timeliness and reliability, but that's a pleasant bonus that you cannot count on. As a review, in the world of IP networking, the UDP protocol suite is used for timely delivery of data while TCP is used to guarantee delivery of data. You can't have both!

Communication Is the Key

To guarantee reliable delivery of data requires the sending and receiving machines to communicate with each other. Critical pieces of information must be exchanged. Important questions, such as "Did you receive that packet I sent you?" must be answered! Otherwise, there can't be any guarantee other than "I'll try once to get it to you, but don't blame me if it doesn't get there." Thus, it becomes obvious that two machines must be talking to each other for reliable delivery to be possible. The more technically accurate phrase for two-way conversation is session.

A *session* is a coherent flow of information between two or more machines. Coherent information flow requires a truly bidirectional flow of information. *Information* includes a whole lot more than just application data! Depending on the type of application you are using, it isn't unrealistic for the flow of application data to be entirely one way. That is, the sender or source machine dumps packets of data onto the network. That would work just fine, and in fact is pretty much how UDP works. However, that one-way flow of information isn't a session.

A session requires the source and destination machines to communicate so that they can coordinate their activities. This is all done through the use of several different but highly specialized TCP/IP packets. Each of these special packets is named for its function. Without getting too far ahead of myself, suffice it to say that these special packets make use of six different flags in the TCP segment's header (which Chapter 5, "Peeking Under the Covers," shows you). You see each one, as well as how they enable a source and destination machine to establish and manage a communications session.

Please keep in mind that this chapter talks about a typical communications session using TCP, not UDP. From the sender's perspective, UDP is a much more streamlined protocol that literally fires off the packets and then forgets about them. That's a one-way data dump! From a recipient's perspective, UDP packets either arrive on time, in sequence, and in good shape or they are either discarded or forgotten about. Communications between machines using TCP are much more complicated and resemble a true conversation. This is where the flags kept in the TCP header (remember these from Chapter 5) also come into use.

Six Little Flags, One Great Adventure

TCP's header contains six fields that are just 1 bit each in length. You can't put much into a single bit; that bit is either on (as indicated with a value of 1) or it's turned off (as indicated with a value of 0). If you were limited to just one-word answers, such as Yes or No, you would have to ask your questions carefully! However, if you were limited to one-word answers and a total of just six questions, your life would be simple!

With TCP, that's exactly the case. It's a complex and robust protocol but you can boil down its operation to just six different questions—each of which is answered with the computer equivalent of a Yes or No. The source and destination machines aren't so much asking questions as they are indicating whether a certain condition exists. If it exists, you wave that flag. If it doesn't exist, you don't wave the flag.

To refresh your memory, the six TCP flags are as follows:

- URG or Urgent

- SYN or Synchronize

- ACK or Acknowledge

- RST or Reset

- PSH or Push

- FIN or Finished Conversation

These six flags are more than enough to enable a source and destination machine to communicate and coordinate their activities. That might not be readily apparent, but it's true! More to the point, these six flags work just as well for you in a verbal conversation as they do in a TCP/IP communications session. Both forms of conversation feature all the same attributes and impose the same type of requirements on both parties.

You walk through both types of conversation and see the similarities in the following sections. In this way, you can better appreciate the different aspects of a conversation, requirements or expectations for communication in that conversation, and some simple tools for facilitating the session. Using the analogy of a human conversation will help you better appreciate the significance of the TCP header's six flags. Take a minute to revisit the names of those six flags and look for where they would come in handy during your verbal conversation. Then rerun that conversation using a different scenario: two computers using TCP/IP.

Communicating in a Crowd

Here's the scene: You are at a ballpark watching a baseball game and get the urge for some liquid refreshment. Initiating a conversation in a crowd can be a daunting affair—especially if you don't know the person you want to converse with! You aren't completely helpless, though. Fortunately, the stadium's management has anticipated your needs and deployed an army of people who walk up and down the aisles yelling "Beer here!" Depending on what wares they are vending, they might opt for a slight variation on that chant. Either way, you get the picture.

The next piece of good news is that chances are both you and the beer industry's answer to Gunga Din speak at least part of the same language. Assuming you've both been to a ballgame before, you both are familiar with the informal protocol that exists for buying beverages from the discomfort of your seat.

Generally speaking, your conversation might undergo three main stages:

1. Initiating the conversation, which includes receiving an acknowledgment that you have, indeed, caught that person's attention and that the conversation can begin

2. Conversing with another person

3. Signaling that the conversation is over

Although this list isn't comprehensive, it does give you a nice overview of the different stages that you can experience during a real-life conversation. During a real conversation, things don't always go as planned. You might contend with outside factors that directly but temporarily impede your ability to converse. Such conditions mean a conversation might experience a couple other minor stages:

- Informally negotiating the pace at which you two can communicate and the sophistication level of each other's vocabulary. Big words don't always impress!

- Occasionally repeating yourself if the noise of the crowd drowns out your words. (Gunga will likely look at you funny or say something clever such as "What?" to indicate the failure of your previous transmission.)

- Pausing the conversation to tend to immediate needs that might arise.

- Restarting the conversation at or around where you left off before you were interrupted.

Take a closer look at these stages. Later sections translate them into TCP/IP for you.

Start It Up!

Your first challenge in your quest to procure liquid refreshment is to actually get Gunga's attention! The good news is that he's a highly trained professional and instinctively recognizes a thirsty fan. That's a good thing because, at least initially, you don't know his name and he doesn't know yours! You might well get to be best friends by the 7th inning, but at first you are just another part of the sea of humanity. Plus, he's got quite a bit of territory to cover and doesn't have the time or patience to go seat to seat asking each individual whether he is thirsty. He merely makes himself available and responds to requests.

The burden is, therefore, on you to initiate the conversation. You can do that in a multitude of ways such as yelling at him, raising your hand, catching his eye and nodding your head, or even just walking up to him. Regardless, you are the one who must start the conversation. When you think about it, that's not much different from the way that your favorite Internet website works! Unless your computer is infected with a virus or spyware, you are the one that must start the communications session using TCP/IP to your favorite website. The website makes itself available via the Internet, and waits for your request to start communicating.

A Little Acknowledgment?

It's not enough to think you have established contact with Gunga; you need to be sure! The only way to be sure is if you can get him to acknowledge your presence and your request. This is easy if you chose to just walk right up to him, but that's not always possible. What would happen if you tried to signal him? You'd have to do something to stand out from the crowd and get his attention. More importantly, you would need some confirmation that your request to initiate a conversation has been received and accepted. Only then can you move on to the conversation itself.

The same basic pattern holds true for TCP. Reliable communications require the source and destination machines to synchronize their activities and to acknowledge that they are communicating properly.

Let's Talk

After you've gotten Gunga's attention, you carefully assess the situation to make sure you are communicating effectively. That means figuring out the following:

- How loudly to speak

- How quickly to speak

- Choosing your words carefully so you're not insulting the man before completing the transaction

In a real conversation with a stranger, much of this happens automatically. You negotiate these finer points without even realizing that you are doing it. This type of negotiation is critical if the two of you are to communicate effectively. In a real TCP/IP communications session, you don't need to worry about many of the subtle points of human communications, but there are some direct analogies. For example, TCP/IP contains mechanisms to regulate the speed of communications. That's important because sometimes a network gets busy and attempts to talk quickly will only fail.

What Did You Say?

Trying to hold a conversation in a crowded ballpark is a lot like trying to access a website on the Internet via a low-grade connection. You have to contend with a lot of noise and will likely have to often repeat yourself to compensate for the poor connection between yourself and your conversation partner.

The two keys to successfully repeating yourself are when to repeat yourself as well as what to repeat. Unless you are a psychic and can read other people's minds, this absolutely requires some interaction with your conversation partner. Most often in this setting you will be told explicitly to repeat yourself via a gruff "What?"

Of course, there's a subtle trap lying in wait in this scenario. What if the request to repeat also gets lost? In such cases, you can infer the need to repeat based on the lack of a response. Gunga hasn't explicitly asked you to repeat yourself, but it's not too tough to tell when someone you are talking to has completely missed what you said. This is equally true in a TCP/IP communications session. The key in both scenarios is to keep track of what you said and how much of that has been acknowledged. TCP allows you to track a session's progress using sequence numbers.

Deal With This: Now!

Sometimes, but not always, something happens that requires your immediate attention. Regardless of how important your conversation with Gunga, you might have to drop it without much warning and pay attention to a more pressing priority.

170   Chapter 8: Guaranteed Delivery: Your Package Will Get Delivered...Eventually!

For example, you have several important things to communicate while negotiating the purchase of your beer: what brand and variety you would like and whether Gunga actually carries that particular brew.

However, during the course of this communications session a foul ball might be hit right at you. As important as your conversation with Gunga is, the news of an impending impact would have to take priority! For example, if someone yells "Duck!" you should probably forget about whatever you and Gunga were discussing to process and act upon this new task immediately. In TCP/IP, the equivalent of that yell is known as an *urgent packet* and qualifies for priority handling.

Where Was I?

After so close a call, you might have temporarily forgotten what you were doing before your emergency self-preservation tactics. Perhaps you put up your mitt and caught the ball, in which case you are now preoccupied with showing off your trophy and hamming it up for the camera crew. Perhaps you merely hid behind your significant other in which case it's now more urgent than ever that you return your focus to your transaction with Gunga.

For the purposes of your conversation with Gunga, how you reacted doesn't matter. What does matter is that the sudden surge of adrenaline and excitement derailed your train of thought. Fortunately, Gunga is still there, waiting to complete the transaction. You can count on him to refresh your memory and facilitate getting the conversation back on track.

The same thing is true with computers that communicate using TCP/IP. You would have lost your session and would need to reestablish it using the Reset or RST flag.

Later!

Eventually all things must come to an end. So, too, must your interaction with Gunga. You might be his most important customer, but you're not his only one. He's probably got thousands of other potentially thirsty customers to satisfy. You and Gunga needn't stand on ceremony or exchange heartfelt hugs of thanks before parting ways, but you do need to convey to each other that both the conversation and transaction are over.

From Gunga's perspective, he's now free to look for other customers to satisfy. From your perspective, you can now get back to the game or merely drown your embarrassment at having clanked that foul ball.

TCP/IP communications sessions, too, must end gracefully. A specific sequence of events allows both the source and destination machines to agree that the session is over.

Recapping the Conversation

This example of an attempt to buy a beer at a ballgame is more than just page filler. It demonstrates all a conversation's stages—major and minor—and strongly resembles a real Internet-based communications session. To briefly recap

1. You found a way to signal to the seller that you needed his services.

2. The seller acknowledged your request to start a conversation.

3. The two of you quickly established the appropriate volume, speed, and vocabulary that would enable you to complete the transaction.

4. The two of you carried out the conversation in which you communicated all your needs to the seller and he responded by providing both confirmation that he received and understood your request, as well as any additional information you might have requested (such as confirming the brands, prices, and so on).

The sample conversation also included error conditions:

- You realized you needed to repeat yourself when the din (pardon the double entendre) of the crowd drowned you out.

- The foul ball caused you to lose track of what you were doing. In fairness, that was a much higher priority and demanded immediate attention, which is why both the rules of etiquette and TCP/IP allow for putting a conversation back on track after so justifiable a distraction.

Now that you are much more familiar with the official parts of a conversation, as well as some of the more common error conditions that could disrupt a conversation, it's time to look a bit more closely at those six little TCP/IP flags and how they are used in a real communications session. Hopefully, you immediately recognize and appreciate the similarities between your conversation with Gunga and the communications session.

Communicating in a Network

The many similarities between communicating in a crowd and communicating in a network are quite startling. The critical parts of a conversation described for you earlier in this chapter are universally required, and that holds true for people talking in a stadium as well as computers talking across a network.

Here's the scenario. Instead of you trying to purchase a beer from a vendor at a ballgame, assume you are purchasing a case of beer directly from the microbrewery via the Internet. Thus, instead of dealing with Gunga the person, you are dealing with an Internet website, which serves a similar purpose for a different audience. The conversation's various stages remain remarkably constant as you make the transition from a live conversation to a TCP/IP communications session.

Getting Started

Your challenge for starting a conversation remains: How do you get the attention of a server that sits on the Internet? By now you should already recognize the futility of trying to guess its IP address. The odds are roughly 4,000,000,000 to 1 against you! Fortunately for you, the Internet Engineering Task Force (IETF) and many other Internet entrepreneurs have anticipated your needs and deployed a wide array of tools for your use.

If you know the name of the microbrewery's website, you could simply enter that in your browser. Or you can search for the name of that company or its products in any one of the countless Internet search engines. That will help you find the server you are seeking, but you still need to get its attention.

Three-Way Handshake

As with Gunga in the stadium, you must also know that you've caught the server's attention rather than simply assume that you have it. This requires an acknowledgment from that distant server. Although that much tracks neatly with your personal conversation, there is an added twist: TCP is a reliable protocol and reliable delivery means confirmation of delivery. Thus, it's not quite enough that you have received an acknowledgment from the microbrewery's website server; you must also acknowledge your receipt of its acknowledgment! That probably sounds a bit complicated, but it is how TCP can guarantee reliable delivery.

That three-part process is how every TCP/IP session begins. In fact, it's known as the ***three-way handshake***. To make this a bit more real, get back to those six flags mentioned earlier. The first step in establishing a communications session using TCP/IP is for you to send out a single packet of data to your intended destination.

That packet bears no application data but instead conveys two critical pieces of information in just the header fields:

- **The pattern of flag bits.** One of the six little flags has been set to 1. That flag is SYN. All the other flags are still set to 0. The pattern of bits in the flags section of the TCP header would look like 000010 because the SYN flag is the fifth of the six.

- **A new serial or sequence number from your computer.** To help you better appreciate the significance and purpose of the sequence number, assume you just sent sequence number 618. Figure 8-1 shows your computer trying to establish a communications session with the microbrewery's server.

Figure 8-1   Step 1 of 3: Your Computer Sends a SYNC Request

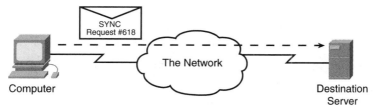

The server's reply would contain two critical pieces of information: that server's sequence number (assume that this number is 916) and both the SYN and ACK flags would be set. The pattern of bits in this response or acknowledgment packet would be 010010. This is shown in Figure 8-2.

Packets that have both the SYN and ACK flags set are known as *SYN-ACK packets*.

Figure 8-2   Step 2 of 3: Your Request Is Acknowledged

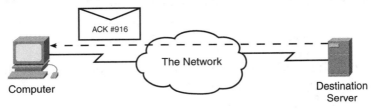

The last piece of the three-way handshake would be for you (or your computer, more precisely) to acknowledge the acknowledgment. Your acknowledgment would be similar to those just shown; it would feature the same two critical pieces of information—sequence number and flags.

The sequence number used would be one digit greater than was used in the original SYN packet. Therefore, if your computer originally generated the SYN packet with a TCP sequence number of 618, this ACK would bear sequence number 619. Each subsequent packet generated in this session between you and the microbrewery would increment the sequence number by 1.

The actual bit pattern in the TCP header's flag field, however, would be different than those you've just seen. That's logical when you consider that this is the third part of the three-way handshake. The pattern of flags in this acknowledgment is 010000. If you reflect back on the structure of the flags field shown earlier in this chapter, you see that the only flag actually set is the ACK or Acknowledge flag. This is illustrated in Figure 8-3.

Figure 8-3   Step 3 of 3: Your Computer Acknowledges the Acknowledgment

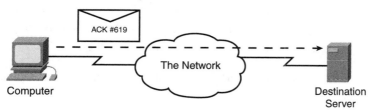

The next part of the conversation features the exchange of information. Even if you're having a conversation with the chattiest person in the world, that person will occasionally pause long enough for you to acknowledge the influx of information…or maybe just prove you are still awake! That confirmation is known as an *acknowledgment*. Acknowledgments are a critical component of a TCP/IP session.

Keeping Track of Things

The TCP sequence numbers do far more than just complicate the establishment of a communications session. They are the mechanism that enables reliable delivery to be reliable. They keep track of data both transmitted and received in a communications session. The sequence numbers don't have to match each other, but each computer needs to track the sequence numbers that it generates and the sequence numbers of incoming packets.

The terminology that describes the chunks of data created by TCP/IP can be confusing and is often misused. The three key terms you need to know are segment, packet, and datagram.

TCP chops up data received from applications into more manageable chunks. Each chunk is known as a *segment*. TCP prepends each segment with a header and hands it off to IP for further processing. Thus, a segment can refer to either a raw chunk of

data or a chunk of data prepended with a TCP header. IP, of course, puts its own header in front of that data segment. That mechanism is known as a *packet*.

A *datagram* is a single unacknowledged packet of information sent over a network as an individual packet without regard to previous or subsequent packets. This definition can apply to packets bearing both TCP and UDP, but the phrase *unacknowledged* implies UDP only. For that reason, UDP packets are often referred to as datagrams, while TCP packets are called segments.

Because IP encapsulates both UDP and TCP, a packet can contain both segments and datagrams.

Keeping track of both sets of sequence numbers forms the basis of reliable delivery. By using a process of elimination, a computer can figure out if it is missing pieces of data that it should have already received. To continue with the previous example, your computer had used sequence numbers 618 and 619 to establish a communications session with the microbrewery's website. That destination computer had started with sequence number 916. Thus, your next TCP packet in this session will be numbered 620 and the next packet you receive from the website should be numbered 917.

Notice that says *should be*. There's no guarantee that the next packet you receive will actually be sequence number 917. You might never receive it if, for example, that packet timed out or was damaged in transit. However, you will notice it's missing when you receive a TCP packet from that same computer bearing the TCP sequence number 918 or higher. By keeping track of which packets have been received, it is possible to deduce which packets have *not* been received.

Your computer indirectly communicates the news about packets not received. Rather than send out the alarm and specifically request a new copy of whatever data was stamped with TCP sequence number 917, your computer acts a bit more discretely. It simply doesn't acknowledge sequence number 917 as having been received. That puts the onus back on the other computer to recognize that 916 has been acknowledged (as has 918, 919) but that 917 must be presumed missing. Consequently, a new copy of it is generated and re-sent. That's what reliable delivery is all about!

Finding Common Ground

One of the more minor aspects of a conversation is gearing your words and rate of speech toward your audience. You need to find a common ground or else the conversation just won't be productive. In human beings, this is almost a subconscious skill. It is ever-present in conversations, particularly when you are talking with people you don't know. You need to figure out how sophisticated that person is, how extensive her vocabulary might be, and even how quickly she speaks. All this useful information helps you tailor your speaking to your audience. Failing to do this risks alienating the person you are trying to converse with and even prematurely ending the conversation.

Computers that speak TCP are no different. It's safe to assume that both computers speak exactly the same language, so there's no worry about vocabulary. However, potential discrepancies lie in the hardware. Using the example of accessing a website across the Internet nicely demonstrates the potential for a hardware mismatch.

You might still be limping along on a Pentium III class machine at home. It has plenty of life left in it, but it's hardly a match for an enterprise-class server such as the one the microbrewery uses. That's perfectly logical. You are just using your computer to surf, e-mail, and chat, but the microbrewery's server is critical to its mission.

If that machine fails, sales stop! So it is perfectly logical for that enterprise to spend a lot more on their computing hardware than you do. Plus, there is a whole lot of networking equipment that makes up the physical path between your PC and that server on the Internet. Each of those devices (known more properly as *routers*) can vary widely in their abilities. Thus, it is imperative that TCP enable two computers to find some common ground as they try to establish a communications session.

The common ground as far as TCP is concerned focuses on how much data the two machines can handle and negotiating a pace that works for both machines. Although that might seem like just one thing, it really has two sides:

- How many TCP segments can be sent without requiring an acknowledgment of receipt from the other machine

- How much data each segment can contain

How Much Can You Handle?

Determining how quickly each machine in a TCP communications session can talk is a prerequisite to a good session. If one machine is much more powerful than the other, it would be easy to overload that smaller, less capable machine. TCP evens out these possible disparities by making sure that both machines agree to a maximum amount of data sent without acknowledgment. This mechanism is known as the TCP window size.

The *TCP window size* identifies the amount of data that can be sent without first getting an acknowledgment. This limit is tracked in terms of octets. An *octet* is 8 bits of data, which is usually the same size as 1 byte of data. Therefore, a window size of 1024 allows you to send 1,024 octets or bytes without receiving an acknowledgment.

Although this is cast as a mechanism to even out differences in computing platforms, this capability has several uses:

- Fine-tuning an application's performance by manipulating the amount of data it can send unacknowledged. When a network is not being heavily used, you can send larger quantities of data. When a network is busy, it has less capacity available for your communications session. Consequently, it is important for a source and destination machine to establish the rate at which they can communicate through a network.

- Reacting to changes in the health of a network. If, for example, the network is suffering severe congestion, reducing the TCP window size can help relieve that congestion by throttling back the amount of data that any given computer sends.

It's important to note that, unlike all other TCP attributes shown throughout this chapter, TCP window sizing isn't set per application or per packet. It is more a computer-level attribute. Thus, when establishing a window size, you are establishing it for all applications on that computer that rely on TCP/IP to communicate.

The term *sliding window* refers to a dynamic approach to controlling *TCP window size*. Rather than hard code the window size, it makes sense to allow TCP to figure out the right window size based on network performance. In other words, the window's actual size can slide up or down in response to changes in the network's state.

How Much Do You Want?

The second aspect of a negotiated data transmission pace is the one more directly useful in negotiating the setup of a communications session. This one is actually an option that can be set in each TCP header and it conveys the maximum size that a segment can be. That limitation, known as ***maximum segment size***, is usually set to the largest possible value by default, but can be modified to fine-tune network performance for a specific application. The TCP header's maximum segment size field tells the destination machine exactly how large a TCP segment it can accept. This value is specified in bytes.

It's important to recognize the relationship between maximum segment size and window size. Any given machine limits the amount of memory available on its network interface card (NIC). The NIC connects a computer to a network. The amount of memory available on that card is what TCP uses to process incoming and outgoing data. Multiplying the number of segments that can be sent unacknowledged by the maximum size of each segment enables you to quickly calculate how much memory you need.

For now, that's all you need to know about negotiating the pace of a communications session, so let's get back to those flags. You still have three left to explore!

Push It Along

Truth be told, some applications just don't tolerate delays well—even those that require guaranteed delivery! For example, you might be using online chat or Instant Messenger software. Those packages work a lot like the old terminal emulation software. In the halcyon days of computing, before Microsoft turned computing into a drag-and-drop video game, you would use a *command-line interface* (CLI) to log onto and use computers.

The CLI would not be data intensive; you would literally type a character and see it appear on the command line. If you were to type with any kind of confidence, it

was imperative that your keystrokes get displayed on the screen promptly! That was the original motivation for TCP's third of the six flags, known properly as the PSH or Push flag. The point is that TCP provides a mechanism for your applications to use when they require a higher priority processing. Packets received with the PSH flag set are processed immediately. Up to now, a simple rule differentiated between TCP and UDP. Applications that require timely delivery use UDP, and applications that require guaranteed delivery use TCP. At first glance, those appear to be almost mutually exclusive goals. They are clearly different enough to warrant the use of different tools (i.e., TCP and UDP), but they really aren't mutually exclusive. There are applications that require both! Applications that operate much like the old command-line interface include text-based communications software such as Instant Messaging (IM) or Internet chat. For such applications, the only real choice is to use TCP and wave the PSH flag.

Packets that have the Push flag set (it's the third of the six bits, so the flag pattern in a Push packet is 001000) require a receiving machine to give it *priority handling*. A machine receiving a Push packet would immediately process and hand it off to the appropriate application, such as chat or IM.

Under normal circumstances, TCP would prefer to hang onto the received data for reassembly with other received data into a larger structure such as a complete file. Hanging onto a packet that contains just a few characters could cause problems for the user of time-sensitive applications such as IM, so the Push flag signals that TCP should immediately pass it on.

 Just like the URG flag, packets marked with the PSH flag actually carry application data. The flag itself is designed to achieve special treatment of an application's data. That makes PSH and URG the only two of TCP's flags to be used inside a packet that also bears user application data (as opposed to an empty packet). Empty packets are used by TCP to coordinate activities between a source and destination machine.

The Do-Over

It's not just children who require a do-over when something goes wrong—TCP does, too! Of course, it's not called a do-over. That wouldn't be professional. Instead, two mechanisms are used when something goes awry in a TCP communications session. These two mechanisms provide the following:

- The ability to retransmit an individual packet if it should time out before reaching its destination

- The ability to reset the session if communications are lost between the source and destination machines

TCP/IP automatically does many things for you when you start a communications session. One of those things is track the time it takes to send a packet to a remote destination and to receive a response. That amount of time is known as *round trip time (RTT)*.

TCP adds a small amount of time to RTT to develop a threshold within which it can safely assume that all acknowledgments will have been received. TCP uses sequence numbers to keep a running tally of packets sent and packets acknowledged. Packets that were sent but not acknowledged within the RTT threshold are considered lost, and must be retransmitted. Packets transmitted but not acknowledged within the RTT are said to have *timed out*.

Remember that the only way a source machine can possibly know that any given packet was actually received is through the receipt of an acknowledgment. It's possible for an acknowledgment packet to have gotten lost in transit even though the packet was, in fact, received.

There is no practical way to distinguish between packets sent/received/ unacknowledged and packets that were sent but not received or acknowledged. Thus, a simplifying assumption is that any packets sent but not acknowledged within a reasonable amount of time are assumed to have been lost in transit and must be re-sent.

Recovering from a lost or defunct connection is a bit different from simply retransmitting a timed-out packet. For one thing, the entire session is at stake rather than just one piece of data. Another thing to remember is that resetting a session requires the use of one of the six TCP header flags. That flag, RST, is the fourth of the six in that header field.

A variety of error conditions can cause a host to reject a session, and an empty RST packet is sent to convey the news of that nameless error. From the other machine's perspective, it doesn't really matter what went wrong; all that's really important is that the session has been terminated and a new one must be negotiated. That means that if the communications between hosts are to continue, a new session must be negotiated via the three-way handshake.

The RST flag might also be used as part of the three-way handshake to reject a request to start a session. For example, instead of replying to an SYN request, a computer can respond with RST. When that happens, the request to establish a connection is rejected.

Stick a Fork in It: It's Done

Lastly, even the best and most enjoyable of conversations must come to an end eventually. When that happens, it's customary to signal to your conversation partner that you're done talking. It doesn't matter how you actually end the conversation, just so long as you signal that you're done talking. So, too, must TCP/IP gracefully conclude its communications sessions. This is done through the use of a Finish packet.

When an application's job is done, either the user logs out of the application or the task of pushing data to a remote computer reaches completion. Either way, the application will tell TCP that it's done. This is TCP's cue to shut down the session. It does so by generating another empty packet (one that contains no application data). This empty packet lets the destination machine know the session is over via the flags.

The last of the six flag bits is known as the FIN or Finish flag. That empty packet bears the flag bit pattern of 000001 and is known as a ***Finish*** or ***FIN packet***. That destination machine must acknowledge that it has received this packet. The response packet, however, is quite special. Its flags are set so that both the FIN and ACK flags are on. This acknowledgment packet's actual flag bit pattern is 010001. That packet is consequently known as a ***Finish-Acknowledgment*** or ***FIN-ACK packet***.

Wait, we're not done yet! The source machine (the one that generated the first FIN packet) must acknowledge this acknowledgment packet. That acknowledgment has to have both the ACK and FIN flags set, too. Only after this pair of Finish-Acknowledgment packets is exchanged can the session be shut down.

In the example you just walked through, there is a subtle but important point that bears further scrutiny: The concept of source and destination machine becomes murky after a conversation has begun! After all, in a true conversation both parties talk and listen. Thus, you could make a convincing argument that both machines engaged in a TCP/IP communications session take turns being the source and destination machines. That is even supported by how the source and destination fields in each TCP/IP packet are used. Each machine that sends out a packet regards itself as the source and the machine it is communicating with as the destination.

With that in mind, it's easy to find an abundance of technical literature that generalizes this source and destination relationship. To many people, the source machine is always the one that started the conversation (that is, the machine that sent the initial SYN packet). Please recognize that the concept of source and destination machines will vary based on who you are talking with and whether you are speaking specifically about packets in a communications session or generally about the communications session itself.

Multitasking with TCP

Now that you've seen how TCP communicates and coordinates activities between a sending and a receiving machine, it's time to turn your attention to a critical but invisible function of TCP. Chapter 4, "TCP/IP: The Networking Protocol That Changed the World," shows you TCP's header structure. The first two fields in the TCP header are the source and destination port address fields. These fields constitute another mechanism for keeping TCP activities coordinated, although they really don't manage the session itself. These mechanisms are used a little later in the process.

TCP is responsible for supporting the needs of a potentially unlimited number of application software packages. They all rely on TCP and might even do so simultaneously. Think about this: When you fire up your home computer, do you really only do one thing at a time? Chances are that you don't. Chances are that you multitask. You probably open up e-mail, check to see which of your IM buddies is online, and then fire up at least one browser window (maybe four or five) so you can stay busy and bounce between your networked applications. You need your communications protocol to keep up with you!

It's easy for you to track the types of communications programs you are using. After all, they are all using a different window on your desktop and probably have a different user interface. There's little chance you will confuse your browser with your IM activities. For TCP, the challenge is quite a bit more daunting. Each application you use represents a different communications session, but all those sessions use the same protocol (TCP) and the same packet structure! How does TCP keep it all straight? With port numbers, of course!

Port numbers function as an address for your applications. If you recall from Chapter 4, TCP's header includes two 16-bit fields in each TCP segment. These fields explicitly communicate the application address—the port numbers—that the computers are using on each side of the communications session. Having walked you through the binary mathematics of the IP address space in Chapter 6, "Pushing the Envelope," you might remember that 16 bits enables 2^{16} power of unique combinations of 1s and 0s. That means that you can have 65,536 different TCP port numbers!

It isn't necessary for you to know all the port numbers in use. Just realize that most of the more common or popular applications have a port number reserved specifically for them. These are known as ***well-known port numbers***. Port numbers enable TCP to forward packets received to the appropriate application every time.

Figure 8-4 shows you how TCP uses port numbers to forward incoming segments to the correct application.

Figure 8-4   TCP Port Numbers at Work

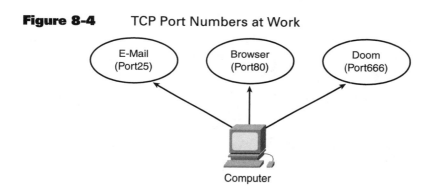

In essence, TCP serves multiple applications at the same time. It knows each application by a 16-bit numeric address. TCP then examines each packet it receives and looks at that same 16-bit numeric destination port address. It decides to which application it should send the data based on that address.

When you run multiple copies of the same application, such as two browser windows, just looking at the destination port address won't be enough; they will both likely be using the same destination port number. Using that same destination port number ensures that the receiving machine knows to which application to send incoming packets, but what about that source machine? How will it track the replies it receives from its two different browser sessions?

The answer is surprisingly simple. TCP uses an internal address known as a ***socket*** to differentiate between the various communications. TCP will use a different source port number for the second and each additional instance of an application

that you might open. The unique combination of your computer's host address plus the TCP source port number is a socket. A socket allows inbound packets to be forwarded to the correct application and session. That's how you can have multiple browser windows open at the same time and keep separate sessions.

Chapter Summary

TCP is a wonderfully feature-rich communications protocol. It needn't be so complex as to defy comprehension. Indeed, the way it operates is much like a normal conversation between two humans. This chapter shows you the key stages of a conversation as well as how people handle unusual situations that might pop up in the midst of a conversation. That analogy helps you more vividly appreciate how TCP works in a typical communications session.

Chapter 9, "Best-Effort Delivery: It's Now or Never," shows you how UDP works.

Chapter Review Questions

The following questions reinforce the key concepts in this chapter:

1. Identify the various stages of a communications session.

2. How does TCP regulate information flow between a source and destination machine?

3. What is a three-way handshake and what is its purpose?

4. What are the three uses for TCP sequence numbers?

5. What is a session?

6. How does a source computer tell a destination computer that the session is over?

7. What are the four special types of TCP packets that do *not* carry any application data?

8. What is a datagram?

What You Will Learn

After reading this chapter, you should be able to answer the following questions:

- ✔ Which of the seven layers in the OSI reference model does UDP occupy?

- ✔ What is the relationship between TCP and UDP?

- ✔ What is meant by the term *best effort*?

- ✔ What is meant by the term *connectionless*?

- ✔ What is the difference between TCP port numbers and UDP port numbers?

- ✔ What are the functions performed by UDP on a source machine?

- ✔ What are the functions performed by UDP on a destination machine?

Best-Effort Delivery: It's Now or Never!

If TCP guarantees that IP packets get delivered safely to their destination, why on earth would you ever need an inferior alternative? The answer lies in exploring the myth that every packet must be delivered. Different applications have different performance requirements. Traditional applications such as online transaction processing, batch updates, or file transfers absolutely require a guaranteed delivery of data. As you saw in the preceding chapter, that sometimes requires some packets to be retransmitted so that you can be assured of their successful delivery.

Other types of applications have radically different network performance requirements. You see, the time required to perform reliable delivery can be quite detrimental to other types of applications. Timeliness is everything for some applications. Quite literally, data arriving late is worthless! That might seem a bit odd or extreme, but it's true. Applications that have such strong requirements for timeliness of data delivery, such as some voice and video applications, rely on UDP. For those applications, it is truly now or never for incoming packets of data.

After having walked you through some of the complexities and sophisticated features of TCP last chapter, you will likely find UDP a refreshing change of pace! This chapter explains what best effort really means and show you how UDP does its best to get data there on time. You see the similarities between TCP and UDP, as well as the many differences.

User Datagram Protocol

The *User Datagram Protocol*, or *UDP*, is another transport layer protocol suite in TCP/IP. You can think of UDP as the unsung hero of TCP/IP. TCP gets all the recognition—it even gets top billing in the protocol suite's name! UDP is a wonderful complement to TCP.

Figure 9-1 shows an overview of the architecture so you can see that TCP and UDP are truly peers. Between them, there's seemingly nothing they can't handle.

Figure 9-1   TCP and UDP Are Functional Peers

TCP/IP Reference Model		OSI Reference Model Layer Description	Layer Number
		Application	7
		Presentation	6
		Session	5
TCP	UDP	Transport	4
IP		Network	3
		Data Link	2
		Physical	1

Functionally speaking, TCP and UDP are truly peers. Both occupy Layer 4 of the OSI reference model and both serve as an intermediary between applications that need to communicate with the Internet Protocol (IP). In other words, UDP accepts data from application software packages and prepares it for handoff to IP. It forms the middle ground between an application that requires network communications and the networking protocol (IP, in this book).

As you see throughout this chapter, both perform their intermediary role using similar tools. UDP just has a lot fewer tools to work with! That simplicity is not a design flaw; it's a design feature. UDP was specifically designed to provide your applications with a type of delivery service that is known as *best effort*.

What Do You Mean, Best Effort?

To some people, giving their best effort means trying as hard as they can until they succeed. Anything less than success isn't their best! UDP, however, doesn't quite work that way. You can take that a step further and wonder how best effort can mean anything but a guarantee of delivery. In other words, having seen the effort that TCP expends to guarantee delivery of data, how can anything less be considered a best effort? Before you can appreciate the solution to that conundrum, you must accept that sometimes less truly is more!

The phrase takes on a completely different connotation in UDP/IP communications. There are no guarantees or complicated mechanisms needed to fulfill any guarantees. UDP's *best effort* is to make one attempt at delivering the data. That's a simple and straightforward goal, so it shouldn't be any surprise that UDP is every bit as simple and straightforward.

Built for Speed

After you see how UDP works, it should be fairly apparent that UDP was built for one purpose: speed! Thus, best effort from UDP's perspective is to make one attempt at delivering application data *as quickly as possible*.

The benefit of a quick delivery mechanism might not be readily apparent. Time is the enemy of some applications. Think back to the last time you made an international telephone call. You probably noticed a slight delay that made conversation a little awkward. That delay is known as *latency*.

In simple terms, latency is the amount of time it takes for a piece of data, such as a TCP or UDP datagram, to pass through a networked device. That device could be the PC transmitting the datagram, a switch in the local-area network (LAN) to which the PC connects, or any one of the seemingly infinite number of routers that make up the Internet. Typically, latency for any given physical device is small, is measured in thousandths of a second, and is referred to in *milliseconds* (ms).

Another component of latency is the amount of time it takes for a piece of data (such as a datagram) to pass through one of the many pipes or transmission facilities. These pipes are the wires that physically connect the Internet together. In theoretical terms, the speed of light (186,000 miles per second) should form the basis for determining how much time it will take for your data to travel over any given pipe in the Internet. Unfortunately, you still don't live in a world of optical computers: You can transmit using light over fiber-optic cables, but all computers and devices at the ends of fiber-optic cables are still electrical. Those devices all form a bottleneck that keeps the speed of light an elusive target.

In practical terms then, the amount of time it takes for your data to travel over a piece of wire is still more closely related to how quickly an electrical current can travel that distance. Fast, but not as fast as light! This amount of time is known as *propagation delay*. Propagation delay measures the theoretical minimum amount of time required for your data to pass through all the network pipes and devices it needs to reach its destination.

Other things, too, can slow down your data. These things are not an innate part of your network (despite what your Internet service provider might tell you!) and, consequently, are known as *delays*. Network conditions such as heavy traffic volumes and the need to retransmit can add greatly to the innate latency of a path between a source and destination machine. Not surprisingly, feature-rich protocols such as TCP can also add quite a bit of time to this process!

Under heavy load conditions is where UDP can really shine. UDP is such a frugal and minimal protocol that it does not add substantially to the total amount of time required to move a packet between a source and destination machine. It will incur a modest amount of time, but not so much that you notice—certainly not when viewed in terms of the latency introduced by the switches and pipes that comprise the physical path between the two machines. Thus, with UDP you have eliminated one potential source of delay. Now all you have to deal with are the congested pipes in your ISP's network!

The Header's Shape

UDP's header is about as concise as any protocol's header can possibly be and still function. It contains just the following fields:

- **Source Application Port Number**—The first 16 bits of the UDP header contain the application port number of the application sending the data.

- **Destination Application Port Number**—The next 16 bits contain the application port number of the application that receives this data.

- **Length**—The next 16 bits identify how long the datagram is in bits.

- **Checksum**—The last 16 bits of the UDP header are reserved for the checksum value. Checksum, if you recall my discussion of this earlier, is an error-detection mechanism. The source machine runs a mathematical algorithm on the datagram. Remember: The contents are inherently binary, so you can run a mathematical algorithm against these Base2 numbers regardless of what they translate into! The destination, or recipient, machine runs the same formula on the datagram. If the results match, you can be reasonably sure that the datagram wasn't damaged en route.

This header gets stuck on the front of application data and that resulting structure becomes known as a ***datagram***. The datagram gets handed off to IP where the IP header gets stuck on it. That structure—datagram plus IP header—is known generically as a ***packet*** and more specifically as an ***IP packet***.

Looking more closely at the UDP header should reveal just how lean this mean machine really is! You have just enough information for the datagram to reach its intended destination application and for UDP on that receiving machine to figure out if the received data is worth passing on.

One could argue that the inclusion of the source application port number is superfluous and could be eliminated. After all, UDP gets used for one-way data dumps! Despite the apparent logic of that claim, UDP can be used for more than just shoveling real-time data in one direction. For those functions, the inclusion of a return address (i.e., the source application port number) is worth the effort.

Yeah, but What's It Good For?

By this point in the chapter, you should have a fairly good appreciation for what UDP does for you. Now it's time to make that appreciation a bit more real. UDP excels at providing a transit service for real-time applications. In practical terms, two broad application categories qualify as real time and need UDP's services. These are voice over IP (VoIP) and streaming video.

It's important to not overgeneralize here. You can't assume that UDP is custom built for delivery of voice and video over networks. Those two, voice and video, are two types of data rather than being two types of applications. Remember: It is the application's network performance requirements that matter, not the data! Just because you know what type of data is being transmitted doesn't mean you know whether you are using UDP or TCP. Let me give a few examples so you can see how fine a line there can be between transport protocol choices.

Video Varieties

Transmitting video across the Internet (or any IP network for that matter) is always an interesting task. A video clip can be generated by at least two different types of applications. For example, one use of video data is downloading a video file from an Internet news site to see what's happening in the world.

Another use is creating and sending video data in real time. For creating and sending video data in real time, the video doesn't live on a hard-disk drive. For example, you might have an IP-based camera installed in your home for security purposes. That would enable you to keep an eye on your home no matter where you go. Of course, that's a proverbial double-edged sword: If you can keep an eye on your home, everyone else on the Internet can, too!

Those two examples of video over IP allow me to show you the spectrum of possibilities for transporting video files. These two applications might use the same file type. For the sake of argument, assume that both use .mpg files. That's not an unreasonable assumption. It will help demonstrate that you can't tell anything about an application's network performance requirements by looking at the data it uses. In general terms, these two application types can be classified based on whether they create their data in real time.

Real-Time Video

The example of a video camera being used for security surveillance is a good one to demonstrate the implications of real-time video transmission. The camera creates video data but does not necessarily store it anywhere. Instead, that data would be immediately available via the network.

Your video-based security system poses some interesting challenges. This data, even though it uses the exact same file type as your downloaded news video, never lives on a hard drive. Its existence is transient, as is its purpose! You probably don't care what happened to your home five minutes ago (assuming, of course, that nothing actually happened). You are much more interested in what's happening right now. Consequently, if a piece of data failed to arrive on time or were damaged you wouldn't want to waste any time getting it delivered correctly. You would simply want to move on to the next picture.

In other words, you wouldn't want or need any of TCP's features. Using those features might even cause you problems! Losing a video frame because of a network problem might mean that you lost one second's worth of video display. That would show up as a temporary glitch or less-than-smooth transition from one video frame to the next. Not great, but not so bad either.

Using TCP to transport live video images would cause two glitches from the viewer's perspective:

- The first glitch would occur when the frame was expected but failed to arrive. Because the application needs this data in real time, you don't have the luxury of waiting until it is successfully retransmitted. The data also doesn't have to be sequenced because it isn't part of a larger file structure (such as a file or series of files). As quickly as data is received, it gets passed onto the application and promptly displayed for the viewer.

- The second glitch would occur when that tardy piece of data finally arrived and was passed onto the application for display. Clearly, the right solution for real-time applications such as this one is to use UDP. You don't want or need TCP's features, and UDP is built for speed, which is exactly what your application requires.

Not-So-Real-Time Video

One of the biggest problems understanding UDP's role in a TCP/IP network is caused by overgeneralizing. It is common to find people, even knowledgeable people, stating that UDP is always used for voice and video communications. Although UDP does excel at transporting real-time communications (including voice, video, and online gaming), it is not always used. In fact, UDP would only be used for real-time transmissions. Transmissions that aren't quite real time would be better off with TCP as the transport protocol.

That means that how you use data is more important than what that data is when it comes to deciding between TCP and UDP as your transport mechanism. Walk through an example to see. The example is downloading a video clip from an Internet news site. That video clip might someday prove to have lasting value. It might be today's news, but it is tomorrow's history. Thus, you might want to save it for future viewing. Alternately, it might be of passing interest and not worth saving.

When you try to download a video clip from an Internet news site, it is not uncommon to get a pop-up box from your Windows operating system. That pop-up box asks if you want to run the file from its current location (i.e., the remote server's hard-disk drive) or if you would prefer to save it to your own computer for running whenever you like.

This decision point is significant: It's the same video clip regardless of which option you choose. What differs, however, is the transport protocol.

You won't see that spelled out for you, nor should you even care. If you choose to save a downloaded file to your hard disk drive, you are tacitly acknowledging that the file has lasting value. Consequently, you want that video to be complete and perfect. You would first save it to disk and then open and run it in your favorite media player. TCP would probably be the best choice of transport protocols for this purpose.

Because you are saving it to disk first, you have the luxury of time to make sure you get all the data intact. That includes retransmitting any data that was lost or damaged in transit and being able to reassemble all the pieces back into the right sequence. In other words, you need all TCP's capabilities for this communications session.

If, however, you chose to just run it from its current location, you are tacitly acknowledging that the clip is of just passing interest to you. You probably won't be looking at it again and again nor do you want to waste storage space on your own computer. Instead, you are choosing to view it in real time.

This set of circumstances imposes a completely different set of network performance requirements! Even though the file and application are exactly the same, the difference is in how you are using them. This approach more closely resembles the usage characteristics of a real-time video stream even though it is a canned file. The data isn't being created in real time as would be the case with live voice or video communications. However, you will be viewing it in real time. Consequently, UDP is much more appropriate.

Sound Options

Although you have seen how network performance requirements can vary for applications that use the same type of data using video, this comparison is valid for other types of data as well. For example, transmitting sounds over a network presents the exact same set of circumstances. Those sounds can be encoded using .wav file type, but used in different ways. Just like video, you can use a .wav as a file that lives on a hard disk and can be sent around just like any other disk-bound file. Alternately, you can convert the sound into a .wav format and play it live over a network.

The days of college students actually having a telephone (as well as a stereo) in the dorms have come and gone. Today, they are much more likely to just have a laptop and a cell phone. Set up properly, both allow them all the functionality of yesterday's stereo and land-line telephone. More to the point, using a laptop instead of a stereo and a telephone demonstrates the use of both TCP and UDP to move sound files across a network.

A laptop can act like a stereo by playing digitized music. (Hopefully, this digitized music was legally purchased rather than just swapped illegally using peer-to-peer software across the Internet.) Regardless of how you acquired it, the fact is that the songs in your collection are digital files that get stored on your hard disk drive. They have lasting value and you will likely play them time and again. Thus, you want to be sure that they are perfect and complete when you download them. The only way to do that is to use TCP.

A laptop can also act like a telephone and, in the process, enable a frugal college student to evade the historically pricey long-distance charges of phone calls home. Unlike digital songs, telephone conversations transmitted over an IP network are of a fleeting nature. They do not get stored on a hard disk drive. The sounds of your voice get digitized in real time as you utter them and are sent in real time across a network. It makes absolutely no sense to recover a half-second's worth of conversation. You and your conversation partner both noticed the glitch and moved on. For this type of application, UDP is your only choice.

These examples illustrate the differences between UDP and TCP as they relate to applications and their network performance requirements. These examples, however, might not be indicative of the way such applications actually work! The bottom line is that you can't judge an application by the type of data it uses. You must look at the application, what it does, and how it does it before you can start figuring out which transport protocol would be best. Fortunately, application developers solve this problem for you but it never hurts to understand what's going on when you launch your favorite applications.

Sound files also can be played across a network from their source location rather than saved locally. In such cases, you are using the file in a manner that more closely approximates real time and are better off using UDP to handle that download.

It Gets a Little More Complicated

I'll reserve my opinion on the increasingly obfuscated nature of today's software and merely point out that it is a rare software package that only performs one function. Instead, each piece of software tends to have a dizzying array of functions. Each discrete function within a software package has its own network performance requirements to consider. The protocol that is right for one application subfunction probably won't be right for all.

The point is that even though this chapter led you to believe that an application is either designed to work with TCP or UDP, the truth is that it is quite common for an application to use both. The catch is that an application can use both UDP and TCP. It would just use them for different functions.

Up to this point, the book presented a rather sanitized perspective of TCP and UDP. This chapter repeatedly points out how you don't have to worry about selecting a transport layer protocol because your applications do that for you. This chapter also suggests that each application has its own performance requirements and that those requirements guide the choice between TCP and UDP. All that is true enough, but there is one small detail omitted for the sake of clarity.

You see, even though an application automatically selects the right protocol to use doesn't mean it must continue using that one protocol for all its needs! Application software has gotten complex enough that it's hard to think of any one piece of software that only does only one thing. Instead, software today tends to have so many bells and whistles hanging that it is sometimes difficult to see the application itself! This is another one of those dangerous generalizations that can lead you astray: You just can't say that this application uses TCP *or* UDP. The truth is most software applications use both TCP and UDP for different functions.

UDP—In Action!

It's easy to get caught up with the comparison between TCP and UDP. The big trap waiting there is that you can become fixated on all the things that UDP can't do and quickly lose sight of all the things that it can do. Explaining what UDP really does implies a two-part answer: the sending perspective and the receiving perspective.

The View from the Source

Transmitting data using UDP is the essence of simplicity. There's nothing but the absolute minimum number of steps in the process to ensure the fastest possible service for the applications that use UDP. After having seen UDP's header, you already knew that!

Take a closer look at the sequence of events needed for a machine to transmit using UDP. The concept of a layered reference model is then correlated to each step to the layers defined in the OSI reference model. Because UDP is a transport layer protocol, don't be too surprised that most of the activity occurs inside Layer 4 of the model.

Figure 9-2 presents UDP's sequence of events for transmitting data.

Figure 9-2   Layered Sequence of Events for Transmitting with UDP

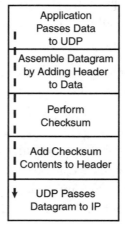

The first step is UDP accepting data from the application.

It uses that data to build a datagram by wrapping a header around it. Unlike TCP, UDP doesn't need to concern itself with segmenting data. The types of applications that use UDP do not pass off large blocks of data. Besides, if you take something apart, you had better be prepared to put it back together again! UDP has no provisions for that, so use of this connectionless, best-effort protocol is limited to applications that don't send large blocks of data at a time or need any other reliable transport protocol features.

The second step is to actually assemble the datagram. To do so requires prepending the UDP header onto the data and populating the header's fields. This includes assigning the source and destination port numbers that function as application addresses.

The last thing UDP does is perform a quick mathematical process on the datagram for quality control purposes. That process creates a ***checksum***. This value gets stored in the UDP checksum field for the recipient.

After that's done, the datagram is handed off to IP for further processing.

The View from the Destination

The other half of the story is what happens on the receiving side. The destination machine, which receives inbound UDP datagrams, has it easy.

On the receiving side of a transmission, UDP's role begins after the LAN delivers a frame of data to a destination machine. That data would have passed through whatever LAN was being used and then processed by IP. IP would have removed its header and then forwarded it to the appropriate transport layer protocol. In this example, that is UDP.

UDP first checks to see if the data contained inside that datagram is the same as it was upon transmission by the source machine. If the data is not exactly the same, it must have been damaged in transit. Determining whether the data inside a UDP packet was damaged is accomplished via the checksum field. UDP performs the same mathematical process as its counterpart protocol did on the source machine and then compares the result it obtained with the value stored in the UDP header's checksum field. If the two values match, you can be reasonably sure that the data is fine and suffered no damage in transit. If the values are different, it can only mean that the data was damaged en route and the entire datagram is simply discarded.

Assuming the datagram's checksum value matched the value calculated by the destination machine, the next step is to strip off the UDP header and hand the data to the appropriate application. That application is determined by examining the UDP port number in the header. Armed with this information, UDP can safely strip off the UDP header and pass on just the enclosed data to the correct application.

That's it! There's no need for reassembling the data into a larger structure or anything else. UDP's job is done. To see this demonstrated that pictorially, please take a look at Figure 9-3. That figure uses a layered model to show you how this works.

Figure 9-3   Layered Approach to Receiving UDP Datagrams

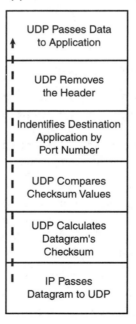

One of the things you might have noticed when reading this section is that there is no complex *three-way handshake* or anything else that would establish a session. Each datagram is dealt with as an individual piece of data. The lack of any mechanism to establish and maintain a session has resulted in UDP often being described as a *connectionless protocol*. It doesn't set up a connection nor does it have the facilities to do so.

UDP Port Numbers

One of the things UDP has in common with TCP is its use of port numbers to keep track of applications. Each application installed on a computer can be identified by a port number. That number works in conjunction with IP addresses to give you the ability to access a specific application on a specific computer.

Both TCP and UDP port numbers follow the same format: They are both 16 bits in length, which means you can have up to 2^{16} power, or 65,536 unique addresses. There is room for some confusion here, though. You must keep in mind that TCP port numbers are different from UDP port numbers even though they look exactly the same. The best way to think about this is that TCP and UDP track their own lists of application port numbers.

You know that TCP and UDP are designed to satisfy different network performance requirements. They satisfy such widely divergent requirements that it would be difficult to imagine one application that could use either TCP or UDP. If each protocol supports different types of applications, why force them to share the same list of port numbers? Doing so would only reduce the number of applications that TCP/IP could support. Instead, each protocol maintains its own list of port numbers correlating to applications.

Having said that, it would be an error to not point out that there is, in fact, quite a bit of overlap between the list of assigned TCP and UDP port numbers! For example, the *hypertext transfer protocol* (better known as http, the protocol on which the Internet's World Wide Web is based) uses TCP port 80. However, http is also assigned UDP port 80.

The same is true for a good many of the well-known port numbers: Regardless of which transport protocol a well-known application might use, it enjoys having the same number reserved on both lists. That might sound inefficient and potentially confusing. After all, if an application or protocol appears on both lists of port numbers, how can you tell which transport (TCP or UDP) it really uses?

Reserving a well-known port number on both lists was intended to help avoid confusion. In practice, applications have been evolving into complex beasts that use both TCP and UDP for different functions. Thus, confusion is avoided by reserving the same number for any given application on both the TCP and UDP lists of reserved port numbers.

Chapter Summary

The User Datagram Protocol, or UDP, is the second transport layer protocol in the TCP/IP protocol suite. It doesn't get the same level of attention as TCP does, but UDP is a wonderfully useful tool that perfectly complements TCP. UDP is ideally suited to providing a streamlined, no-frills transportation for applications that require a timely—not guaranteed—delivery of data.

By including just a minimalist set of functions, UDP effectively trades reliability for speed. That's quite useful for any and all real-time applications such as live voice, video communications, or even online gaming.

UDP isn't a substitute or alternative to TCP: It is a completely different tool designed for a completely different set of functional requirements. TCP/IP needs both TCP and UDP to satisfy all your networking needs.

Chapter Review Questions

The following questions reinforce the key concepts in this chapter.

1. Which of the seven layers in the OSI reference model does UDP occupy?

2. What is the relationship between TCP and UDP?

3. What is meant by the term *best effort*?

4. What is meant by the term *connectionless*?

5. What is the difference between TCP port numbers and UDP port numbers?

6. Identify the functions performed by UDP on a source machine.

7. Identify the functions performed by UDP on a destination machine.

PART III

Network Services: Making Your Network Easy to Use

What You Will Learn

By the end of this chapter, you should be able to answer the following questions:

- ✔ What does the acronym ICMP stand for?

- ✔ Which layer of the OSI reference model does ICMP occupy?

- ✔ What is the purpose of ICMP?

- ✔ Is ICMP useful to end users?

- ✔ What are some of the tools that you can use that rely upon ICMP?

- ✔ What does PING do and why is it useful?

- ✔ Which ICMP message types does PING utilize?

- ✔ What does TRACEROUTE do and why is it useful?

- ✔ Which ICMP message type does TRACEROUTE utilize?

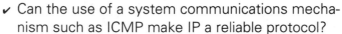

- ✔ Can the use of a system communications mechanism such as ICMP make IP a reliable protocol?

CHAPTER 10

Special Delivery for Special Messages

After having seen that TCP/IP offers two options for data delivery—best effort by UDP and reliable delivery by TCP—you might be wondering what else you could possibly need in a communications protocol! The answer is simple: You still need a mechanism for delivering system messages.

System messages are a bit different than the types of applications discussed in the previous two chapters. Instead of originating at a user machine, *system messages* originate inside the network. User applications let users communicate with each other, share data, run application software, and so on, but system messages let the network devices communicate, coordinate their activities, and actually run the network. The mechanism that transports these special messages is the ***Internet Control Message Protocol (ICMP)***.

ICMP is designed to transport system-level messages between network devices. Generally speaking, ICMP helps disseminate information about error conditions between systems and network devices in an IP network.

In this chapter, you take a look at ICMP, its mechanisms and how they work, and the role that this transport protocol plays in a network. You find that ICMP plays an interesting and critical but behind-the-scenes role in an IP network's normal operation.

ICMP: A Protocol for System Messages

The last architectural component of the TCP/IP protocol suite that you need to know about is ICMP, which is an abbreviation for *Internet Control Message Protocol*. That's a real mouthful! Unfortunately, it's not meaningful or descriptive. Whoever thought up that name surely felt it was perfect, but it is awkward at best and meaningless at worst!

Without casting aspersions on whoever came up with the name, ICMP was first described way back in September 1981. It was published by the *Internet Engineering Task Force (IETF)* in RFC 792. You can still check out the original document at the following URL: http://www.faqs.org/rfcs/rfc792.html.

ICMP rounds out the TCP/IP protocol suite. One could argue that it's redundant given that you have both TCP and UDP, but those protocols are user tools. Okay, you caught me: Those users can't directly use those protocol suites, but they are used directly by applications that users use. ICMP, on the other hand, is designed to carry system-level traffic.

System-level communications, like two routers letting each other know about congestion in the network, are also carried inside IP packets. Those packets are sent from one machine in a network to another but *not* on behalf of a live user. Thus, ICMP lurks in the shadows and remains almost completely transparent to people using IP networks.

In theory, packets that carry a user's data are a higher priority than system packets. Without philosophically exploring whether your online Doom packets are more important than two routers communicating information about a failure in the network, suffice it to say that you will miss the data if it gets dropped. Systems, on the other hand, won't miss a thing. Thus, when a network gets so busy that it can't keep up with all the generated packets, it can easily differentiate between user and system packets by looking at the protocol. If a packet uses either TCP or UDP, it's a user's packet. If a packet is ICMP, it's a system message; the network can lighten its load by dropping every ICMP packet it receives until the conditions on the network improve.

 IP was not designed to be a reliable delivery mechanism. Reliable delivery is only possible when you add the higher-level capabilities of TCP. Thus, it is important to note that the purpose of ICMP messages is *not* to make IP reliable! The ICMP messages, however, allow networked devices to provide feedback to each other about various error conditions in either the network or with specific IP packets.

Because ICMP uses IP, it is inherently unreliable. That means you aren't guaranteed to receive an ICMP message, nor will you ever receive an ICMP message about another ICMP message! ICMP messages are reserved strictly for network error conditions or error conditions within packets bearing user application data.

The Architecture

ICMP is a lightweight protocol that hardly qualifies for its own layer. A common misperception is that it's the third transport layer protocol suite in TCP/IP. If you read the introduction to this chapter carefully, you saw that it came close to calling ICMP a transport layer protocol—but it didn't! After all, IP is the only network layer protocol in the TCP/IP suite and ICMP does use IP packets to operate across a network—but the argument ends there!

In fact, TCP and UDP are the only two transport layer protocols in the TCP/IP suite. ICMP is a lightweight protocol—hardly a suite of protocols unto itself. ICMP is most properly described as being an integral component of IP, although it operates only at the top of IP, which is why it probably feels like a Layer 4 protocol.

Figure 10-1 shows you how ICMP fits in the TCP/IP architecture relative to the OSI reference model.

Figure 10-1   ICMP and the TCP/IP Architecture

TCP/IP Reference Model		OSI Reference Model Layer Description	Layer Number
		Application	7
		Presentation	6
		Session	5
TCP	UDP	Transport	4
ICMP IP		Network	3
		Data Link	2
		Physical	1

Visually, ICMP fits within the boundaries of the IP protocol suite. That's because it is an integral component; one of the IP protocols. It lies toward the top of the IP stack because it is a higher-layer function. That is, its functionality is close to transport protocols instead of network protocols.

Fields and Functions

ICMP uses the basic IP header structure to travel through a network. Much like how a TCP segment of data gets wrapped inside an IP packet, the ICMP message occupies an IP packet's data field. It's not considered part of the header and it is treated the same as TCP and UDP, which helps explain some of the confusion that surrounds ICMP.

The ICMP message contains the following structure:

- **Type Indicator**—The first 8 bits of the ICMP message indicate the ICMP message type. This 8-binary field (bits) yields the ability to identify 2^8, or 256, unique message types. Relax: There aren't that many message types defined and this chapter is limited to a subset of the most useful message types. Each message type is specifically designed to perform a special task. Table 10-1 identifies each of these message types for you.

- **Code Field**—The next 8 bits are called the code field and they enable even more information about this particular ICMP packet and type to be supplied to the receiving node. The use of this field varies based on the ICMP message type. If you really want to know more about code field options, please read RFC 792!

- **Checksum**—The next field is a 16-bit checksum. If you recall from earlier chapters, a *checksum* is a mathematical function that helps ensure that the contents of a datagram don't get changed en route to its destination. If a datagram gets damaged, the result of a common mathematical algorithm will be different for the destination and source machines. This difference tells the recipient, or destination, machine that the packet is damaged and to discard it.

ICMP has many different message types and you are introduced to them. Each message type is designed for a specific purpose and, consequently, has a slightly different structure to suit that purpose. The different structures share a common foundation, which is comprised of the fields just described.

Each message type can contain hundreds more bits of information, but some things vary greatly from message type to message type: the length, how those bits are carved up, and what each field does. For right now, consider these three fields—a whopping 32 bits—the ICMP "header." The rest of the ICMP structure is better thought of as data. The actual functionality of each ICMP message is determined by the message type and the contents of some of its code field.

Types of Messages

As mentioned, ICMP supports the creation of many types of messages. Each message type is designed for a specific purpose. These messages are listed in Table 10-1.

Table 10-1   ICMP Message Types

Message Number	Message Description
0	Echo Reply
3	Destination Unreachable

continues

Table 10-1 ICMP Message Types (continued)

Message Number	Message Description
4	Source Quench
5	Redirect
8	Echo
11	Time Exceeded
12	Parameter Problem
13	Timestamp Request
14	Timestamp Reply

That probably didn't make much sense. Those really are all the types of special-purpose messages that you can create—or that can be created by ICMP. If nothing else, looking at each message type enlightens you as to precisely what ICMP does!

Echo and Echo Reply

Echo and Echo Reply, two interrelated ICMP message types, are extremely useful. Their structures are remarkably similar so it wouldn't make sense to treat them separately. An Echo message contains two addresses: the sending computer's address and the destination machine's IP address.

Echo's purpose is to test whether any given machine is reachable through the network. Of course, this isn't a perfect test because, again, ICMP messages are the first to be dropped whenever a network gets congested. Consequently, testing reachability to any given destination using an ICMP Echo message only gives you an idea of that machine's reachability. It cannot, however, give you an understanding of that machine's status.

The Echo Reply message is virtually identical to the Echo message except that in an Echo Reply message the source and destination IP addresses are reversed. Thus, the Echo message's source IP address becomes the Echo Reply's destination address, and vice versa for the Echo message's destination IP address.

Destination Unreachable

When a destination is unreachable, it might be due to a wide variety of reasons. ICMP's job is to tell the source machine (whose packet failed to reach its intended destination) that it failed and to supply as much information regarding why it failed. To do that, ICMP must have some way of letting the source machine know exactly which of its packets failed. Thus, the failed IP packet's original header and the first 64 bits of the packet are tacked onto the ICMP header and sent back to the source machine.

When a machine in the network determines that a destination is unreachable (usually when trying to forward a packet addressed to that destination), it generates an ICMP Destination Unreachable message. The code field in that message uses its options to identify where the failure occurred. For example, the destination machine could be powered off or the network it is connected to could have suffered a major failure. Alternately, the network and the host could be perfectly fine, but the protocol (as identified by the destination port number in the TCP header) might not be configured.

Communicating the source of the problem is important. For example, if the entire network were unreachable, you want to spread the word broadly so that everybody's network knows about the problem and stops trying to send IP packets to machines within that unreachable network. If, however, the problem were that just one machine was turned off, all the other machines in that network would still be reachable. Thus, you wouldn't want to continue sending IP packets addressed to that network.

The possible code field options are listed in Table 10-2.

Table 10-2   Destination Unreachable Code Values

Code Field Value	Failure Location or Type
0	Network Address Unreachable
1	Host Address Not Responding
2	Protocol Unreachable
3	TCP Port Not Reachable
4	Fragmentation Needed
5	Source Route Failed

Although the code field values in this section are identified in decimal numbers, the actual field in the ICMP header is a binary field. The decimal values are given to make life a little easier.

Networks are remarkably complex and lots of things can go wrong. The code field helps you understand which packet failed to get where it was going and why! After seeing Table 10-2, you should have a fairly good appreciation for how that happens.

Source Quench

Source quench is another classic example of a name that must have made sense to some nerdy bunch of engineers locked inside a conference room for too many consecutive hours. The ICMP Source Quench message requests that the source machine in a TCP/IP communications session slow down.

Sometimes, a router or switch in the network or even a destination computer might become overloaded. That's a bad thing because it means the device will start dropping packets due to its inability to keep up with the incoming packets. Rather than sit back and wait for the inevitable, that troubled machine can start sending out ICMP Source Quench messages that tell sending machines to throttle down their packet transmission.

When (or if) network conditions improve, TCP/IP might allow networked devices to increase the rate of packet transmission. That's a function of TCP, not ICMP— but both protocols must work together to determine the most appropriate rate of transmission. ICMP handles the throttling back via source quench messages while TCP always tries to increase its rate of transfer using its sliding window mechanism.

Redirect

It's better to have something that you probably won't ever need than to need something you probably won't ever have! The redirect message falls into the former category. Under normal operating circumstances you won't need this function. However, things can and do change in a network. When changes occur, packets sometimes get caught midstream! This is where the ICMP Redirect message can come in handy.

To better understand this, a couple of pictures are required. Please take a look at Figure 10-2. This shows a sample internetwork that consists of Networks 10.1.1.0/ 24, 10.1.2.0/24, 10.1.3.0/24, 10.1.4.0/24, and 10.1.5.0/24. Rather than show you a complicated network topology, you see the network engineer's old standby: a cloud! Clouds are commonly used to portray networks from an architectural per- spective.

Figure 10-2   A Router in a Network Accepts an IP Packet

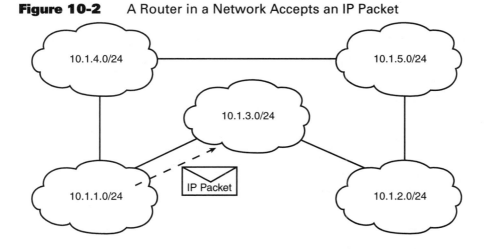

In Figure 10-2, a router inside Network 10.1.3.0/24 accepts a packet that was sent by a computer connected to Network 10.1.1.0/24. This packet is bound for Network 10.1.4.0/24. Unfortunately, Network 10.1.3.0/24 doesn't have a direct connection to that network. To get that packet delivered, it would have to be passed through Networks 10.1.2.0/24 and 10.2.5.0/25 before finally reaching its destination. There's nothing wrong with that.

Quite often when you surf the Internet, your packets pass through 20 or more networks; passing through five should not be a big deal. The real problem is that Network 10.1.3.0/24 doesn't have a direct connection to Network 10.1.4.0/24, but Network 10.1.1.0/24 does! The fact that Network 10.1.1.0/24 has a more direct connection to the destination network but didn't use it indicates that something is wrong. It is likely working with obsolete information as a result of a recent change in the network. Believe it or not, information flows quickly—but not immediately—throughout devices in a network.

In situations like this one, the right thing to do is let Network 10.1.1.0/24 know, "Hey! There's a better way!" with the hope that future packets will take the more efficient path. That "Hey" message is really an ICMP Redirect message. This is shown in Figure 10-3.

Figure 10-3   Network 10.1.3 Sends an ICMP Redirect Message

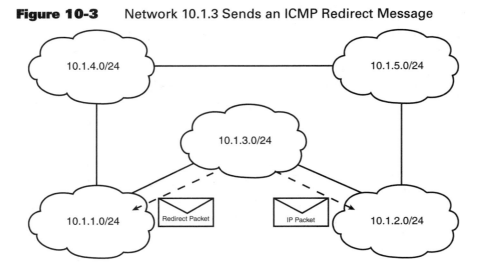

The router on Network 10.1.3.0/24 sends that packet along, but takes the time to notify its peer network using an ICMP Redirect message. Redirects can be a difficult topic to understand, but after you understand them you develop a greater appreciation for just how much goes on behind the scenes in a TCP/IP network. This simple example should give you a sense of how ICMP and redirects actually work.

Time Exceeded

Time can be exceeded two ways with respect to transmitting TCP/IP. The first, and most obvious, is that the packet wandered around a congested or ailing network for too long without finding a route to its destination. Eventually, the IP packet's *Time-To-Live (TTL)* timer expires and the packet is destroyed. Rather than wait until TCP figures out that a segment has gone missing, the machine that destroyed the segment sends a courtesy note back to the source machine. That note comes in the form of an ICMP Time Exceeded message! That message has a code value of 0.

The second way is a bit more subtle. Remember that TCP segments might require reassembly at their destination. Thus, incoming TCP segments are stored in a section of memory until enough consecutive segments are received to completely reassemble a larger piece of data that the application can actually use. A file, for example, might require dozens or more segments/packets. It is entirely possible that the destination machine loses patience and declares the segments in memory too old to be useful. That machine would generate an ICMP Time Exceeded message to inform the source machine of its actions. That message bears a code value of 1.

Parameter Problem

Sometimes IP packets just don't get formed properly. Other times, a well-made IP packet gets damaged in transit by electromagnetic interference. Either way, the result is the same: A machine receives an IP packet that just doesn't make sense!

The contents of the IP header are not consistent with valid value ranges in one or more of the fields. When this happens, your best bet is to just throw it away!

IP packets that have header parameters with problems can be identified either at the destination machine or at any network device between the source and destination. Regardless of who finds the problem, the right thing to do is request a retransmission. The ICMP Parameter Problem message is the right way to accomplish this task.

To make sure the source machine knows exactly which packet was damaged and then discarded, the machine that generates the ICMP Parameter Problem message must include some information about that damaged packet. As with any ICMP message dealing with a specific IP packet, this is accomplished by taking the header of that IP packet plus the first 64 bits of its payload and appending them at the back of the ICMP message. Upon receipt of such a message, the source machine knows precisely which packet to retransmit.

In all fairness, today's network and computing devices are sophisticated and manufactured to strict specifications. They operate extremely reliably and rarely generate a poorly formed IP packet. Thus, the ICMP Parameter Problem message type probably sees less use than any other. Still, it is nice to know it's there!

Timestamp and Timestamp Reply

Timestamp and Timestamp Reply are the last message types covered. It takes some time and a few more chapters to fully appreciate the purpose for the functionality enabled by these two messages.

This pair's goal is to establish not only the date and time, but how many milliseconds have elapsed since midnight, Universal Time. Although that might sound esoteric, if not completely silly, that capability allows you to establish a common point of reference throughout a network. That common point of reference forms the foundation for timing events such as computing roundtrip times in a network. Imagine trying to perform that task in an environment in which there were no consistent time from device to device. That would truly be an exercise in frustration. It is important to note that the ICMP Timestamp message doesn't keep track of time in your network. The message enables you to check the time on a given system.

 Now that you know what the Timestamp and Timestamp Reply messages do, it might interest you that there is a time-related protocol in TCP/IP. That protocol is the *Network Time Protocol (NTP)*, which is responsible for maintaining the synchronicity of time throughout a network.

Using ICMP

The beginning of this chapter says that ICMP is mysterious because it lurks in the shadows and remains almost completely out of sight. The key word in that sentence is *almost*. For the most part, ICMP is invisible to network users. It is, after all, a mechanism for systems to communicate with each other, so there is little to be seen by the carbon-based life forms that infest the edge of a network.

You can use, however, a couple of tools that enable users to directly use ICMP. These tools are PING and TRACEROUTE. They are similar, but use different ICMP messages and perform different functions.

PING

PING is an oddly named utility native to TCP/IP. The acronym derives from *Packet Internet Groper*. They're not made up—just passed onto you! PING allows you to see if any given IP address is on the network and reachable. Thinking back through the ICMP message types explained earlier, it should be obvious that PING is nothing more than a small program that allows you to specify an IP address for testing and then feeds that address to an ICMP Echo message. The response is received courtesy of an ICMP Echo Reply message, formatted appropriately, and dumped onto your computer's video screen.

That's a simplification, but you get the point. PING is creating a series of Echo messages so you can see if a host is reachable. If that host is reachable, you can see the average roundtrip times that it takes for packets to reach that host and receive an acknowledgment. This can be quite useful information!

If the host doesn't respond to your PINGs, you have some thinking to do—and perhaps a bit more investigation. All you will know for sure is that the host didn't reply. Some reasons for not getting a response might include

- It might not have replied because it is down.

- Your PING packet might have hit a congested part of the network and gotten dumped before it reached its destination. The Echo Reply packet generated by the machine you PINGed met that fate.

- There might be some serious trouble in the network and you just can't reach that host!

Clearly, the failure of a PING indicates something is amiss; you'll have to do more diagnosis before figuring out what happened.

 In this era of spyware and other unwanted, malevolent software (which you can inadvertently acquire via the Internet), it is increasingly common for people and organizations to block ICMP at the border separating their network and the Internet. In such cases, PING will fail for no other reason than it is not allowed! Thus, you might find your attempts to troubleshoot using PING impeded.

TRACEROUTE

TRACEROUTE or TRACERT, depending on which operating system you use, is a marvelous tool and diagnostic mechanism for IP networks. This utility allows you to map out the entire route that your packets will take to their destination. Along with identifying each network device in the path, you also see how long it takes to progress to each step of the way! A TRACEROUTE's cumulative results are that you know the path your packets take and the relative speed (or lack thereof) of every device in the path.

TRACEROUTE, as you might have guessed, uses ICMP Time Exceeded messages. It uses a *lot* of them! Unlike PING, TRACEROUTE doesn't generate an ICMP message as much as it causes one to be generated. The way it works is quite simple: TRACEROUTE creates a series of packets that get launched into the network bearing the destination IP address that you stipulate. These packets are created with a small TTL.

When the packets expire, the network device that noticed their expiration sends you an ICMP Time Exceeded message. Tallying up the values enables TRACEROUTE to show you the cumulative delays in the path and where they were incurred. This is an incredibly useful tool. With a little practice, you can use TRACEROUTE to map out how a network is constructed and see how well—or how poorly—it is performing at any given time.

Chapter Summary

Even though ICMP is not something you would directly use on a daily basis, it is quite important to the operation of an IP network. It provides a mechanism for many critical system-level functions and can even provide end users with some interesting and useful information about the network they are using. Everything from notifying a source machine about damage to an IP packet's header to deletion due to expiration of its TTL timer is communicated using ICMP. Network congestion and news about better routes to specific destination networks also can be shared between network devices using ICMP.

Some of ICMP's mechanisms can be exploited by real live users, if you know how to use them. Such mechanisms enable you to tap into network information to find out just how well the network is performing. All this courtesy of the unsung hero of TCP/IP: the Internet Control Message Protocol!

Chapter Review Questions

The following questions reinforce the key concepts in this chapter:

1. What does the acronym ICMP stand for?

2. Which layer of the OSI reference model does ICMP occupy?

3. What is the purpose of ICMP?

4. Is ICMP useful to end users?

5. What are some of the tools you can use that rely upon ICMP?

6. What does PING do and why is it useful?

7. Which ICMP message types does PING utilize?

8. What does TRACEROUTE do and why is it useful?

9. If you know what you are looking at, you can map out all the connections that make up your network and get a good perspective on how busy or idle each connection is at any given time.

10. Which ICMP message type does TRACEROUTE utilize?

11. Can using a system-communications mechanism such as ICMP make IP a reliable protocol?

What You Will Learn

After reading this chapter, you should be able to answer the following questions:

- ✔ What is a router?

- ✔ What are a router's six primary functions?

- ✔ What are two approaches to calculating best paths?

- ✔ Which portion of an IP address does a router use to route?

- ✔ What is a routing protocol?

- ✔ What does a routing protocol do?

- ✔ At what layer(s) of the OSI reference model does a router separate different networks?

- ✔ At what layer(s) of the OSI reference model does a router interconnect networks?

- ✔ What is a hop and why is it significant in routing?

- ✔ What is a distance vector?

CHAPTER 11

How Do I Get There from Here?

A whole other set of protocols exists that isn't exactly part of the TCP/IP suite, but is absolutely indispensable to an IP network. These routing protocols determine how to get your IP packets from your machine to where they need to go.

Routing protocols provide the critical functions that enable two or more networks to communicate by sharing information about machines connected to each network, compare notes about different ways to reach any given destination machine, and pick the best path to those destinations. Without trying to cause a philosophical debate regarding what "the best" actually means, suffice it to say lots of valid ways can solve the same problem—usually with different "correct" answers! This chapter shows you some of the different options for routing between networks and kicks around their benefits and weaknesses.

Routers Route!

It's true: Routers route—but that's not all they do. Despite all outward appearances, routers live complicated, hard-working lives. Routers continuously perform these functions:

- Communicate information about known destinations with their neighboring routers

- Discover new destinations

- Compare different paths to the same destination

- Select the best path to each known destination

- Store that path in a table filled with other best paths

- Send packets of data en route to their destination via the best known path

That sounds like quite a load for the router, and it is. Luckily for you, it's easier understanding how a router works. Start by looking at what a router is, what it does, and what it doesn't do.

Routers actually perform a multitude of tasks, but not all are directly related to routing. For example, routers can filter unwanted packets that might try to enter your network, keep detailed event logs, and translate addresses. As important as these tasks are, they are not an integral part of routing. Thus, they were left out of the bulleted list on critical router functions.

What Is a Router?

A router is a specialized device designed to push IP packets (or other protocols' packets) through a network. Routing is actually a function that can be performed on a variety of physical platforms. A PC, for example, can be configured as a router, but it isn't a good or robust one. A software routing application can be run on a general-purpose computer such as a PC. Such routers are known as software-based routers. Cisco Systems makes a highly specialized line of routers, known as hardware-based routers, of all shapes and sizes to fit any network niche.

Regardless of its form, a router interconnects networks and regulates the flow of IP packets between those networks. For that to occur, a router must have the ability to interface with many types of physical networks.

For the purposes of routing, a network is defined as the collection of end systems and networking equipment bound by a common IP network address. Routers sit at the edge of that network and decide what to do with each packet it receives based on the IP network address in each IP packet's destination address field.

What Does a Router Do?

To route, a router must form the boundary, or edge, of a network so it can pass IP packets back and forth between two or more networks or subnetworks. So far, so good. What's not so clear is what a *network* is.

A network could be a local-area network (LAN). Ethernet has become the dominant type of LAN in the world today and is found in homes, small offices, and large enterprises. A network could also be a wide-area network (WAN). A WAN is a collection of LANs interconnected with routers, so you can think of a WAN as being a network of networks. Recall the example network in Chapter 7, "More Fun with IP Addresses," which shows how a router can create a series of subnetworks from within a single network. That's yet another example of a different type of network.

Regardless of a network's shape, a router has a paradoxical role in a network. It must simultaneously separate yet interconnect networks. Figure 11-1 illustrates this.

Figure 11-1   A Router Interconnects and Separates LANs

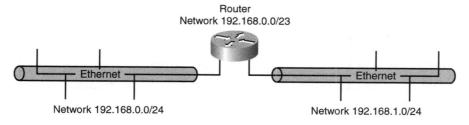

In Figure 11-1, you see a simple network consisting of two LANs interconnected by a small router. All share the same IP network address of 192.168.0.0/23, but that network address is subdivided into two subnetworks of equal size. The LAN on the left uses 192.168.0.0/24, which gives it host addresses that range from 192.168.0.1 to 192.168.0.255. The LAN on the right uses the other half of the /23 network, which forms the subnetwork 192.168.1.0/24. The valid host addresses in

that subnetwork range from 192.168.1.0 through 192.168.1.255. The router's paradoxical job is to separate yet interconnect these two LANs.

The key to understanding the seemingly self-contradictory role and, subsequently, routing's function, is to recognize that the separation and interconnection occur at different levels.

Recall the OSI reference model mentioned throughout this book. Remember that IP operates at Layer 3—the network layer—of that model. LANs, such as Ethernet networks, operate at Layers 1 and 2 of that same model. Take a look at Figure 11-2, which is an abstract view of the network illustrated in Figure 11-1.

Figure 11-2   An Abstract View of the Network Using the OSI Reference Model

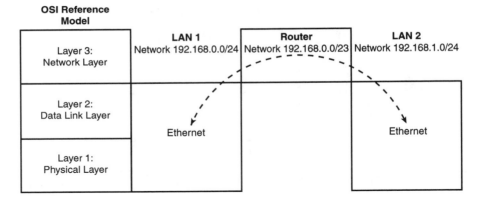

In Figure 11-2, you see that each LAN is just an OSI reference model's physical and data link layers. The router interconnects them at the network layer, but maintains separation at the physical and data link layers.

Now that you have the abstract perspective, take another look at the network itself. In Figure 11-3, you see the same network from Figure 11-1. The difference is that Figure 11-3 has dotted squares around the different network environments, indicating how a router both interconnects and separates.

Figure 11-3 The Router Separates Layers 1 and 2, but Interconnects at Layer 3

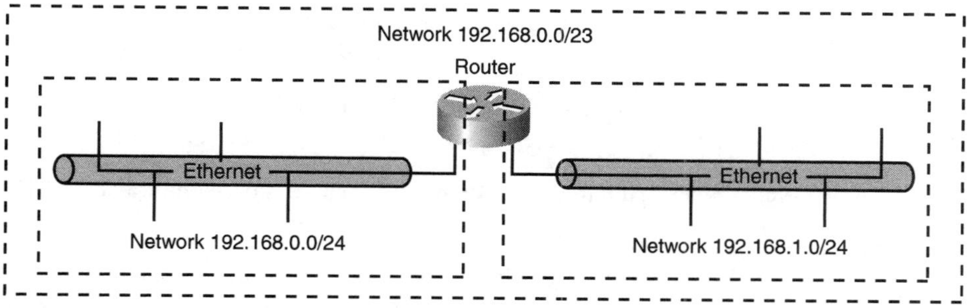

Network 192.168.0.0/23
Router
Ethernet
Network 192.168.0.0/24
Ethernet
Network 192.168.1.0/24

By comparing Figures 11-1, 11-2, and 11-3, you can see that a router physically interconnects different networks using IP, but logically separates those networks at Layers 1 and 2. The big question is how that works.

How Does That Work?

Dig a little deeper and see how that router in Figure 11-3 does what it does. Reflecting on a router's six primary functions, you can see that not all those functions apply in this little network. Several functions are only apparent when you have a network with two or more routers working together. Table 11-1 recaps those primary functions and shows you which apply in a single-router network.

Table 11-1 Router Functions in a Single-Router Network

Function Number	Function	Applicable in Single-Router Networks?
1	Communicate information about known destinations with neighboring routers	No. There are no neighboring routers in a single-router network.
2	Discover new destinations	Yes. The mechanism for routing is configured on each cable port or interface on a router. Thus, even a single-router network could have at least two ports configured with an active routing protocol.

continues

Table 11-1   Router Functions in a Single-Router Network (continued)

Function Number	Function	Applicable in Single-Router Networks?
3	Compare different paths to the same destination	No. There is only one way to reach each destination network.
4	Select the best path to each known destination	No. There is only one way to reach each destination network.
5	Store that path in a table filled with other best paths	Yes. Depending on how you configure the router, it automatically builds a routing table of best paths to known destinations.
6	Send packets of data en route to their destination via the best known path	Yes. Forwarding packets is a router's primary purpose.

In a network that consists of just a single router, the primary functions that the router provides are limited to learning about new destinations, tracking the best paths it has found, and forwarding packets.

Table 11-1 identifies the six critical functions of a router. A router can perform more functions, but these are the most important for the sake of routing in a network.

A router's ability to perform these functions implies that a router communicates with other routers. That's a function of a *routing protocol*. Routing protocols, just like every other protocol in the TCP/IP family of protocols, is a highly specialized piece of software. These protocols don't run on desktop computers or other devices that humans use. Instead, they run on routers. Routing protocols enable routers to do the first five of the six critical functions identified in Table 11-1. The last function, forwarding packets, is a native function of a router's hardware and operating system and is independent of a routing protocol's presence.

There are many routing protocols and at least two schools of thought about what constitutes a best path. Focus on the mechanics of a router using the same small network used throughout this chapter; then you are ready to look at different ways to interpret the best way to get there from here!

Please remember that as you read the remainder of this chapter that routing is an extremely complex science. The goal isn't to make you an expert at all the nuances of routing, but rather to impart a basic understanding.

Learning About New Destinations

One of any routing protocol's basic functions is enabling routers that use the same protocol to communicate with each other. That communication enables a router to essentially tell its neighbor, "Hi! I'm connected to network 192.168.5.0/24. What networks do you know about?" In this chapter's example, the neighbors aren't two different routers, but two different ports or interfaces on the same router. Each interface must be configured to use the same routing protocol. That's just like telling them to speak the same language. Each interface keeps its own track of best paths to known destinations and shares its list with its neighbors. In the real world you wouldn't set up a network this way, but this simple example helps get the point across.

Figure 11-4 shows this first basic step in the routing process. The two interfaces on neighboring routers establish contact with each other and share what they know about destinations they can reach. This contact is limited to direct neighbors, but those neighbors share all they know about the rest of the network. The arrowed lines interconnecting the network clouds in Figure 11-4 indicate the two-way exchange of information between direct neighbors in a network.

Figure 11-4   Step 1: Saying Hi!

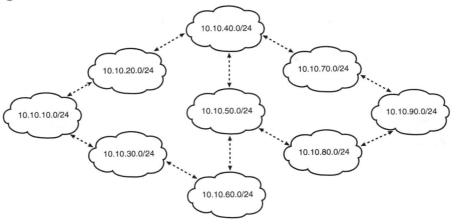

Routers don't actually say "Hi" to each other, but router interfaces that speak the same language do talk to each other. How they do that varies by the specific routing protocol. You understand later what they say when they communicate.

Remembering Best Paths

As a router's network interfaces exchange information with other routers, each one begins piecing together a picture of what the network looks like. That picture consists of just three basic pieces of information:

- The destination network IP address.

- The router interface used to get to that destination network.

- Some measure of that path's cost. Cost is not necessarily a financial term in this sense, but it does indicate some measure of the reachability of known destination networks.

These pieces of information are stored and kept correlated in a structure known as a *routing table*. Whenever a router needs to forward a data packet, it checks each packet's destination address against the contents of this table. That's how it knows where to send each packet.

Using the sample network depicted in Figure 11-4, it is time to see what information might be communicated between neighbors. Although the actual information exchange is dictated by the routing protocol, it is useful to understand the function of information exchanges between neighbors without the complexity that specific routing protocols can introduce.

 Many routing protocols use the concept of cost to compare different routes to the same destination. The lower the cost, the better the route. That much is logical. However, the cost metric often has nothing to do with money! Instead, routing *cost* measures the number of routers that lie along the path between any given source and destination networks.

Table 11-2 shows the simple set of routing tables that exist in the example network. Rather than map out all routing table updates for all the networks, simplify the chore and look only at what the router in network 10.10.20.0/24 would share with its neighboring router in network 10.10.10.0/24.

The 10.10.20.0/24 network is a good example because it only contains two direct connections: one to 10.10.10.0/24 via its serial interface #0 (S0) and another to 10.10.40.0/24 via its serial interface #1 (S1). These two connections enable it to reach every other network, albeit indirectly. Table 11-2 shows what the information updates would look like.

Table 11-2   Step 2: Communicating Best Paths to Known Networks

Interface Number	Reachable Networks	Routing Cost
S0	10.10.10.0/24	1
S0	10.10.30.0/24	2
S1	10.10.40.0/24	1
S1	10.10.50.0/24	2
S1	10.10.60.0/24	3
S1	10.10.70.0/24	2
S1	10.10.80.0/24	3
S1	10.10.90.0/24	3

There might be many ways to reach a given destination network, but the routing protocol has selected these as the best or shortest path. That's a simple, if not trivial, example. This network's extreme smallness means you probably wouldn't use a routing protocol in real life. Still, it makes for a marvelous example absent the clutter of detail.

You return to calculating routes a bit later in this chapter. For right now, finish exploring the functions of a router. The next step in routing is the easiest piece of all: forwarding packets.

Forwarding Packets

A router's mission in life is to route packets. That is, it accepts packets sent by devices at the edge of a network, such as your computer, and forwards them to their intended destination. You already say how routers communicate and use that ability to build routing tables. The last piece of the puzzle is what they do with packets. You see, routers don't create packets—they can create frames.

Generally speaking, routers do not create IP packets. Their reason for being is to ensure that IP packets created by end-user applications get delivered safely and efficiently to their destinations. But, as explained in Chapter 10, "Special Delivery for Special Messages," routers are capable of creating IP packets that contain system-level information. Those packets are delivered to other systems (not end-user applications) using Internet Control Message Protocol (ICMP).

The point about routers creating frames and not packets might sound like word games. Frames and packets are critically different. Both function as an envelope and carry a user's or application's data through a network, but that's where the similarities stop! Packets are persistent and are created once. Frames are only good for one link in a network.

In Figure 11-5 you see a computer connected to network 192.168.0.0/24 sending a packet addressed to a server in the 192.168.1.0/24 network. Although the computer can create an IP packet (thanks to its TCP/IP protocol stack), it cannot place the IP packet on that network. At least, it can't do that directly. The network is an Ethernet network, so it wraps that IP packet inside an Ethernet frame and places that frame on the network. That Ethernet frame is addressed to the Media Access Control (MAC) address of the router's E0 interface.

This is a subtle but important point: The IP packet embedded in that Ethernet frame bears the destination IP address of the server in network 192.168.1.0/24. However, Ethernet doesn't look at, use, or understand IP addresses. Ethernet uses MAC addresses.

Figure 11-5   Ethernet Frame Is Launched

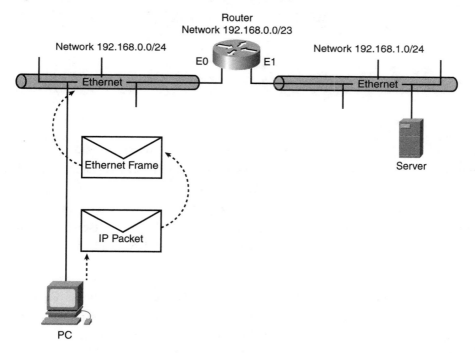

Figure 11-6 shows you the next step in the process. Upon arrival at the router's E0 interface, the IP packet is pulled out of the frame and the frame is discarded. It has done its job! The IP packet, however, has some work to do. Specifically, it needs to get its data to its intended destination—the server in network 192.168.1.0/24.

Figure 11-6   IP Packet Is Extracted from the Ethernet Frame

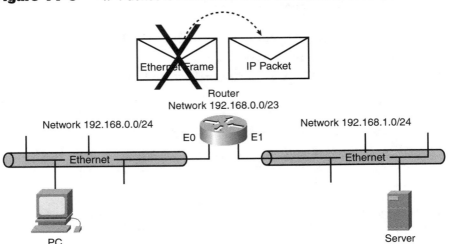

The routing protocol on the E0 interface takes a look at the destination IP address and sees that it is the network connected via its E1 interface. The packet is handed off to the E1 interface. The E1 interface must again wrap that IP packet in an Ethernet frame for transport through the next Ethernet network. This time, the Ethernet frame bears the destination MAC address of the server itself, rather than an intermediary network interface (as shown in Figure 11-5). This step is illustrated in Figure 11-7.

The server accepts this incoming Ethernet frame, strips it to reveal the IP packet inside, and processes that packet's contents. If nothing else, this sequence of illustrations shows you that packets are persistent, that frames are transient, and how that applies to the process by which routers forward packets.

Figure 11-7   IP Packet Is Wrapped in a New Ethernet Frame

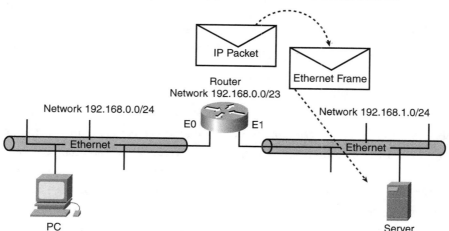

Packets forwarded by routers must be rewrapped in a network frame, such as an Ethernet frame. Remember: IP packets operate at Layer 3 of the OSI reference model and network frames operate at Layer 2. Packets are persistent and, unless damaged or lost in transit, remain intact from source to destination. Network frames, on the other hand, are highly transient creations good for only one trip through a network. This iterative process of wrapping and unwrapping continues until the packet reaches its destination or is discarded.

Calculating Routes

Now that you've been exposed to the basics of routing and packet forwarding, prepare for a bit more detail. Routing is just a complex set of mathematical algorithms that you trust to pick the best route through a network. Picking the best route is critical because, as you saw in earlier chapters, each IP packet only has a certain amount of time to live. When that expires, it is discarded! Consequently, it is in your interest to pick the best possible route to your destination.

The phrase *best possible route* is a bit nebulous. What does "best" measure? That depends on what's important to you, and how you define *best*. For example, if you drove from your home to a nearby park, you might have several options for getting there. Generally speaking, the farther away that destination, the greater the number of routes.

Assume that park is 20 miles away when measured in a straight line. It's highly doubtful that a road would run in such a straight line. In fact, you would most likely have to figure out a combination of different, interconnected roads that get you to that park. The total mileage is likely to be quite a bit more than just 20 miles, depending on the route you select. Speaking of routes, a seemingly infinite number of ways get you there. Your challenge is to pick the best route between your home and that park. You can evaluate those routes with at least two different, plausible criteria. These criteria can be directly applied to networks, so the analogy is quite fitting.

First, you might be in a hurry, in which case you would prefer the route with the most high-speed roads or highways. That high-speed route might be a bit longer. You need to decide what is more important to you: time or distance? The easy answer might be to minimize total drive time. That's a valid approach. However, that can be a problem. If, for example, you were driving your antique Mustang convertible, you would be keenly interested in keeping the miles low. Total drive time, in this case, is immaterial. Perhaps you would choose a slightly longer route if you knew the roads were in better condition and you wouldn't risk damaging your vintage vehicle. What's the right answer? It depends on what is important to you!

Now translate that scenario into a network. In a network, routers can select best paths to destinations based on either some arbitrary measure of distance or on some measure of the quality of the links that compose that route. The approach is totally up to whomever is responsible for running the network. Take a closer look at both approaches.

Measuring Distances

Distance-vector routing is the discipline that attempts to make best-path decisions based on distance. Distance-vector routing is the oldest and least sophisticated method for selecting best-path routes. Its roots go back to an academic exercise conducted at Princeton University in the late 1950s. Those exercises proved that you could select optimal routes through a network that offered many different paths to any given destination using some arbitrary measure of distance. That measure is known as a ***hop***.

How It Works

Counting hops to a destination is the simplest approach. Rather than bore you with a detailed network topology, gaze upon that time-honored classic symbol of networks: the puffy cloud. Figure 11-8 shows an internetwork. A puffy cloud symbolizes each network.

When counting hops through a network, it is necessary to see those hops, or routers, before you start counting. Thus, a detailed network topology diagram is required. However, detailed network topology diagrams can get confusing. In contract, a puffy cloud in a network symbolizes an entire network, and the cloud allows you to focus on routing between networks without worrying about the details of how each network was constructed. Figure 11-8 combines two perspectives: The puffy clouds symbolize networks, but hops are counted at the rate of one per cloud. Although not a practice that works in the real world, this shortcut helps you appreciate the mathematics of routing.

Figure 11-8   Counting Hops to a Destination

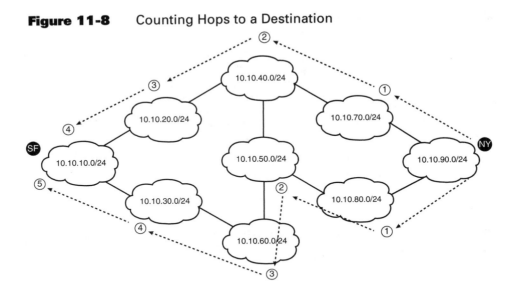

As you can see in Figure 11-8, at least a few different paths can get you from New York to San Francisco. Which one is the right one? If you assume that all the transmission facilities are the same type, the best path is the one touching the fewest number of networks. Of the two paths indicated, the best is the one that gets you to San Francisco with just four hops.

Although counting hops might seem like a trivial approach to a complex problem, the reality is that it works and works well! Hop counting has become so successful as a basis for routing because it offers both stability and simplicity.

Stability is important for a network. If you base your routing decisions on volatile information, the routers in your network will never reach any consensus about what the network looks like or what the best path is. They will spend all their time reacting to temporary changes in the volatile information. Hop counting is a remarkably stable way of calculating routes. The only time a hop count changes is if new routers or transmission facilities are added to the network, or if there is a failure and some part(s) of the network become unavailable.

The second beneficial attribute of hop counting is its simplicity. That translates into less work for each router, so it can spend more time processing packets than calculating routes. That's good news for end users.

The Downside

Counting hops (routers) completely ignores the transmission facilities or lines that interconnect them. In the 1950s (and even as late as the 1980s), it was reasonable to generalize network connectivity because there wasn't that much variety between transmission lines. When figuring out the best path it was more important to count the pieces of hardware than it was to fret over the quality of the lines that connected the routers.

At least two potential problems can occur with this simplification:

- There is no good correlation between actual distance and the number of routers in a network.

- Transmission facilities' performance differences are ignored.

Today, networks have become quite sophisticated and can vary tremendously in terms of speed and performance. Using something as abstract as a hop to calculate and compare distances these days is hardly a recipe for accuracy. Consider, for example, that one common WAN transmission facility is a T1. That circuit type offers 1.5 megabits per second (Mbps) of bandwidth. A hop-counting routing protocol wouldn't differentiate that T1 from a 100-Mbps Fast Ethernet connection, even though there's a 600-percent difference in speed and capacity between them.

The other source of possible inaccuracy is that there isn't necessarily a good correlation between a hop and actual distance. If you reflect back on Figure 11-8, you know that your packets are spanning approximately 3500 miles en route to their destination, but without knowing where exactly each of the intermediate routers is located, that journey could be substantially longer. Just counting the hops is a poor indicator of actual distance. The fewest hops might actually be the longer route or the one across the slowest parts of the network.

Recognize this device for what it is: a simplifying assumption. However, it is a highly successful simplifying assumption! Even with the introduction of more sophisticated ways to calculate and compare routes, hop counting continues to soldier on. It's not the most accurate approach, but it offers the best combination of stability in operation with a serviceable level of accuracy.

You can get a more accurate solution, but is it worth the effort? The answer depends on your network. If your network features widely different types of transmission facilities, think about using a link-state routing protocol. If, however, your network is constructed using mostly the same type of transmission facilities, a distance-vector protocol might be just the ticket for you.

 This chapter presents an overview of routing. The subject is sufficiently complex that you could write an entire book on it. In fact, it's been done! If you'd like more information on routing, please check out *IP Routing Fundamentals* published by Cisco Press.

Measuring Quality of the Connections

Another routing approach is based on the quality of the individual connections, or links, that comprise the total route. This approach is known as *link-state routing*. You could measure and evaluate a network link's status several ways:

- **Link speed**—Known more properly as *bandwidth*, the link speed gives a good indication of how fast any given link can be.

- **Traffic quantity**—Another good way to make a routing decision based on link states is to see how heavily utilized it is. Known as *load*, this metric can help you avoid congested areas when making routing decisions.

- **Delays**—It makes perfect sense to pick a route based on how large or small an expected delay is. Many things can cause network delays. A heavily loaded link adds a considerable amount of delay, but so can a sickly router or Denial-of-Service (DoS) attack. Rather than waste time figuring out why a network link might be slow, routers track the average delay you can expect to encounter on a per-link basis.

■ **Error rate**—Yet another thing you would probably want to check is a link's reliability. Reliability can be measured by counting all the transmission errors that a link has incurred in recent history. By avoiding links with high error rates, you can increase your chances of safely delivering packets to their destination.

You can evaluate a link's status other ways, but this is a nice set with which to start. The network administrator explicitly configures one of these pieces of information on the router: bandwidth. That is, when you bring up a new link in a network, the person running the network must tell the router what kind of pipe it is and how much bandwidth it offers. A router keeps a running tally of the other information as part of its operating routine. Thus, a router has or tracks all the information it needs to make good decisions about routes based on the state of the links in its network.

How It Works

How link-state routing works depends directly on which routing protocol you are using. For the sake of example, please refer to Figure 11-9. The network used in the preceding figures has been updated to show more detail about the transmission lines that interconnect these networks. All these lines are either T1s, which have 1.5 Mbps of bandwidth, or T3s, which offer 45 Mbps of bandwidth. Obviously, if you have a choice you use the T3s whenever possible; they are faster and have more bandwidth available. The pipe speed means that T3s won't get overloaded as quickly as T1 circuits.

Figure 11-9   Differences in Transmission Facilities

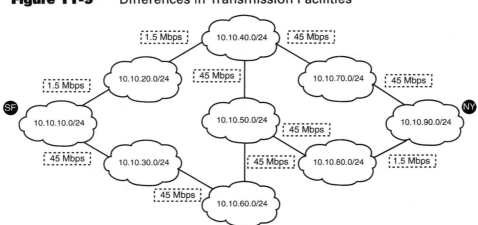

If you program your routers to always pick a T3 whenever possible, the network picks a route that meets those criteria. Figure 11-10 shows the slightly convoluted route (which a distance-vector routing protocol would *never* select!) that satisfies the requirement. This path uses only T3 links, but takes a total of six hops to reach San Francisco.

Figure 11-10   Same Goal, Different Outcome

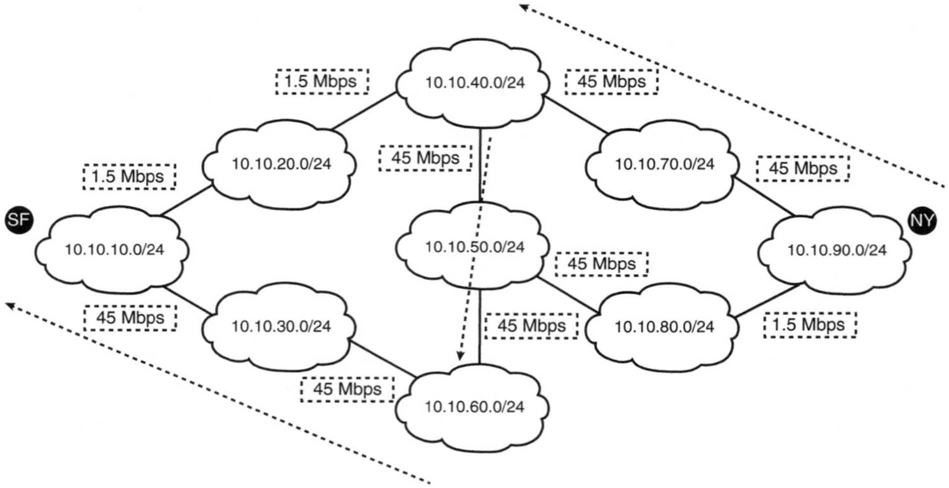

You could similarly choose to emphasize other link-state data, such as selecting the best path based on lowest cumulative error rates per link, least delay, or load per link, or even a combination of these things. Using different criteria might result in different best paths between any given source and destination network, but the approach remains the same. Decisions about the best path are not based on the routers; they are based on the links that interconnect the routers.

The Downside

If you think about link-state routing on a strictly superficial basis, it makes all the sense in the world. What could be better than making decisions about potential network paths than basing it on the network's current state? Making decisions about relatively constant states would be ideal. Unfortunately, many of the introduced attributes (which you can use to assess a link's status) are volatile pieces of information. They can even vary one second to the next. Quite simply, they are too volatile on which to base your routing decisions.

Some link states, such as cumulative error rates or available bandwidth, are relatively stable. Others, such as delay and load levels, can vary by the millisecond. Generally speaking, if it takes your network's routers 5 minutes to complete the iterative process of sharing what they know about best paths with their neighbors, you wouldn't want to begin that process using data that could change more frequently than 5 minutes. If you did, your network would remain forever mired in that update process and the network's users probably wouldn't be happy! Fortunately, mechanisms built into each link-state routing protocol can help mitigate against the volatility of data to ensure your network remains as stable as can be.

Another potential issue is that link-state routing protocols can be quite complex. That can translate into a computationally intensive workload for routers. If your network is constructed with old, slow routers, or routers that don't have a lot of physical memory, they might be unable to meet the resource requirements of a link-state routing protocol. This can be a real problem. Don't think of that as a reason to avoid link-state protocols, however. Consider that another reason you should use the right tool (both router and routing protocol) for the job.

Applying Rules

You just read that you have two main approaches to route calculation. That's a true statement, but a third option exists. Sometimes a network is so large that identifying—much less calculating and comparing—all the routes between a source and a destination is impossible. The Internet is just such a network. It's truly global and so vast in scope that you just can't count all the possible paths between two points, much less try to compare any of them mathematically.

When forced to make routing decisions under these circumstances, your best approach is not to make routing decisions. Instead, apply some rules or policies for handling IP packets in the aggregate rather than making a routing decision for each individual packet.

The Internet's routing protocol is the *Border Gateway Protocol, version 4 (BGP4)*. BGP4 is a remarkably complex protocol. For the purposes of this chapter, please recognize that routing by rules or policies is a valid option that provides massive scalability. It isn't used in home networking or even in large corporation networks. It is used exclusively to drive Internet routing decisions.

Basically, BGP4 allows the network engineer to specify a set of rules or policies. Routing protocols typically keep track of each network address that might be connected to the Internet and then makes routing decisions based on that information. BGP4 allows you to set rules for routing packets as a group without having to decide for each packet. The result is a much more efficient and scalable approach to routing that lets you build truly global networks.

You can compare the relative efficiency of different routes to the same destination two primary ways. The most commonly encountered are distance-vector routing and link-state routing. A third approach to routing applies rule or policies. This approach is intended only for massively scalable networks such as the Internet and is known as *policy-based routing*.

Chapter Summary

Routing protocols are the tools that figure out how to get IP packets from their source to their destination as quickly and efficiently as possible. Generally speaking, routing protocols run on network devices known as routers and communicate continuously with neighboring routers. That communication enables routers to piece together a comprehensive view of the larger network in which they function. Part of that view includes identifying IP network addresses reachable via the network, as well as all the ways to reach those networks. Some logic must be applied to figure out which of those alternative routes to each destination network is best.

Each router stores a collection of best routes in a routing table that forwards IP packets efficiently to their destination.

You can calculate a route's efficiency two main ways. The first is known as distance-vector routing. Distance-vector routing protocols count the number of routers in each path and choose that with the fewest number of routers between it and the destination network. The second way to calculate routes is kind of the opposite approach. Instead of focusing on the routers, this approach focuses on data that measures the quality of the links interconnecting the routers. This approach is known as link-state routing. A third approach exists, but doesn't calculate routes. Instead, it enables you to develop rules for forwarding IP packets in the aggregate rather than making decisions individually. Policy-based routing, as this approach is known, is only useful for networks that require massive scalability, such as the Internet.

Chapter Review Questions

The following questions reinforce the key concepts in this chapter:

1. What is a router?

2. What are two different approaches to calculating best paths?

3. Which portion of an IP address does a router use to route?

4. What is a routing protocol?

5. What does a routing protocol do?

6. At what layer(s) of the OSI reference model does a router separate different networks?

7. At what layer(s) of the OSI reference model does a router interconnect different networks?

8. What is a *hop* and why is it significant in routing?

9. What is a distance vector?

PART IV

User Services: Making the Most Use of Your Network

What You Will Learn

After reading this chapter, you should be able to answer the following questions:

- ✔ How are TCP/IP and networks such as Ethernet related?

- ✔ How many components are needed, at a minimum, to build a local-area network?

- ✔ What is the difference between a hub and a switch?

- ✔ Is coaxial cable obsolete or does it still serve a purpose?

- ✔ What is a Category of Performance?

- ✔ What is currently the fastest speed at which a wireless network can operate?

- ✔ What is the fastest speed at which an Ethernet wire-based local-area network can operate?

- ✔ Which is more reliable: wire-based networks or wireless networks?

- ✔ What are the main drawbacks of wire-based networks?

- ✔ What are the main advantages of wire-based networks?

- ✔ What do wireless networks use to transmit signals?

- ✔ What are the main benefits of wireless networks?

CHAPTER 12

Connecting to TCP/IP Networks

Now that you have learned most of the theory and mechanics that are TCP/IP's foundation, it is time to make things a bit more real. By now you should know that TCP/IP is not a network. You run TCP/IP over networks, but it isn't a network unto itself. TCP/IP absolutely requires a network of some type to run.

This chapter introduces the two most commonly used networks technologies: wire-based Ethernet and wireless. These network technologies serve double duty as they can be found in both professional and home networks. Learning a little about them will provide you with a double advantage.

Such networks are the mechanism that enables you to use TCP/IP. You see how to configure these networks and how to connect to them using TCP/IP. That leaves you more than ready for the remaining two chapters of the book, which show you how to use TCP/IP networks and how to figure out what's wrong when they don't work as expected.

Anatomy of a Local-Area Network

Local-area networks (LANs) aren't as hard to understand as you might expect. It's true that they can be quite large and complex. In fact, entire books have been written on both wire-based and wireless LANs. For the purposes of this book, however, this chapter focuses on the basics.

In its simplest form, a LAN really needs only four components:

- Two or more computers or other devices
- A *network interface card (NIC)* to connect your machine to the network

- A transmission medium

- A hub (or switch) that interconnects multiple end-user machines

Figure 12-1 shows you how these pieces fit together to form a simple LAN.

Figure 12-1   A Simple LAN

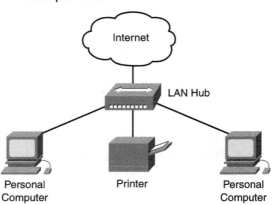

As you can see in Figure 12-1, the shape of your typical wire-based home network begins with a hub. A **hub** is the mechanism that interconnects all the devices on your network. It forms the center of your network and everything radiates from there. A simple LAN is illustrated for you. This is the type you might build and use in your own home.

Figure 12-1 shows you something else; it reveals the LAN's architectural components. There is a computer connected to a hub (which is sometimes called a **switch**) that physically interconnects another computer, a printer, and a connection to the Internet. Each device that connects to the network uses a NIC to do so.

A NIC can take many different forms. It can be a circuit board that you install inside your computer or be built right into your computer. A NIC can even come in the shape of a PC card for laptop computers. Regardless of its physical shape, a NIC forms the interconnection between your computer and the network.

Each NIC connects to a *transmission medium*—a copper wire, in this case—to the hub. The hub brings together multiple computers and enables them to communicate with each other. That's it! By using these basic mechanisms, you can build virtually any type of LAN. It is possible to use other things to build a larger, more complex network, but these are the building blocks. You can't build a network without them!

Two words that too often get used interchangeably are *hub* and *switch*. Both serve the same function: to interconnect multiple end-user devices in a LAN. There is a technical distinction between a hub and a switch. Both serve the same function, but a switch offers much higher performance. A hub forces all the devices that it interconnects to share the same bandwidth. For example, an eight-port 10-megabit (Mb) Ethernet hub forces all eight devices to share those 10 Mb. An eight-port Ethernet switch provides each of those eight devices with its own 10-Mb connection.

Looking at a hub and a switch, you would be hard pressed to tell them apart. Operationally, however, a huge distinction exists. Because all devices connected to a hub share the same bandwidth, only one device can talk at a time. A switch offers each connecting device a dedicated connection so that each device can talk simultaneously without degrading performance.

There are, however, some ways to vary the network's actual shape or technology base. For example, the type of transmission medium you use can have a profound effect on the network's shape and performance. That's true for both wire types as well as for wireless.

Wire-Based Networks

When you look at Figure 12-1, you really can't see the NIC. Usually, it is an internal component of a computer, printer, or other device attached to a network. All you see when you look is a port or cable interface. The most commonly used cable interface looks like a double-wide telephone jack. You find the same type of interface on the hub.

The transmission medium can be almost anything. The most common is twisted-pair wiring (which uses the telephone jack-like interface), but there are many other types of media. In addition to twisted-pair copper wire, you can use fiber-optic cables, coaxial cables (the same type used to deliver cable TV service to your home), and radio waves.

For the purposes of a home network, you can skip fiber-optic cables. That allows you to focus on just twisted-pair copper and wireless transmission technologies. The remainder of this section introduces your two main options for a LAN's physical transmission media (coaxial cables and twisted pair) and shows you how they are used.

Coaxial Cables

Coaxial cables were the original copper wire used in LANs. Although successful in this role, over time they fell into disuse. Coaxial cables are thicker and less flexible than twisted-pair wiring, as well as more expensive.

The first generation of Ethernet LANs used two different types of coaxial cable: thick and thin. The thick cable formed your hub or backbone and the thin cables were spliced into that backbone to enable individual computers to connect to that network. Both thick and thin coaxial cables have almost completely disappeared from the landscape due to the emergence of less expensive and less bulky alternatives. Although coaxial cable continues to enjoy one functional niche, it is hardly ever used in LANs today.

Twisted-Pair Wire

Twisted-pair wiring started out as just the wire used for telephones. It has been repeatedly enhanced over the last decade or so for even greater performance.

Twisted-pair wiring slowly but steadily overtook coaxial cables as the preferred transmission medium in LANs around the world. The market was quick to perceive two main advantages of twisted pair versus coaxial cable: The former is less expensive to purchase, installation is much easier, and it takes up less room in cable trays and ducts.

Twisted-pair wiring has many different grades. These grades are known as Categories of Performance, although that is usually shortened to just Cat-x (where x is a number). For example, Cat-3 can support a 10 megabit per second (Mbps) connection for up to 100 meters. Cat-5 is the next step up and it can support 100 Mbps up to 100 meters. There are higher categories, too, but Cat-5 is the most commonly used in LANs.

When you go shopping for cable, you might notice some newer alternatives to Cat-5 cable. An enhanced version known as Cat-5e is now available as is a whole new category: Cat-6.

The Best of Both Worlds

Today, coaxial cables are enjoying a minor renaissance thanks to the emergence of high-speed Internet service delivered over cable TV networks. If you buy Internet access from a cable company, the company installs a coaxial cable (better known as *coax*) in your home. Of course, they also connect it to a network device that allows you to connect your home computer to it using twisted pair. The point is that coaxial cable is still alive and well. It is just living in a much smaller niche.

Figure 12-2 shows you this hybrid of a wire-based home network built using both twisted pair and coaxial cable.

Figure 12-2   Topology of a Wire-Based Home Network

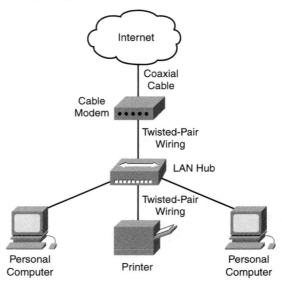

Perhaps the best way to think of the two choices for a LAN wire is that you have two different tools designed for two entirely different purposes. Although they are used interchangeably, time and experience have sorted them into different roles. Coaxial cable has met all the needs of a community's cable TV service and can even do a nice job of delivering high-speed Internet access to your home. Twisted pair has proven itself far superior to coax when it comes to connecting things to your LAN.

Benefits of Wire-Based Networks

Wire-based networks, such as any of the Ethernet variations (10 Mbps Ethernet, 100 Mbps Fast Ethernet, and 1 Gigabit Ethernet), offer two main benefits: speed and reliability. Although both wireless and wire-based networks seem to continuously get faster, the wire-based media have a distinct advantage when it comes to speed. You can purchase relatively inexpensive switches for your home or office that support Ethernet at either 10 Mb, 100 Mb, or even 1 Gigabit (which is 1000 Mb or 1 billion bits per second).

With wireless LANs, your options are limited to 2 Mbps, 11 Mbps, or (if you have one of the new wireless networks) 54 Mbps. Although that's not bad, it's far short of the 1 Gigabit (Gb) that you can get with a wire-based network. Plus, a wireless network operates much more like a hub in that the amount of bandwidth must be shared by all the devices. Thus, your 54 Mbps wireless network actually doesn't operate as fast as the published operating speed.

 Ethernet can actually run at speeds of 10 Gbps, but that is typically reserved for network backbones. You can get NICs and switches that allow 10, 100, or 1000 (1 Gb) connections for individual computers.

The other advantage of a wire-based network is reliability. That might sound a bit odd, but it's true. Many things can disrupt a signal that's traveling over something as fragile and unprotected as radio waves. Unless you're sporting a new XM radio, chances are good you've experienced static on your car radio during an electrical storm or when you approach the edges of that radio station's transmission area. That static is really a breakdown in the reliability of the transmission. Wire-based networks are more of a closed system and not as susceptible to such interference. Interference can still happen, it just doesn't happen as easily as with a wireless network.

Drawbacks of Wire-Based Networks

You should be aware of wire-based networks' two drawbacks: tidiness and inflexibility. Having worked with and around telecommunications gear for a couple of decades, rest assured that properly installed wiring is beautiful. Unfortunately, aside from the professional technicians who install *carrier-class networks* (top-level interstate or international networks), precious few people even know how to install wire the right way. Even fewer people would take the time to actually do so in a home network!

That might sound counterintuitive. After all, if you are going to install something that will remain in place for years, you would want to do it right. Unfortunately,

logic takes a back seat to convenience when it comes to network wiring. Consequently, home networks that interconnect more than just two or three devices tend to get really messy. For one thing, all wires (power cables as well as network cables) tend to come in standard sizes that often have nothing in common with where you install them. That means that you have to coil up the excess and hide that unsightly mess.

The other drawback to wire-based networks is that after you have installed the wiring, making changes becomes difficult and possibly even expensive. Depending on how widespread your network is, your cabling can be limited to a single room or spread throughout a campus environment. In larger environments, changes might mean ripping out the old wire and reinstalling new wire. Those are small and manageable problems, but they are inherent in every wire-based network.

Wireless Networks

I'll be the first to admit that *wireless networks* can be a bit of an oxymoron. It is rare to find a truly wireless network. Some useful networks were built, however, with less wire than the more traditionally constructed networks. Wireless networks employ either radio waves, microwaves, or light waves to carry their signals through the air. That's in contrast to wire-based networks, which use electricity to carry a signal over a wired (usually copper or fiber optic) median.

The notion of a wireless network is compelling: You are spared the expense of purchasing and installing cables. Moves and rearrangements are easy, because you don't have to rip up or reinstall any network wires. At least you won't have to worry about cabling between the computer and the hub. That's the only part of a network that benefits from the wireless technology in a typical home network.

Although it is possible to build a completely wireless network at home, such networks are not the norm. Wireless technologies are maturing, but they certainly aren't ubiquitous, nor can they match the features and performance of a wire-based network. That is made a bit clearer in Figures 12-3 and 12-4. Figure 12-3 shows a typical home network constructed using both wire and wireless technologies. Figure 12-4 shows a purely wireless network.

Figure 12-3   Topology of a Typical Hybrid Home Network

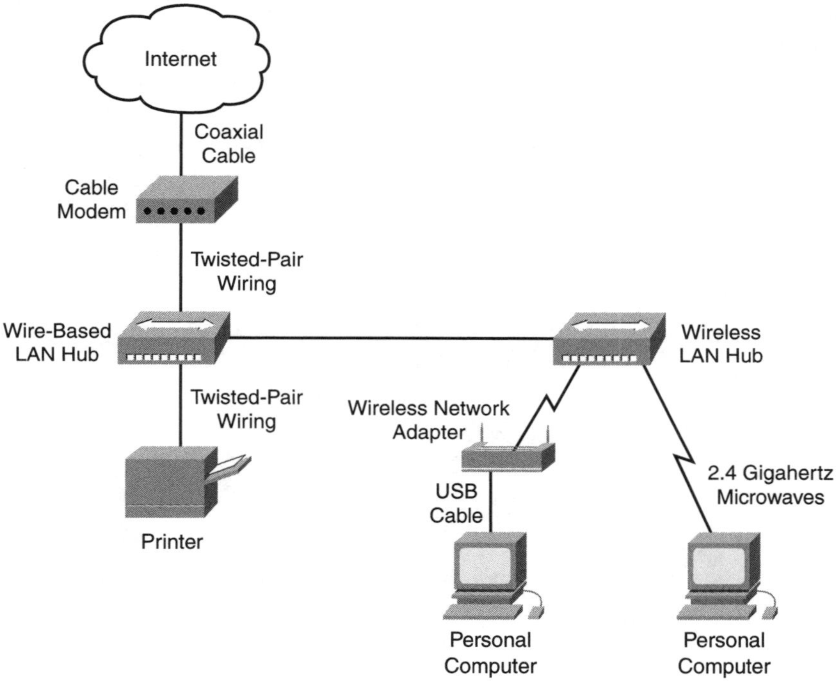

As you can see in Figure 12-3, most wireless home networks are only wireless from the computer to the network. Many other devices tend to require physical wiring, including the Internet router and the printer. These physically wired connections use Fast Ethernet (100 Mbps) technology and operate at 100 Mbps. This "wireless" network is really a hybrid constructed of a coaxial cable from the Internet service provider, a twisted-pair wire from the cable modem to a wire-based Ethernet switch, and a twisted-pair wire from the Ethernet switch to the wireless hub.

Although you can't see this in the illustration, one of the home computers in this illustration uses an external wireless access point that conforms to the Wireless G standard and operates at 54 Mbps. To physically connect the computer to that access point requires the use of a *Universal Serial Bus (USB)* cable. It might not be long, but it's still a cable. Arguing from a purist's perspective, that USB cable between the computer and the wireless access point—not to mention all the other wires—makes this a "less wire" rather than a truly wireless solution.

For the sake of comparison, Figure 12-4 shows you an example of a purely wireless home network. This network can't do much, but it is completely wireless!

Figure 12-4   Topology of a Pure Wireless Home Network

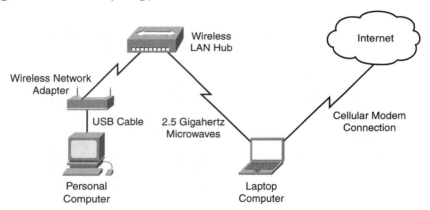

In Figure 12-4, there is no printer, no Network Attached Storage, nor anything else connected to the network besides a laptop and a PC. Internet access is courtesy of a cellular modem built into the laptop computer. This network was built using Wireless G technology and operates at 54 Mbps. About the only things you can do with this small but completely wireless network are share files and—when the laptop is on the network—share the Internet connection.

When you compare the networks in Figures 12-3 and 12-4, it becomes easy to see that you do pay a fairly heavy price for truly wireless technology. Sure, it's easy to install a wireless network, but the performance pales in comparison to a wire-based

Ethernet. You will likely find your options limited unless you are willing to look at mixing wire and wireless technologies.

Please don't misconstrue this as wireless networks bashing. This is an attempt to show you the limits of the technology. If you are willing to not be a purist, a hybrid network with wireless access points and a modest amount of wire connecting certain peripherals can give you as feature-rich a network as you can hope to have!

Benefits of Wireless Networks

Now that you know a couple ways to build a home network, you should easily identify the benefits of a wireless network. They are easy to install—no cables or cable-management worries. They also help you keep a tidy house. You don't have to worry about pre-cut cable sizes not quite matching your home environment. Nor will you have to pay extra for a custom-made cable that is the perfect size for your environment.

The greatest benefit of all is mobility. There is no end to the ways wireless network technology can enhance your mobility. Companies are quickly moving toward wireless access for their conference rooms and other public spaces. You may enjoy being able to just pick up you laptop and move to quieter areas of the house without breaking the network connection (or your train of thought).

Drawbacks of Wireless Networks

If the advantages of a wire-based network are speed and reliability, it is logical to conclude that the drawbacks of a wireless network are speed and reliability! Wireless LANs are becoming faster, but so are wire-based LANs. In the time it took for wireless to go from 2 to 54 Mbps, wire-based LANs stretched from 10 to 100 Mb and then up to 1 Gbps. Wireless networks are designed for flexibility and mobility, not speed or reliability.

Wireless transmissions are also quite fragile. Depending on the technology, rain, fog, and smoke can impede your outdoor wireless technologies. Thunderstorms, other forms of electrical interference, and even other electrical devices can all impede your indoor transmissions. Remember: You bought it for flexibility and mobility, not reliability!

Security is another drawback inherent in wireless networks. Let's face it: You are transmitting over public radio waves. Just as anybody can listen to a radio station if they are within its range, anybody close enough to your wireless network can pick off your transmissions. Wire-based LANs aren't perfect, but it is a little harder to intercept data transmitted in a wire-based network than it in a wireless LAN.

Goose Alert

The drawbacks of wireless networks aren't limited to equipment designed for the home or small office. A few years ago my employer had a data center on the edge of a marsh. Let's not discuss the wisdom of the location; it was also located directly on top of a major fault line in California. Suffice it to say they are now out of business.

Due to the location, we used a microwave system instead of fiber optics to connect to the nearest telephone company's switch facility. All worked well for a while and then an intermittent failure crept in. Each day at approximately 4 p.m. we lost connectivity almost completely. The problem would last for a minute or two and then clear up. All the hardware tested clean and we were stumped as to a cause.

One day, an engineer was enjoying a smoke break outside the building at that time and noticed a large flock of geese flying in tight formation out of the marsh and through the beam connecting the data center and telephone company. Upon reentering the building, he was told that the "problem" happened again! Wireless transmissions are fragile!

You might categorize this as either a benefit or a drawback, but many of today's wireless LANs operate at the same frequency as a microwave oven. The wireless LAN transmits at low power levels while the oven operates at a much higher power level. That's fairly logical; you can't cook food with a wireless LAN even though it uses the same frequency as a microwave oven.

If your microwave oven leaks waves, they will stomp on your wireless LAN. Your wireless LAN will become almost completely useless. You won't be able to send or receive anything while the oven is in use.

If your wireless LAN sometimes seems to slow down or you can't use it at all, check to see if your microwave oven is in use. If you can correlate the oven's usage with slowdowns in your wireless LAN, it is time to buy a new oven! Please note that if you live in an apartment, condo, or otherwise in close proximity to your neighbors, your wireless LAN might suffer if their microwave oven has seen better days. There's not much you can do about that unless you are willing to buy a new microwave oven for all your neighbors!

You decide whether the microwave oven integrity test is a benefit or drawback of wireless LANs!

Configuring a Network Connection

Now that you know a little bit about how networks are constructed, it's time to show you how to actually configure your computer to connect to a network and communicate using TCP/IP. It should be somewhat obvious that what you need to configure on your computer is the ***network interface card (NIC)***. After you do that, you need to tell that NIC you will be using TCP/IP to communicate. In the old days that required two separate steps. Today, it is assumed that you will want TCP/IP on your network.

Regardless of whether you are using a laptop or a desktop computer, the operating system provides a common graphics-based tool for configuring the network connection. Thus, the operating system buffers you from differences between these two types of computers. The physical differences between a desktop and a laptop computer, however, have a greater impact on your hardware choices for a NIC. That's something that can't be hidden by the operating system!

The following sections explain some of those differences and then show you how to configure a wireless and a wire-based network connection.

Laptop Versus Desktop Computers

Desktop and laptop computers were designed for different purposes. Essentially, the tradeoff can be summarized like this: Are you willing to trade performance for portability? From the perspective of adding network connectivity, you will find that these types of computers are different in terms of your ability to add hardware. However, the logical process for configuring a connection to a LAN is remarkably similar thanks to the fact that both desktop and laptop computers can run the same operating system.

Your challenge in configuring network connectivity begins with determining which type of LAN is best for you: traditional wire-based Ethernet/Fast Ethernet or wireless network. After determining this, you need to figure out how to provide that connectivity on your computer. That last decision is where laptops and desktops can differ.

Laptops

Laptop computers are a bit different from desktop computers because they are specifically designed for mobility. In fact, many aspects of a laptop computer's performance are traded for portability and longer battery life. When you consider that one of the biggest benefits of wireless network technology is how it enables mobility, it isn't much of a surprise to see that virtually all today's laptop manufacturers are including wireless access capabilities as a native feature.

Another implication of a highly portable computer is that the act—carrying it—can be hostile to its innards. Laptop manufacturers know this and go out of their way to make a laptop as durable as possible. What does all that have to do with connecting your laptop to a network? It means you probably can't just crack open the case and start adding internal peripheral devices. If your laptop didn't come with a specific feature, you aren't going to be able to install it yourself. Your only options for add-on functionality are to use an external add-on device that connects via either a USB port or a PC card.

Desktops

Desktop computers are like monuments: They get installed once and stay in that one spot seemingly forever. They don't move around and, generally speaking, can't enjoy the benefits of a wireless connection. Such machines get hard-wired to a wire-based network and stay that way. Given that one of the inherent tradeoffs between wire and wireless is speed versus mobility, it makes sense that desktop computers wouldn't be built with wireless access capabilities. Instead, desktop computers typically are built with 10/100 Mb Ethernet as a native feature. Connecting to a network can be as simple as just plugging in the network cable.

If you want a desktop computer to access a wireless network, you must purchase some type of aftermarket network access device. Two types are on the market. The first is a circuit board that you have to plug into one of the expansion slots on your computer's motherboard.

The second type is external and connects to one of your computer's USB ports. This type of device gets both its electrical power and its network connection over the same wire to your computer. More importantly, you can place the antenna in a spot that enhances its network connection. Because it is an external device, you don't have to install as you would a card on the motherboard. You simply plug it in.

Connecting to a Wire-Based Network

If you are connecting to a wire-based network, chances are you are connecting to either a 10 Mbps or 100 Mbps Fast Ethernet hub or switch. That hub or switch is an external device; you don't need to configure it as far as your computer is concerned.

You do need to configure the NIC that connects to that hub or switch. That's not as daunting a task as you might expect. For one thing, assuming your laptop isn't an antique, the operating system will automatically detect the NIC as well as whether it is actually connected to a network.

The following series of figures from a computer running Microsoft Windows XP shows this.

1. Start by opening your computer's Control Panel, which is shown in Figure 12-5.

Figure 12-5   The Control Panel Organizes Network and Internet Connection Options

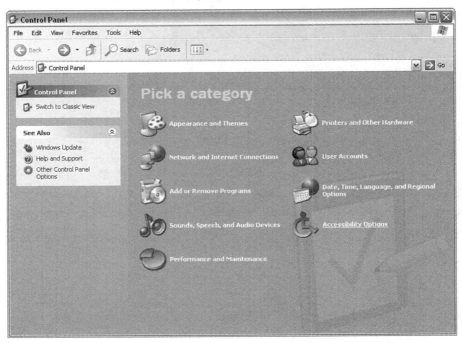

2. From the Control Panel screen, click the line that says Network and Internet Connections. That brings up a screen that organizes your connectivity options and offers three options for setting up or changing those options using a wizard.

Wizards are special software programs that "think" for you by asking questions and configuring software or services based on your answers. It makes sense to first configure your network connection and then configure your Internet access because you can't get to the Internet without a network connection! Chapter 13, "Smiling and Dialing," shows some ways to configure your Internet connection.

3. Click Network Connections to see all your computer's network interfaces. Figure 12-6 shows you all the network interfaces on one computer.

Figure 12-6   A Computer's Network Interfaces

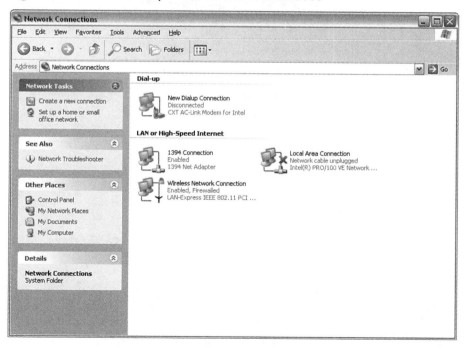

As you can see, this computer has three network connections: a Firewire 1394 interface (which typically connects to peripheral devices), a wireless network, and an unused Fast Ethernet interface. The red X indicates that the Fast Ethernet interface isn't connected to anything.

4. Clicking that red X brings up a new screen that lets you configure what services you want to run over that LAN connection. Figure 12-7 shows you that screen.

As you can see in that figure, TCP/IP is already selected for use on this network interface even though that interface isn't active. That should reinforce what the chapter is saying: TCP/IP has become the world's first choice in network protocols. The default settings are good enough to get you going.

Figure 12-7   LAN Connection Properties

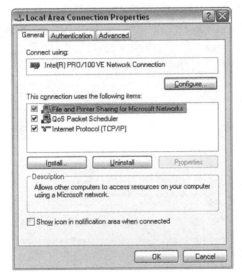

5. All that remains is to actually plug in the wire. You don't have to change a thing; just plug a modular twisted-pair cable into your network interface. The operating system acknowledges and starts using it. Figure 12-8 shows you how the red X on the Network Connections screen updates automatically when you physically connect to the network.

Figure 12-8   The Ethernet Connection Activates Automatically

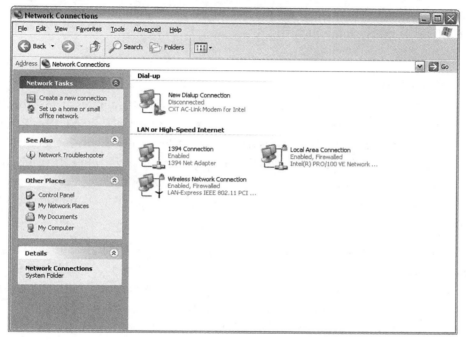

That's really all there is to configuring and activating a LAN connection on your computer. Getting a wireless connection working is just as easy!

Connecting to a Wireless Network

There are an abundance of acronyms that creep into wireless networking. For the sake of practicality, this exploration is limited to the wireless networks that are most commonly used to support TCP/IP communications. Those wireless networks include the following:

- IEEE 802.11a, which is also known as Wireless A

- IEEE 802.11b, also known as Wireless B

- IEEE 802.11g, better known as Wireless G

The user-friendly aliases ("wireless something") aren't much of an improvement on the official alphabet soup that the Institute of Electrical and Electronics Engineers (IEEE) gives each standard.

Wireless B and G

Wireless B is the older standard established by the IEEE. It operates at 11 Mbps. *Wireless G* operates at 54 Mbps and is ***backward-compatible*** with Wireless B. In other words, if you have a Wireless B laptop and a Wireless G network, that laptop will connect at 11 Mbps even though the network can run at 54 Mbps. If you have a Wireless G laptop and a Wireless B network, that laptop will connect and operate at the 11 Mbps rate of Wireless B, even though the laptop can communicate at much higher speeds.

A subtle implication of this type of interoperability between Wireless B and G is that both use the same radio waves. If Wireless B and G technologies didn't use the same radio waves, a Wireless B laptop wouldn't communicate with a Wireless G network or vice versa. In fact, both Wireless B and G use the 2.4 gigahertz (GHz) frequency range. Interoperability is a simple matter of figuring out how fast each device can talk.

Because both of these wireless technologies communicate at the same radio frequency, both enjoy similar distance limitations. With products conforming to both B and G, you can stay connected to the wireless LAN up to about 100 meters away. Obviously, depending on what lies between you and the wireless network in those intervening 100 meters, your mileage will vary!

Wireless A

Wireless A is a different animal. For one thing, instead of using the 2.4 GHz frequency, it communicates at the 5 GHz range. All by itself, that should tell you that although Wireless B and G can interoperate, Wireless A stands alone!

Wireless A can offer speeds up to 54 Mbps, which is equivalent to the Wireless G standard. Thus, it clearly outperforms Wireless B but offers the same performance as G for a *lot* more money! For your extra investment, you might be pained to realize that you sacrifice a great deal of distance: Wireless A networks lose signal after about 20 meters compared to the 100 meters of Wireless B and G. That's a function of the radio frequency they use.

Connecting Without Wires

Virtually all the laptops made today come equipped with some form of wireless LAN capability. Using that capability isn't a matter of installing a new feature—it is a matter of activating it. No need for PC card add-ons or external plug-ins! You sure won't have to look for a cable interface lurking behind one of the myriad hatches adorning your laptop's sides. You might, however, have to find the physical switch that turns it on.

When you power up your wireless connection, the first thing that device does is seek out wireless networks within its range.

1. Click the wireless network icon (which looks just like two desktop computers side by side) in the lower-right corner of your screen by the digital clock.

   This is a circuitous journey! Figure 12-9 shows you the first screen you see upon clicking that wireless LAN icon in the status bar.

Figure 12-9   Seeking Out Wireless LANs

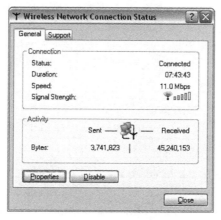

This screen offers a lot useful information. First of all, it confirms whether you are actually connected to the network. Next, it lists the signal strength (good, in this case) and the speed with which are you connected to the wireless LAN. This screen also tracks how many bytes you have sent and received since that session became active.

Notice that the laptop, even though of recent manufacture, only connected at 11 Mbps. That would indicate that the connection uses the IEEE 802.11 B standard instead of the more robust G standard. Clicking the Properties button on that screen brings up the aptly named General Wireless Network Connection Properties. That screen is illustrated in Figure 12-10.

Figure 12-10   General Wireless Network Connection Properties

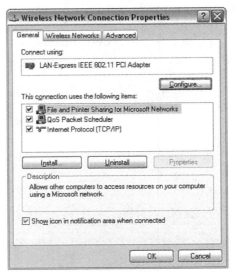

As was the case with wire-based Ethernet, the operating system assumes that you are using TCP/IP to communicate across that network interface. It is already selected for you.

2. More information is available about your wireless LAN connection by clicking the Wireless Networks tab at the top of the screen. This screen shows you how many wireless networks your computer is able to access. That screen is shown in Figure 12-11.

Figure 12-11   Wireless Network Connection Properties

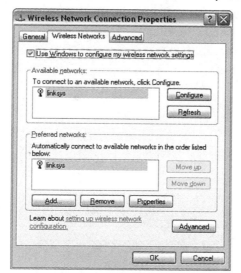

Figure 12-11 shows you a laptop, when operated from home, only finds one wireless network. Fortunately, that's the correct network! It is given the rather unimaginative name of linksys in honor of the hardware's manufacturer.

Go ahead and laugh for the unimaginative network name. Then think for a minute about how much information you would like to give away to anyone within radio range of your home network. Perhaps a generic name isn't so bad after all!

Assuming that your wireless network itself was configured properly, you should change two things about the default settings that Microsoft uses for wireless LANs. Both help to better secure your laptop and any data you might be transmitting. The first step is to enable your computer's firewall. Although a poor substitute for an industrial strength firewall, Microsoft's free version is better than nothing.

3. Click the Advanced tab at the top of the screen. (Do not click the Advanced button at the bottom of the screen.) Figure 12-12 shows you the screen you get when you do this properly.

Figure 12-12   Enabling Your Computer's Firewall for Wireless Connectivity

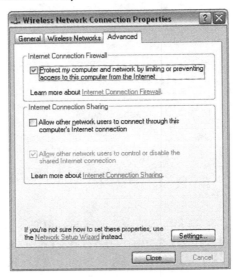

4. All you need to do to activate the firewall is check the box! That protects you from most unwanted intrusions from the Internet.

The next thing you want to do is to protect the data that you are sending and receiving across the radio waves. You can do that by encrypting the data that you are sending and receiving between your computer and wireless network.

5. When you are at the Wireless Network Connection Properties box, click the Configure button. That brings up the Wireless Network Connection Properties screen.

6. Check the box that says Data Encryption (WEP Enabled) and you are done! Figure 12-13 shows you this screen with that box selected.

 For wireless encryption to be activated, it must be enabled at both ends: the computer and the radio access point. This section assumes that the access point was already configured and just shows you how to configure your computer.

Figure 12-13   Encrypting Your Computer's Data Transmissions

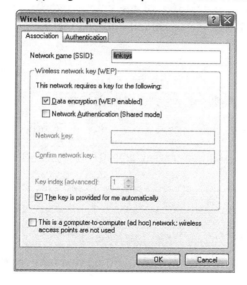

That really is all there is to it. By following these simple steps, you can configure and secure a wireless network connection.

Chapter Summary

TCP/IP absolutely requires a network of some type to communicate. That network can be any shape or size; it might even be multiple interconnected networks. This chapter introduces you two types of LANs: wire based and wireless. Each of these network types has its own unique combination of benefits and limitations. By understanding those benefits and limitations relative to your needs, you can be sure to pick the right solution for you. You can follow the instructions in this chapter for actually configuring your computer's connection to that network.

Now you are ready for the next step: using your network connection to access the Internet. Your options and how to actually do that are revealed in Chapter 13.

Chapter Review Questions

The following questions reinforce the key concepts in this chapter:

1. Explain the relationship between TCP/IP and networks such as Ethernet.

2. How many components are needed, at a minimum, to build a local-area network (LAN)?

3. What is the difference between a hub and a switch?

4. Is coaxial cable obsolete or does it still serve a purpose?

5. What is a Category of Performance?

6. What is the fastest speed at which a wireless network can operate?

7. What is the fastest speed at which an Ethernet wire-based network can operate?

8. Which is more reliable: wire-based networks or wireless networks?

9. What are the main drawbacks of wire-based networks?

10. What are the main advantages of wire-based networks?

11. What do wireless networks use to transmit signals?

12. What are the main benefits of wireless networks?

What You Will Learn

After reading this chapter, you should be able to answer the following questions:

- ✔ What is the Internet?

- ✔ What is the Internet's official network communications protocol?

- ✔ What are your options for accessing the Internet from home?

- ✔ Is the fastest access technology always the best choice for you?

- ✔ Under what circumstances might you find yourself still using a modem with a dedicated connection to a cable TV network?

CHAPTER 13

Smiling and Dialing

The previous chapter shows you how to connect your computer to a TCP/IP network. Truth be told, there are other ways to connect. Those ways might seem a bit antiquated, but are still quite useful and necessary: good old-fashioned dial-up modem and telephone line.

This chapter explains a bit more precisely what the Internet is and why that's important to you. Then you see some of the ways you can connect to the Internet. You also learn some of the ups and downs of each approach and how to set up your computer to connect to a TCP/IP network using a dial-up connection.

What, Exactly, Is the Internet?

The largest and most successful TCP/IP network ever built is the Internet. Within just a few short years, the Internet has gone from a quirky, complex network with arcane tools that only a geek could love, to a powerful, global utility that features user-friendly tools for all. Today's TCP/IP networks users have it so easy that they almost don't realize when they are using a network.

Before you can use the Internet (or any other TCP/IP network, for that matter), you first have to know how to connect to it! Since the Internet commercialized during the early 1990s, it has experienced a phenomenal rate of growth and acceptance. Today, access to the Internet is available at homes, libraries, motels, and even cafes and coffee shops. Even those who use the Internet routinely might be unable to tell you exactly what it is.

The *Internet* is a collection of networks that communicate via TCP/IP. Despite what some large ***Internet service providers*** (ISPs)—who shall remain nameless but whose name likely contains three initials—would have you believe based on their advertising and service, no single ISP has every host and every user connected to its network.

The Internet services industry has consolidated quite a bit, but there are probably still more than 10,000 ISPs around the world. Even though all sell essentially the same service, each ISP tries to differentiate itself from its peers through marketing and customized services. This is especially true of the large ISPs and the small ones that serve only local markets.

All ISPs Are Not Created Equal

Some ISPs focus on providing high-bandwidth pipes to businesses. Others specialize in providing low-bandwidth connections to residential consumers. Still others focus on residential consumers in general and try to add value beyond the connection. In general terms, these types of providers function as on-ramps to the Internet and are often referred to as such.

Some ***on-ramp providers*** try to lock you into their service by offering proprietary chat and instant messenger services. Others focus on hosting services. The one thing that all these types of ISPs have in common is that they don't cover the world.

You can think of the top-level providers as an ISP for ISPs. This small group provides Internet connectivity to smaller or regional ISPs. They form the backbone of the Internet and, as a result, are sometimes referred to as ***Internet backbone providers***. To give you a visual of how all this fits into perspective, take a look at Figure 13-1.

Figure 13-1   The Internet Is Made from Tiers of Networks

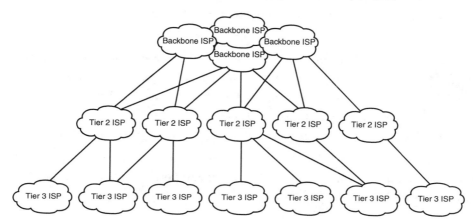

As you can see in Figure 13-1, the Internet is made up of lots of ISPs organized into functional tiers. Some providers play a game as they strive to appear bigger than they really are. For a while, the investment community favored Tier 1 ISPs as less risky than Tier 3 ISPs.

Although nobody ever clearly delineated what separates the tiers, Tier 1 was universally accepted to mean a backbone provider and Tier 3 was accepted to mean an on-ramp. Tier 2 generally means an ISP with a presence in multiple regions and a limited backbone interconnecting those regional networks. The distinctions between these three tiers became blurry over time because many providers embodied aspects of all three.

The important point here is that no single ISP can offer you universal connectivity alone. Even though any given pair of ISPs compete, they rely upon each other to support the Internet user community's need to reach every possible destination via one network connection. That's the real beauty of the Internet: For ISPs, it is simultaneously a competitive yet cooperative environment.

 Notice that Figure 13-1 is illustrative in nature and not an attempt to show you the actual architecture of the Internet. In general terms there are a lot of Tier 3 providers, an order of magnitude fewer Tier 2 providers, and just a handful or so of true Tier 1 providers.

Now that you know a little bit more about how the Internet is pieced together and have seen that not all ISPs are created equal, the important decision facing you is how to pick an ISP.

Picking an ISP

Almost everyone is affected by peer pressure and ISPs know this. They know that anyone can respond to a media advertisement or be swayed by the influence of a friend or family member. In fact, some ISPs count on that to increase their sub-scriber base and convert those new users into long-term users. That's just good business. What's good for an ISP might not be good for you! Your approach to selecting an ISP should be more of a logical process than a falling-for-peer-pressure process. You should understand your needs and then search for an ISP that can satisfy you.

You already walked through some of the differences between ISPs, and in those differences lie the clues to your decision-making process:

- Find an ISP that provides service in your area.

- Consider the access technologies that the ISPs in your area support. One question you need to answer is whether they support residential consumers. Remember: Not all on-ramp ISPs market to homes. Some only market high-speed connections for enterprises. Do they support only dial-up or can you get a faster connection? Is a faster connection important to you?

- Consider what, if any, amenities are offered by those ISPs. ISP amenities are things like a home page environment, utilities for contacting and interacting with others on the net (such as instant messaging or chat), and whether those are important to you.

  For some users, a high-speed connection without any home environment is perfect—but that's me. You need to evaluate your particular needs and weigh your options carefully. For example, you might actually have friends, in which case knowing when they are online might be important to you.

- How solid are they financially? The Internet as an industry has undergone tremendous consolidation in the last five years. Many ISPs are no longer around and many are still around but not necessarily here to stay.

  You can take some comfort in knowing that of all the assets an ISP has, its customers are its most valuable. In a merger, acquisition, or bankruptcy, it is the customer base (not circuits, shareholders, hardware, or employees) that is most highly valued. This criterion should be the least of the data points that you consider when making this decision, but it should be one of your data points. No sense in signing on for a year's service when the ISP is about to shut its doors. Especially if they are offering discounts if you pay for that year's worth of service in advance!

There are many telltale signs of an ISP in trouble, not the least of which is the financial information that a publicly traded company must publish. If your ISP has been losing money for several quarters in a row, if its stock price is sinking steadily, or if it has been making local headlines for laying off employees, you should beware! If it is a company you wouldn't invest in, you should be wary of being its customer, too. Generally speaking, smaller ISPs are more vulnerable than larger ones, but even major ISPs have gone bankrupt during the implosion of the ISP industry. Caveat emptor!

Picking an Access Technology

Before you can use the Internet, you have to connect to it. Fortunately, you have a few options. Those options reflect the different technologies for connecting. Some technologies are just a bit beyond the budget of most residential users, while others are custom made for the small office/home office (SoHo) market.

You have two basic choices for connecting to the Internet:

- Dial-up

- A dedicated broadband connection (such as Digital Subscriber Line [DSL] or cable service)

Of those two options, the first one requires you to establish a connection each and every time you want to use the Internet. The other option is known as **_always-on_** or **_dedicated access_**. Your connection to the Internet is active as soon as you turn on your computer. Configuring a dedicated connection is much like configuring a connection to a TCP/IP network, which is what you see in Chapter 12, "Connecting to TCP/IP Networks." What you haven't yet seen is how to use a dial-up connection to get on a TCP/IP network.

It is quite tempting to just say that faster is always better when it comes to connecting to the Internet. As a general rule, that is true enough. However, there might be more to deciding how to connect to the Internet than you might have at first believed. The next section gives you inside scoop about some of the different access technologies and lets you see why smiling and dialing is still a popular pastime.

More Power!

Perhaps Freud was right: The quest for bigger, better, and faster says interesting things about the person engaged in said pursuit. There are real benefits for a bigger, better, faster connection to the Internet. The Internet, with rare exception, has become increasingly graphic intensive. Although websites with a lot of graphics might look pretty, they can take a while to download— especially if you don't have a robust connection.

The shift toward graphic-intensive websites drove the development of new transmission technologies. These new technologies were designed specifically for carrying data traffic. After emerging, they quickly surpassed the performance level of dial-up technologies. These alternatives to dial-up service are known generically as **broadband connections**. Unlike dial-up service, which requires you to establish a connection when you want to go online, a dedicated connection is always on and available. In that regards it functions precisely as a local-area network (LAN).

The two main types of dedicated connectivity available to residential Internet users are some form of DSL and cable. Both afford much faster transmission rates than dial-up can, although your actual speed might vary.

What's the Catch?

Dedicated connections save you the time to connect to the network and run faster than dial-ups…so what's the catch? Simple! The strength of dedicated connections is also their weakness. If the connection is always on TCP/IP is running whenever you turn your computer on. You already know that TCP/IP communicates bidirectionally. It also doesn't really need much, if any, input from you to function properly.

That means that the catch with a dedicated connection is that your computer is always connected to a hot connection and is making decisions without your explicit knowledge and consent. That might not seem like such a big deal, but it really is. Your computer answers incoming requests and might even let a virus or other nasty software into your computer.

For example, one of the myriad utilities embedded in TCP/IP is designed to facilitate file transfers. There are actually two versions of that utility. The first is known, somewhat obviously, as **File Transfer Protocol (FTP)**. FTP is a wonderful little tool, but it requires your specific input to work. You log on to a computer through a TCP/IP network, start the FTP session, and use that protocol's features to send or receive files. That's fine, but FTP has a sinister sibling. That sibling protocol is the **Trivial File Transfer Protocol (TFTP)**. Maybe it wasn't intended to be sinister, but it gets misused more often than properly used.

With TFTP, you don't have to log on to the other computer to start the file transfer session. As long as that computer is up, running, and using TCP/IP to communicate, a TFTP session can be initiated without any other intervention. As a result of that "feature," TFTP has become one of the tools that virus writers exploit. Using TFTP, a virus can be put on your computer without you even knowing about it. That's just one more reason to configure a good firewall and an even better reason to be particularly cautious about always-on connections.

Potential security threats aside, dedicated broadband connections can provide a satisfying Internet experience. None of the dedicated broadband technologies has yet to put the final nail in the coffin for dial-up Internet access. The reasons are varied but easy enough to understand. Keep reading and I'll fill you in on the story with dial-up connections.

What's the Story with Dial-Up Connections?

Dial-up connections are made using *plain old telephone service (POTS)* and a modem. A POTS line, as the name indicates, is a regular telephone line. You might have noticed that telephone lines excel at carrying sounds. That implies that when you use a POTS line to establish a data connection, you need some device that converts your computer's digital signals to sounds. That device is a *modem*. You might have heard those sounds—a collection of rapid pulses of whistles and beeps—if you have ever picked up an incoming fax call.

Now that you know what a modem and a POTS line are, it's time to take a look at how they work together. Then you see how to decide whether they are for you and, if they are, how to configure a dial-up connection on your computer.

How Does It Work?

How does it work? An excellent question! The beginning of this chapter tells you about some of the differences in ISPs and how they really serve different markets within the Internet. Some of those ISPs that function as residential on-ramps would have to support dial-up connectivity to the Internet. Think about it this way: Cable network operators want you to access the Internet using their cable network, whereas local telephone companies want you to use their telephone lines. Independent ISPs (those that aren't a cable or telephone company) are at a distinct disadvantage when it comes to connecting your home to their network.

Independent ISPs have been consolidating (translation: going out of business) at a frightening pace. They still exist and still serve a useful purpose. Such ISPs rely upon your home's telephone line as a way to connect you to their network. To support this, they buy hundreds of modems and install them in a series so when you dial the main telephone number, your call is routed to the next available modem in the pool.

The modems would need to be connected to the telephone company's network. Instead of buying hundreds of POTS lines, it's better to buy trunk lines. A *trunk line* is a generic term for a high-capacity telecommunications line that can carry multiple dial-up sessions simultaneously. These modems aren't connected to a computer; they are connected to a network. After you prove your identity as a paying customer (by correctly responding to the ID and password challenge), you have free run of the network.

Figures 13-2 and 13-3 show you how this type of Internet access works.

Figure 13-2   Topology of a Dial-Up Internet Service Before a Call

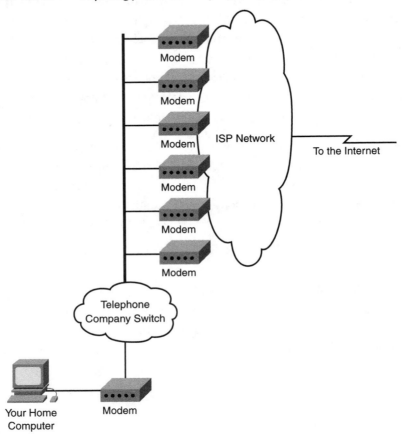

Figure 13-3   Topology of a Dial-Up Internet Service During a Call

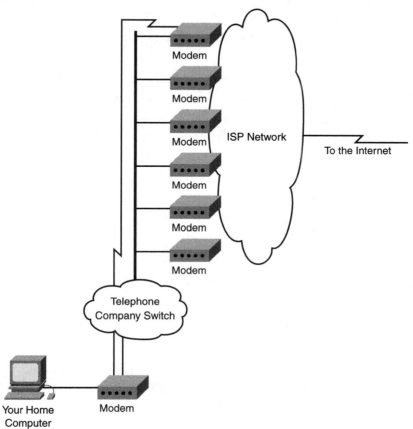

As you can see from comparing Figures 13-2 and 13-3, no permanent connection
exists between your computer and the Internet. Instead, there is a physical link
between your computer and your local telephone company's switch. That switch
makes a temporary physical connection to your ISP when you initiate a dial-up
session. The dial-up session is indicated with lightning bolts.

You have two main choices with respect to modems. Modems have become so inexpensive that they are frequently built into today's computers. Internal modems require only that you plug a modular telephone cord into a telephone jack and then configure your dial-up connection.

If you have an older computer or bought a new computer that didn't have a modem built in, you can add an external one. Setting up an external modem is only slightly more complicated than setting up an internal modem. You need to plug it into an electrical outlet, cable it to your computer using, and then connect it to the modular telephone jack.

Later, this chapter walks you through configuring a dial-up connection logically on your computer.

Dial-Up Today

One of the questions that must be running through your mind is "In this era of residential broadband service, does anybody really still use dial-up technology to access the Internet?" That's a fair question.

Dial-up technologies used to be the only game in town. If you wanted to make a data connection to the Internet from home, you were smiling and dialing. Over time, the quality of the connection increased greatly from just a few hundred bits per second (bps) to about 56,000 bps. That's about where it has stalled.

Remember: You are using a telephone line that was only designed for carrying voice signals, so there is a finite amount of bandwidth available. Over time, modems became capable of processing up to 115,200 bps, which is great over voice-grade telephone lines, but still paltry in comparison to the performance offered by other dedicated transmission technologies.

Modems that communicate over POTS lines are restricted to just 56,000 bps because a POTS line can only carry 64,000 bps. You need some of that capacity for managing the connection, so the theoretical maximum throughput of a modem is 56,000 bps. Modems that transmit at any rate greater than 56,000 bps use compression to reduce the number of bits that need to be sent. Thus, more data gets sent per second even though the modem still only transmits at 56,000 bps.

The other drawback to dial-up service might seem trivial. Still, it is worth mentioning. The process of initiating a communications session can take a little while, although certainly a matter of seconds, not minutes. Think about that. While dedicated connections are always on, with dial-up you have to actually dial the receiving end, wait for the receiving modem to answer, and then negotiate how fast the two modems can talk. All that can occur in less than a minute, but you must suffer that wait every time you want to connect.

When All Else Fails...

...there are still good old modems and POTS lines! Modems and POTS lines are still used in areas where dedicated Internet access technologies aren't available. Let's face it: Cable companies still don't have the same global reach of wire-based telephone companies. Some neighborhoods are just too sparsely populated to make it worthwhile for cable companies to extend their networks there. For such neighborhoods, modems and POTS lines are still the only game in town.

Even if Cable Is Available...

...there might still be a use for modems and POTS lines. Even in neighborhoods where cable companies have built a network, modems and POTS lines might play a role. You see, not every cable company has built a network capable of transmitting and receiving data.

The original cable TV networks were designed just to send signals to their customers. In areas where there is only a one-way network, cable companies offer a service known as an asymmetric cable service. Connecting to the Internet via an *asymmetric cable solution* requires you to use a modem and POTS line as your uplink and the cable as the downlink. As Figure 13-4 shows, you transmit to the Internet using the modem and POTS line and receive via the cable.

Figure 13-4 Modem and POTS Line in an Asymmetric Cable Modem Connection

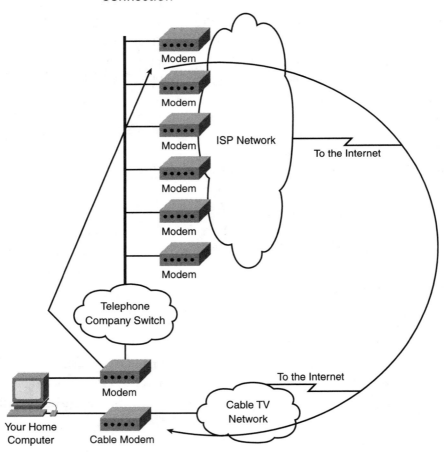

This solution might seem a bit awkward, but it actually makes a lot of sense. Asymmetric service was conceived as a cost-effective way of providing cable-based Internet access without incurring the cost of upgrading the cable network to two-way capability. The asymmetry is in the performance capabilities of the two connections. Cable service is high bandwidth; sometimes as fast as 1 million bps per second on the connection to your home. Dial-up is slow in comparison and is frequently hard pressed to hit more than 50,000 bps in actual throughput.

That might seem like a tragic mismatch of technologies until you stop and think about your Internet usage habits. You open a browser and type in a tiny little command to access a website. That command might be as simple as typing http:// www.cisco.com in your browser's address bar. That paltry amount of data easily fits inside just one packet. However, you receive an entire web page filled with lots of information and pretty pictures. Depending on where you go on the Internet, it is possible that the one packet you sent results in the receipt of hundreds of packets. In other words, the nature of web browsing is asymmetric, so why not build a network that way?

The bottom line with dial-up technologies is this: Their best days are behind them but they are not dead yet! Until broadband technologies become as widely installed as telephones, there continues to be a need for modems and POTS lines.

Configuring a Dial-Up Connection

Now that you have learned a little bit about how dial-up Internet access works, it's time to get your computer ready for this. Before you start dialing, tell your computer that you have attached a modem and are using it to connect to the Internet. The good news is that is easy to do.

Configuring a dial-up connection can be as simple as letting a Microsoft Windows Wizard do the work for you. However, the wizard isn't a mind reader. It gets you a functional connection but not necessarily an optimal connection. Later, this chapter

returns to that point. For right now, take a look at how you can get the wizard to
work for you.

1. From your computer's Control Panel (assuming you are using a Microsoft
   operating system), select Network and Internet Connections. The Network
   and Internet Connections menu is illustrated in Figure 13-5.

Figure 13-5   Open the Network and Internet Connections Menu

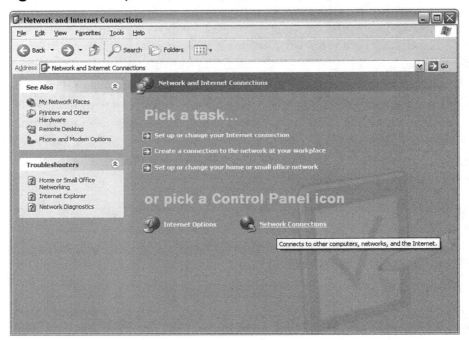

2. Under the Pick a Task section, click Set Up or Change Your Internet Connection.
   That brings up the Internet Properties Connections tab shown in Figure 13-6.

Figure 13-6   Connections Tab of the Internet Properties Dialog Box

You are probably thinking: Where's the wizard? Fear not—this is where the wizard lives.

3. Click once to select the New Dial-up Connection item and then click the Add button to the right. That brings up the New Connection Wizard screen illustrated in Figure 13-7.

Figure 13-7   New Connection Wizard

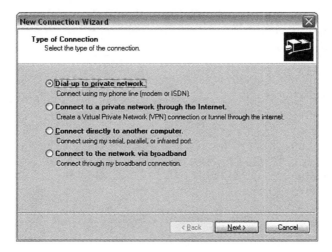

4. Select Dial-up to Private Network and press Next, as indicated in Figure 13-7.

5. Enter the telephone number that you will dial. As reminded by the wizard, this is the actual number that you feed to your modem, so you might need to preface it with a 1 or a 1 and an area code. When in doubt, dial the number from a regular telephone to figure out exactly what your modem needs to dial.

6. When you have entered the number, press Next at the bottom of the screen.

7. The next screen you see lets you name your dial-up connection for future reference. The name Dial-up My ISP is shown here. This is illustrated in Figure 13-8.

Figure 13-8   Naming Your Dial-Up Connection

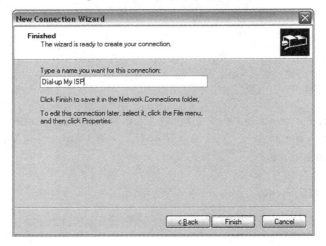

8. Click Finish. After clicking the Finish button, you might be surprised to learn that you really aren't finished with the creation process. Instead, you get yet another screen that asks you to furnish some more personal information.

9. Provide the information (such as your network logon and password for that dial-up ISP).

10. On this screen, you also need to check the box that instructs your computer's operating system to automatically detect your modem's settings. This is the safest way to configure a modem and takes the guesswork out of your chore.

11. Press the OK button at the bottom of the screen when you are finished entering your personal information. This screen is illustrated in Figure 13-9.

Figure 13-9   Adding Personal Information

12. After you press OK, you are returned to the Connections tab of the Internet Connections menu. The difference is that now you can see the dial-up connection you just configured.

From now on, whenever you want to modify your connection, all you have to do is click that named connection and press Settings.

There! You've done it. You have successfully set up a dial-up connection on your computer. Will you be happy with it? Probably. Just to make sure, you are shown how to track the wizard and see just what decisions it made for you.

Tracking Down the Wizard

As said before, most of the default settings selected by the Network Setup Wizard get you up and running. It is still a good idea to check on the wizard and make some important refinements. To do that, you need to know what settings the wizard modifies and how to modify them without his help.

1. Go back to the Network and Internet Connections menu you saw illustrated in Figure 13-5.

2. Click the Network Connections option. The Network Connections Menu you see next offers a choice of managing either dial-up connections or LAN/high-speed connections.

3. Select the Dial-Up Connections option. Figure 13-10 shows you this screen.

Figure 13-10   Network Connections Menu

As you've seen throughout this chapter, dial-up connections are established on demand. Thus, it shouldn't be a surprise to see that the dial-up connection just configured shows a disconnected state while two of the three high-speed connections are enabled, or active.

Now turn your attention to a couple of settings.

4. From the Network Connections Menu, double-click the Dial-Up My ISP (or whatever name you have chosen for your dial-up Internet connection). This brings up a box you probably haven't seen before. That screen appears for you in Figure 13-11.

Figure 13-11   Checking Your Dial-Up Configuration

That screen is simple enough: It shows a user ID but hides the password for the sake of security. Also, for the sake of security, you have the option of limiting this ID, password, and dial-up connection for just yourself. In fact, that's the default that the wizard selects for you. Windows XP allows you to establish multiple user identities. Thus, even though this could be your computer, your wife and children could use it via their own logons. The default setting prevents anyone else from using my connection to the Internet.

The next interesting field is the telephone number to be dialed. Under normal circumstances, this number shouldn't change. However, you might be traveling or experience network difficulties that require you to either modify or change the telephone number. If so, here's your opportunity to do so.

If you are trying to connect from an office or hotel, you might be dialing through a privately owned telephone switch (known as a **PBX** or **private branch exchange**) that services the entire building. If so, a special numeric signal must be sent to indicate your wish to dial outside that local switch. Typically a 9 is that signal, but that is not universally true.

If you are having trouble connecting from a large building or hotel, you might want to ask what number to dial to get out of that building! Put that number in front of the number you are dialing.

5. When it comes time to actually establish a dial-up connection to the Internet, this is the screen that you use. Click the Dial button at the lower left of the box and away you go!

If, however, you are interested in seeing what other decisions the wizard has made on your behalf, you might want to explore other buttons and tabs on this box first. Click the Properties button at the bottom of this box to continue exploring.

General Tab

The first tab you get to explore comes up automatically when you click Properties in the General tab. Figure 13-12 shows you this screen.

The General tab is where you can add other, alternate dial-up telephone numbers. Remember: The wizard lets you stipulate one but you might need more! Clicking the Alternates button lets you do this.

Figure 13-12   The General Tab

The wizard also figured out what type of modem was installed and selected that manufacturer and model number. If you want to change that modem's settings, this is the screen that lets you do that, too. Simply click the Configure button to see what your options are. Fortunately, this is one area where the wizard does a good job and you shouldn't need to change any modem settings. Unless you like to live dangerously, it is time to move on to the Options tab.

Options Tab

Earlier, this chapter told you that one of the disadvantages to dial-up connections is the amount of time required to actually set up the call. Under normal operating conditions, call setup time is seconds, not minutes. However, some conditions such as busy signals can cause you to wait seemingly forever to establish a connection. The Options tab shows you how to manage your dialing and redialing options. This tab is shown in Figure 13-13.

Figure 13-13 The Options Tab

The dialing options are there for your peace of mind. Somehow, it always feels better when you can see your call setup attempt making progress. Launching the task and not getting any feedback at all during the setup leaves you wondering if the call is really being set up.

The selected redialing options are those you hope never to use. If these rules come into effect, it is because your attempt to set up a call to the Internet failed. Multiplying the number of retry attempts by the amount of time between the redial attempts shows you just how long it can take to get onto the Internet using a dial-up connection.

The Options tab has a button labeled X.25. That's an ancient network technology you will probably never have to worry about unless you travel to lesser developed nations. If you limit your travels to North America, you probably can go a lifetime without ever having to worry about that button or technology!

The only option on this menu that you might want to change is the one labeled Redial if Line Is Dropped. That's fairly self explanatory: If you check this box, Windows automatically starts redialing your Internet access connection if your session is disconnected while in use. Why the wizard doesn't select this for you is a mystery to me, but that's why it is important to track down the wizard.

Security Tab

Despite its important if not ominous name, the contents of this tab are really anti-climactic. Surely there is more to securing a TCP/IP connection than this paltry set of options indicates! Indeed, there is more to securing a TCP/IP connection than Microsoft would have you believe. I'll vacate my soapbox for now and help you understand why this tab exists.

Figure 13-14 shows you the Security tab.

Figure 13-14   Security Tab

As you can see in Figure 13-14, you really have only two Security options available on this tab. The first set is labeled Typical (which evokes the reaction, "My thought exactly!") and Advanced. The wizard sets just three Typical settings:

- To use just an ID and password as opposed to more rigorous authentication. The wizard defaults to the least secure method of authenticating you.

- Whether you want to use your Windows logon as the logon ID when dialing remote networks. The wizard doesn't activate this feature.

- Deciding if you want to encrypt all data that you send and receive. The wizard leaves this feature off. If you activate it and then try to dial a network that doesn't support encryption, your dial-up session is always automatically terminated. It's probably best to leave this turned off.

The advanced settings requires—as the box says—a knowledge of security and security protocols. If you select the Advanced settings and then click the Settings button to its right, your efforts are rewarded with a handful of options for other authentication protocols. For the sake of connecting to the Internet, these authentication protocols probably won't be necessary. However, if you were to ever connect to a private network (such as your employer's wide-area network) using a dial-up connection, you might find these options necessary.

Overall, the wizard does a decent job of selecting security options for you. My only gripe with this tab is that there is more to securing a TCP/IP communications session than just encryption and authentication.

Networking Tab

If you click the Networking tab, you see yet another screen that lets you configure communications protocols. Notice that Windows assumes you are using TCP/IP. It is conveniently selected for you.

Figure 13-15 shows you the Networking Properties menu. On this menu you can specify just two things: whether you are connecting to a Microsoft or UNIX system and which protocols you use to communicate with that remote system.

Figure 13-15 Networking Properties Menu

The default values on the Networking Properties menu likely do just fine. Clicking this menu's Properties button brings up another screen, which allows you to stipulate IP address information. The default is that your computer gets an IP address for you automatically when you dial up to your ISP. The same is true for a *Domain Name System (DNS)*. Unless you have an IP address permanently assigned to you by your ISP (which is extremely unlikely, especially when you connect via dial-up), these two options are perfect for you. Figure 13-16 shows you the default values.

Figure 13-16   The Internet Protocol (TCP/IP) Properties Menu

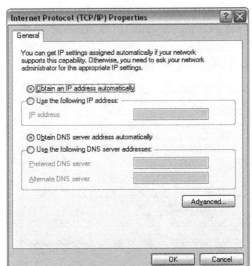

Advanced Tab

The last configuration setting for your dial-up Internet connection is hidden under the Advanced tab of the New Dial-up Connection menu. You can choose only two options here and the first one is really important. Figure 13-17 shows you this screen.

Did you notice that the first option isn't checked? Apparently the wizard doesn't believe it is necessary to protect your computer and network from unwanted intrusions while you are connected to the Internet. That option is really a roundabout way of saying "Would you like to activate the firewall that comes bundled with Windows?" The answer is: absolutely!

A *firewall* can be either a physical device or a piece of software that protects you from unwanted Internet intrusions. When it comes to the Internet, what you don't see absolutely hurts you. Remember: TCP/IP is always running when your computer is turned on. That means it is always available for your communications needs, but it is also always available for answering any inbound communications attempts.

Figure 13-17 Advanced Properties Menu

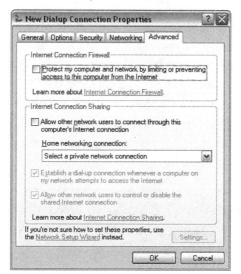

For example, virus writers often rely upon TFTP to plant a virus on your computer's hard drive. A properly configured firewall prevents that TFTP session from reaching your computer. Similarly, a firewall can make your computer "invisible" to the Internet by hiding your IP address and preventing any ***Internet Control Message Protocol***-based messages that originate outside your network. Such steps are small, but all contribute to your protection.

At a minimum, the "Would you like to activate the firewall?" box in Windows XP should come checked for you as a default. If nothing else, this option is important enough that it should be the first option in the Security tab. This critical feature should not be hidden under the Advanced tab. Doing so sends the message that if you don't consider yourself an astute user of networked computers, you don't need anything tucked away on that tab. This is the biggest reason of all to not trust the wizard.

Now that you have put up with the ranting, rest easy knowing that you learned how to properly configure a dial-up connection to the Internet. The key word in the preceding sentence was *properly*. Anyone can follow the wizard, but you know how to keep him honest, too. That's really all there is to it!

Chapter Summary

Residential consumers can choose from different ways to connect to the Internet. Each access technology has its own abilities and limitations, which can bias your decision. An even greater influence in your access technology selection is a bit more pragmatic: What's available in your neighborhood? Despite all the technological advances in networking technologies, dial-up access using modems and POTS lines continues to soldier on. In this chapter, you learn some of the reasons modems and POTS lines are still quite necessary and how you can use them to access the Internet.

You also learn how to set up and configure your computer for a dial-up connection, as well as how to keep the wizard honest! Chapter 14, "Taking the Next Step," shows you what to do when things don't quite go as expected!

Chapter Review Questions

The following questions reinforce the key concepts in this chapter:

1. What is the Internet?

2. What is the official network communications protocol of the Internet?

3. What are your options for accessing the Internet from home?

4. Is the fastest access technology always the best choice for you?

5. Under what circumstances might you find yourself still using a modem with a dedicated connection to a cable TV network?

What You Will Learn

After reading this chapter, you should be able to answer the following questions:

- ✔ What is troubleshooting?

- ✔ What command verifies that TCP/IP is configured correctly on your computer?

- ✔ Which TCP/IP utility tests the reachability of any given destination on the Internet?

- ✔ Which tool would you use to see if your computer's Ethernet connection is working properly?

- ✔ Which tool would you use to see if your computer's TCP/IP protocol suite is working effectively?

- ✔ How would you find out if the computer you are trying to access (or the network it is connected to) is experiencing heavy congestion?

- ✔ Which tool tracks the path your packets take through a network?

CHAPTER 14

Taking the Next Step

Nobody with any measure of self respect wants to abdicate responsibility for their own lot in life. When it comes to TCP/IP networks, most users unfortunately do just that. When something doesn't work, they simply swallow their pride, reach for the phone, and put themselves at the mercy of the local support organization. With a little bit of guidance, there is no reason every single user of TCP/IP networks can't take the next step and assume some responsibility for his or her own internetworking actions. If nothing else, your local support organization will appreciate a more carefully thought-out trouble call instead of the usual "Help! My network doesn't work."

To assist you in taking that next step, there's another group of tools that almost defy categorization (except that they are quite useful)! This collection of miscellany can help you find out the exact path your data takes to any given destination, find out if a server is reachable or in service, determine the name of a remote device, and discover how your computer is configured with respect to its TCP/IP settings. All this information can come in handy and can even help you transition beyond being just a user of TCP/IP networks. They are quirky utilities, to be sure, but they can help you take the next step into diagnosing network troubles.

This chapter introduces you to some of those quirky utilities and shows you how to use them. These utilities might be a bit obscure and are probably also not as feature rich or user friendly as some of those you've become accustomed to, but they are invaluable if you know what to do with them.

Information, Please!

Your first step in taking responsibility for your own internetworking success: becoming adept at gathering all the information you really need. This is what separates the newbies from the veterans. The veterans won't be satisfied with just knowing how to use a network. They want to figure out a little more clearly what happened if they suddenly can't connect to their favorite network destinations. Before you can figure out what's going on, you need to gather any information pertinent to your connection and destination.

The two tools that you need to start this information gathering exercise are **whois** and **ipconfig**. They are different tools and not necessarily even part of TCP/IP, but they are *the* place to start.

Checking Your Configuration

If you are a Windows XP user, your operating system comes with what's known as a command prompt. The command prompt used to be the old DOS prompt, but let's face it: DOS is dead, so why keep its name alive?

Accessing your command prompt is relatively simple:

1. Click the **Start** button in the lower left of your screen.

2. Select **All Programs**, which brings up a menu of all programs installed on your computer.

3. From there, slide your pointer or mouse to select **Accessories**. That brings up another submenu of applications, one of which is the command prompt.

   Figure 14-1 shows you this last step of the process. Alternatively, depending on your version of Windows, you can also click **Start > Run**, and type **CMD**. Either way will work.

4. Clicking the **Command Prompt** opens a new window on your desktop. Inside that window is a *command-line interface (CLI)*. Although it seems quaint, if not just plain crude, in comparison to the *graphical user interfaces (GUI)* found in today's applications, the CLI used to rule the world. In fact, the command prompt is all that's left of the original PC operating systems.

Figure 14-1   Select Command Prompt from the Accessories Menu

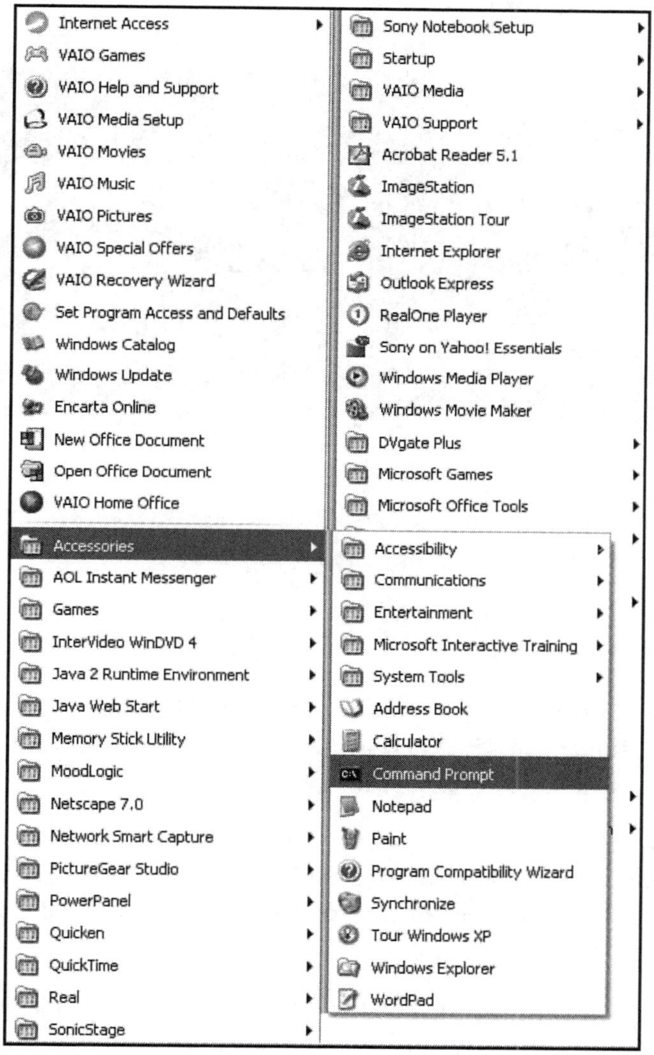

Internet Access ▶	Sony Notebook Setup ▶
VAIO Games	Startup ▶
VAIO Help and Support	VAIO Media ▶
VAIO Media Setup	VAIO Support ▶
VAIO Movies	Acrobat Reader 5.1
VAIO Music	ImageStation
VAIO Pictures	ImageStation Tour
VAIO Special Offers	Internet Explorer
VAIO Recovery Wizard	Outlook Express
Set Program Access and Defaults	RealOne Player
Windows Catalog	Sony on Yahoo! Essentials
Windows Update	Windows Media Player
Encarta Online	Windows Movie Maker
New Office Document	DVgate Plus ▶
Open Office Document	Microsoft Games ▶
VAIO Home Office	Microsoft Office Tools ▶
Accessories ▶	Accessibility ▶
AOL Instant Messenger ▶	Communications ▶
Games ▶	Entertainment ▶
InterVideo WinDVD 4 ▶	Microsoft Interactive Training ▶
Java 2 Runtime Environment ▶	System Tools ▶
Java Web Start ▶	Address Book
Memory Stick Utility ▶	Calculator
MoodLogic ▶	Command Prompt
Netscape 7.0 ▶	Notepad
Network Smart Capture ▶	Paint
PictureGear Studio ▶	Program Compatibility Wizard
PowerPanel ▶	Synchronize
Quicken ▶	Tour Windows XP
QuickTime ▶	Windows Explorer
Real ▶	WordPad
SonicStage ▶	

5. Type **ipconfig** in this window and your computer's operating system gets all the information it has on how IP was configured on your computer.

Figure 14-2 shows you the results of running **ipconfig** on my personal laptop computer with the Windows XP operating system.

Figure 14-2   Using the Command Prompt to Run the **ipconfig** Command

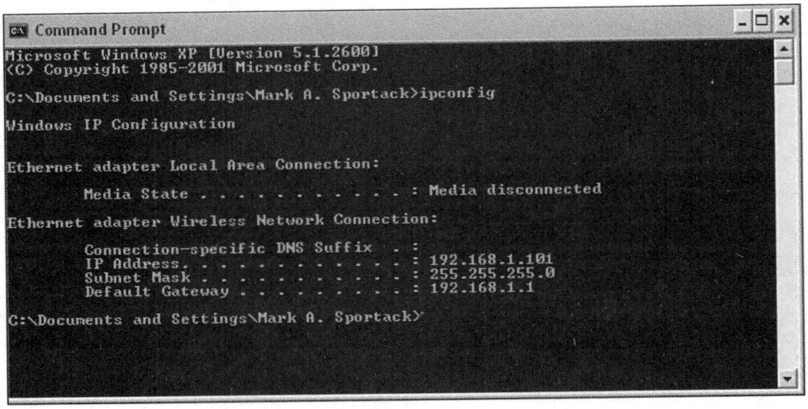

```
Command Prompt                                                    _ □ ×
Microsoft Windows XP [Version 5.1.2600]
(C) Copyright 1985-2001 Microsoft Corp.

C:\Documents and Settings\Mark A. Sportack>ipconfig

Windows IP Configuration

Ethernet adapter Local Area Connection:

        Media State . . . . . . . . . . . : Media disconnected

Ethernet adapter Wireless Network Connection:

        Connection-specific DNS Suffix  . :
        IP Address. . . . . . . . . . . . : 192.168.1.101
        Subnet Mask . . . . . . . . . . . : 255.255.255.0
        Default Gateway . . . . . . . . . : 192.168.1.1

C:\Documents and Settings\Mark A. Sportack>
```

The **ipconfig** command gives you some fairly important pieces of information. The things you can learn using this command include

- Your computer's IP address. My IP address, at the time of this snapshot, was 192.168.1.101.

- The size of the subnet being used by the network to which you are connected. Using a 255.255.255.0 subnet mask gives the ability to create 254 devices in a home network, for instance.

- The IP address of the network device that connects you to the outside world. Known as a *default gateway*, this device is typically a router that connects your network to either the Internet or another network. My default gateway's IP address is 192.168.1.1.

There is even more vital information presented in this concise little tool. It tells you whether your computer is actually connected to the network. If you refer back to Figure 14-2, you see that my laptop has two network connections defined: One is a traditional Ethernet interface and the other is a more modern wireless Ethernet interface. To show you both the normal state and the error condition, the home network was connected to using a wireless connection and the Fast Ethernet connection was left disconnected.

The result is that all the current IP configuration data shows up under the wireless network connection. The wire-based Ethernet local-area network (LAN) connection shows this error message: media disconnected. If you are ever unable to access a network destination, first run **ipconfig** to determine whether your computer is actually connected to the network! Nothing is more embarrassing than opening a trouble ticket only to find out that you failed to physically connect to the network.

After you ascertain that you really are connected to the network, the rest of the information is of use to your network administrator: You will have saved that person some effort and she will probably hold you in higher esteem for that.

Internet's Yellow Pages

Now that you know how to get your own computer's IP address information, your next challenge is to learn more about the organization that owns the IP address of the destination you might be trying to access via the Internet. This is useful in many ways. It is most useful in figuring out if an Internet domain is legitimate or suspicious. It's not unlike using a phone book to look up a contractor or other business whose services you are considering employing.

The Internet doesn't really have a phone book, but it does have an incredibly useful tool that lets you find organizations connected to it. This tool is the utility called **whois**. That's spelled correctly. Remember, this is a text-based tool that predated the ability to insert spaces in filenames.

whois is a command that lets you search the Internet's databases to find organizations, their contact information, what IP address block(s) they use, and which Internet domain names they use. Unfortunately, most people never even realize that this tool exists, much less what types of information are contained in Internet databases. Consequently, **whois** often is relegated to just the engineering community. That's a shame because **whois** is remarkably easy to use and can be invaluable.

To be perfectly honest, **whois** really isn't a TCP/IP utility as much as it is a standardized naming convention for accessing data about Internet user communities.

There are actually two main types of **whois** queries. Both use the same command name (**whois**) but search different databases and return different information. The two databases are maintained by different Internet organizations, although many other groups maintain **whois** databases. The main two are maintained by *American Registry for Internet Numbers (ARIN)* and the InterNIC.

InterNIC's whois

InterNIC is the Internet's Network Information Center. InterNIC tracks such useful data as the name of the company that registered any given Internet domain, the date it created that domain, whether it is an active domain, and when that domain name expires. This information can be useful in a wide variety of ways.

I personally use it to track down spammers, but you might find it equally useful in checking to see if that nifty domain name you thought up is actually available (or if someone else had that same brilliant thought before you did). It might be easier to just guess and enter your guesses repeatedly in your browser, but this takes some of the risk out of that venture.

Guessing URLs used to be a safe and convenient way to find a new website. As the Internet matured, darker forces appeared. Consequently, guessing URLs is no longer as safe as it used to be. Many pornographers intentionally register domain names that are an easy typographical error away from globally recognized names. Another trick is to register variations of popular names. In these days of spyware and rampant viruses, it doesn't make as much sense to just guess at URLs. Thus, the InterNIC **whois** query is more valuable than ever!

1. To run an InterNIC **whois** query, enter **www.internic.org** in your browser. Figure 14-3 shows you the InterNIC home page.

2. Clicking that **whois** link takes you to another screen, which gives you the opportunity to specify which domain name in which you are interested in finding out more information.

For the sake of this example, assume you want to know more about Cisco Systems' Cisco.com domain. This is illustrated in Figure 14-4.

Figure 14-3 InterNIC's Home Page

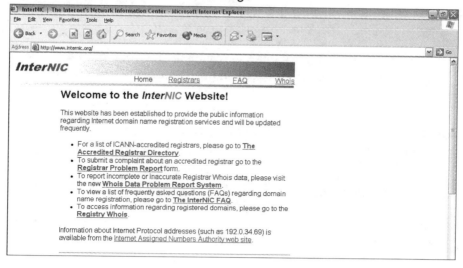

Figure 14-4 InterNIC's whois Query Screen

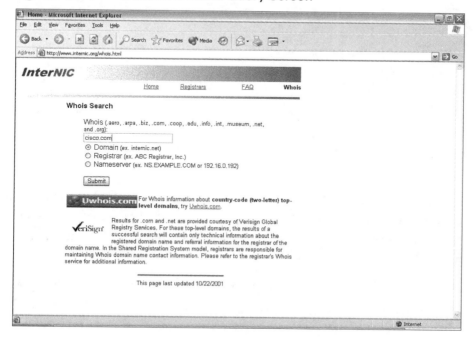

3. After entering the domain (Cisco.com in this example, as indicated in the preceding figure), click the **Submit** button.

This performs looks up that piece of data in the InterNIC database. The results of an InterNIC **whois** query on the Cisco.com domain are presented for you in Figure 14-5.

Figure 14-5   InterNIC's whois Query on Cisco.com

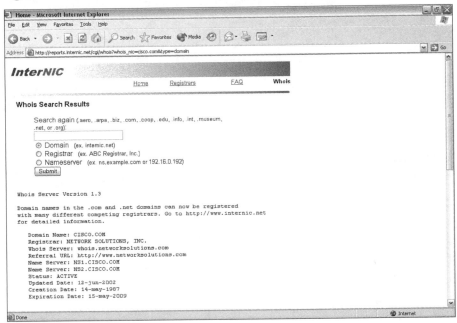

As you can see in the preceding screenshot, Cisco.com is a valid Internet domain that dates all the way back to 1987. All by itself, that creation date should assure you that clicking Cisco.com will bring you to the website of a true Internet pioneer.

Recent creation dates should be a warning sign to you that the organization you just looked up is either a brand new entity or has just decided to do business under that Internet domain. Either way, it should ratchet up one's discomfort level with respect to any website associated with that domain.

Packet Internet Groper

Before you see the other **whois** function, it's time for a little detour. Here's another trusty tool for checking out destinations on an IP network. Its full name shows that someone had a twisted sense of humor, which is why it goes by its acronym (which also shows its creator had a twisted sense of humor!).

The *Packet Internet Groper (ping)* is an awkward name with a negative connotation. However, it is a remarkably accurate description of what the utility actually does. This utility is better known by its abbreviation, **ping**, which forms a marvelous double entendre. You see, **ping** lets you feel your way through a network to see if any given destination is actually reachable.

A Little History

Ping, if you ever watched any old World War II Navy films, is the sonar sound emitted by a submarine when it uses sound to detect other ships in the vicinity. Sound emitted under water keeps traveling until it hits something. Then it is reflected back to its source. That reflected sound lets the sender know what's in the vicinity even though it can't physically see anything.

ping in an IP network works much the same way a Navy boat's ping works. It lets you reach out and test connectivity to a device that you cannot see.

1. To use **ping**, you have to open up the trusty old command prompt window.

2. Type the word **ping** followed by a space and either the IP address or fully qualified domain name of the computer you are trying to reach.

3. Press **Enter** and watch the results.

To show you just how useful **ping** can be, get back to the example of www.cisco.com.

I showed you how to use InterNIC's **whois** to determine if Cisco.com was a valid domain and worth the risk of accessing. Figure 14-6 takes this to the next step by running **ping** in a command prompt window to test whether the host of the Cisco Systems website is accessible.

Figure 14-6   Pinging Cisco.com

```
Command Prompt                                                    _ □ x
Microsoft Windows XP [Version 5.1.2600]
(C) Copyright 1985-2001 Microsoft Corp.

C:\Documents and Settings\Mark A. Sportack>ping www.cisco.com

Pinging www.cisco.com [198.133.219.25] with 32 bytes of data:

Reply from 198.133.219.25: bytes=32 time=94ms TTL=241
Reply from 198.133.219.25: bytes=32 time=94ms TTL=241
Reply from 198.133.219.25: bytes=32 time=94ms TTL=241
Reply from 198.133.219.25: bytes=32 time=94ms TTL=241

Ping statistics for 198.133.219.25:
    Packets: Sent = 4, Received = 4, Lost = 0 (0% loss),
Approximate round trip times in milli-seconds:
    Minimum = 94ms, Maximum = 94ms, Average = 94ms

C:\Documents and Settings\Mark A. Sportack>
```

As you can see in Figure 14-6, the IP address assigned to the Cisco Systems Internet website is 198.133.219.25. This bit of information will become useful shortly. Curiously, as important as it is to be able to translate a name to an address, this is little more than just a fringe benefit of **ping**. Its main purpose is to test accessibility of network-attached resources.

The way **ping** works is actually quite simple. The **ping** utility creates a series of *Internet Control Message Protocol (ICMP)* packets that get sent to the destination you specified in the command prompt. The command prompt window displays the results of these test packets in terms of whether the packet was successfully delivered and how long it took to get there. **ping** is also nice enough to tally up the minimum time, maximum time, and average delivery times for that series of tests. All this is evident in Figure 14-6.

ping is one of the more useful of the native TCP/IP utilities that you will find. One of its nicer features is that it works with either fully qualified domain names (FQDNs) such as www.cisco.com or with IP addresses. If you feed **ping** an FQDN, it goes out and finds the corresponding IP address for you.

Figure 14-6 showed you how **ping** translated the IP address of www.cisco.com into an IP address. Now that you know the IP address, you can take advantage of the other Internet yellow pages: the ARIN **whois** service.

ARIN's whois

ARIN, the American Registry for Internet Numbers, is the official Internet registry service for IP addresses, autonomous system numbers, and other special-purpose numbers that are either reserved or registered for use in North America. Their **whois** service is available via their Internet home page on www.arin.net. Please be sure to use the .net suffix instead of .com or .org. That would result in a URL that brings you to someone else's site.

ARIN's charter is limited to North America. For checking on Internet numbers registered in other parts of the world, you need to rely upon **whois** queries via ARIN's counterparts. These counterparts are

- APNIC for Asia Pacific at www.apnic.net

- LACNIC for Latin America and some Caribbean countries at www.lacnic.net

- RIPE at www.ripe.net for Europe, the Middle East, Central Asia, and African nations north of the equator

All have the same mission and maintain the same data for Internet customers in their respective regions.

Figure 14-7 shows you the ARIN home page. As you can see, there's quite a bit of information about ARIN. So much information that it won't all fit in one screenshot. For right now, just focus on the **whois** query in that upper-right corner.

Figure 14-7   ARIN's Home Page

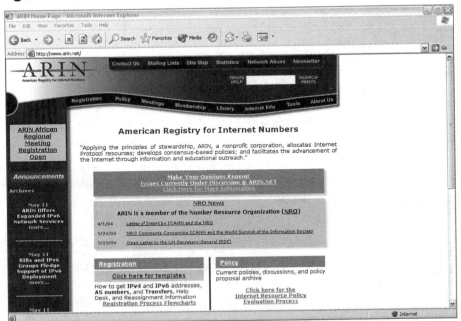

That query box is where you can plug in the IP address that you were able to glean courtesy of **ping**. To refresh your memory, the Cisco Systems website's IP address is 198.133.219.25. Figure 14-8 shows you the results of an ARIN **whois** query on this IP address.

The differences between an ARIN **whois** query and an InterNIC **whois** query are immediately obvious when you compare Figures 14-8 and 14-5. Both use the same name for the command to query Internet databases, but the data contained is quite different. They are two different tools for two different jobs. Together, they enable you to find out quite a bit about any organization that connects to and uses the Internet.

Figure 14-8   Results of ARIN's Query on 198.133.219.25

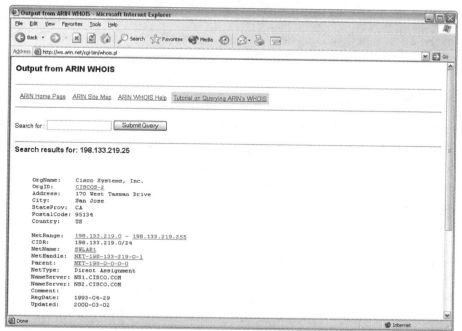

TCP/IP's Bugshooting Tools

Troubleshooting is the fine art of figuring out what precisely is failing when a complex system isn't working to your expectations. A complex system has many parts—just like your connection to a TCP/IP network. If any one part breaks, the overall connection between you and your destination is broken. When that happens, you can reach into TCP/IP's bag of tools and start testing one component at a time in the network until you find exactly where the problem lies. Then you can hold your head up high and call in an informed trouble report to your network's help desk.

Map It Out

The first step in diagnosing a problem is to map out the system. After you have identified all its parts, you can then start systematically testing each one. By testing each component, you can start isolating the source of the problem by eliminating the components that still work. This process of elimination is a simple but effective way to find a problem's source.

To see how this works, walk through a basic example and see how to use some of TCP/IP's tools to start that step-by-step process of eliminating potential causes. For the sake of example, assume you are just communicating across a LAN with a nearby web server. That web server should be serving up a web page but isn't. Figure 14-9 shows you all the components in this scenario that could be causing this problem.

Figure 14-9   Potential Sources of Failure

Application Software
TCP/IP
Operating System
Ethernet LAN

Check the Browser

As you can see in Figure 14-10, everything starts with the application software: your web browser. Immediately below that is your network protocol: TCP/IP. TCP/IP runs on top of your operating system, and the operating system relies upon a LAN (Ethernet) for connectivity to the web server.

The web server features almost the same set of points of failure in reverse: Ethernet, operating system, TCP/IP, and the web service. Any one of these components, on either machine, could cause the entire communications session to fail. Trouble-shooting should always begin at the top, close to home, and iterate outward toward the destination. At the top of the stack is the application software. In this case, that's the browser. Figure 14-10 shows you which of the potential problem areas you check first.

Figure 14-10   First Step: Check the Application

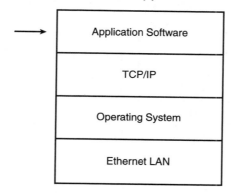

Your browser is a fairly bulletproof piece of software. Chances are really good that unless you have been deleting files at random from your hard drive, your browser is just fine. It is, however, still a good habit to systematically test and eliminate the potential sources of failure by starting at the top and working your way down through the stack.

You can check the integrity of your browser by using it to access a file on your own computer. This type of test allows you to check whether the browser is working by testing it—not it plus a whole bunch of other things. Figure 14-11 shows you how to do this.

In a Windows XP environment, it is as simple as opening up an Internet Explorer or Netscape Navigator session and entering **c:** in the address bar. Figure 14-11 shows an entered c: in Internet Explorer's address bar. Figure 14-12 shows what you can expect to get *after* you press Enter.

Figure 14-11   Use the Browser Locally

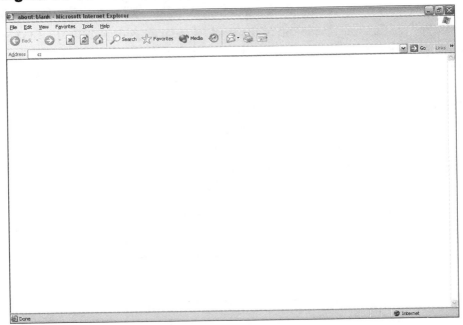

If you can successfully browse your hard drive and see your local folder structure and files, you have proven that both your browser and computer's operating system are working just fine. Notice that when troubleshooting, you don't always have the luxury of working systematically from the top down. This example rules out the operating system and the browser but not exonerating TCP/IP. That's okay because a systematic approach of eliminating possible causes is followed. A process of elimination, when carefully applied, gradually leads you to the source of the problem regardless of the order in which you have eliminated the possible causes.

Figure 14-12   Use Your Browser to Check Local Information

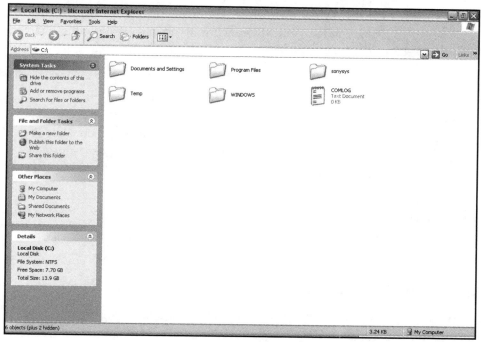

Check TCP/IP

The next level down in your stack of potential problem areas is TCP/IP. A quick look at Figure 14-13 shows you visually which area to focus on next.

Figure 14-13   Second Step: Check TCP/IP

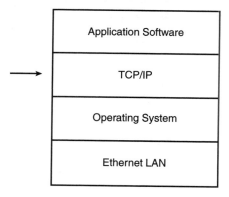

TCP/IP, too, is fairly reliable. However, it is possible to misconfigure it. Thus, your next step should be to run the **ipconfig** command to verify that your connection is set up properly. You have already seen how to do that earlier in this chapter. Some of the things to check are whether TCP/IP is actually running, what your IP address is, and whether you are using the right subnet mask.

If you never run **ipconfig** or any other diagnostic utility until after experiencing problems, you will never know what settings are normal. It's best to start familiarizing yourself with these tools during normal operating conditions rather than waiting until there is a problem.

After you have ascertained that TCP/IP is configured properly, your next step is to start collecting statistics about your computer's network usage.

Show Me the Numbers

netstat is one of the more versatile tools available for diagnosing TCP/IP networks. That's just an abbreviation for *network statistics*. Perhaps not surprisingly, many different statistics are available for measuring a TCP/IP network, and this one universal tool can be used to evaluate just about all of them. Consequently, **netstat** can be a bit of a chameleon; depending on how you use it, the results can vary tremendously! Consider that a sign of its strength and versatility.

Figure 14-14 shows you all the different options that you can use with **netstat**. These options are revealed to you when you open a command prompt and enter either **netstat ?** or **netstat -?** at the prompt.

Figure 14-14   netstat Help Screen

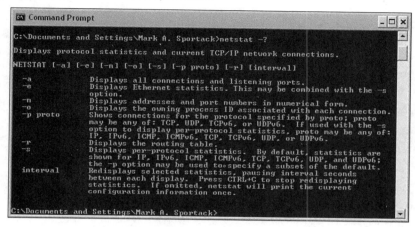

The more useful **netstat** options are summarized in Table 14-1. All the options are quite useful, but the basic set identified in Table 14-1 is *most* useful. The others are a bit more sophisticated and beyond the scope of basic troubleshooting. They are options that you can grow into, but are hardly appropriate for someone just venturing into the world of troubleshooting TCP/IP networks.

Table 14-1   Useful Netstat Options

Option Name	Description
- e	This option allows you to check the health of your connection to the local Ethernet network through the use of several statistics. In other words, running **netstat –e** enables you to determine whether the LAN is okay.
- s	The –s option shows all the TCP/IP statistics broken out per protocol. You see a separate set of statistics for TCP, UDP, and IP. Thus, you can use this option to determine whether TCP/IP is working properly.

Read on to see how you can use **netstat –s** and **netstat –e** to make sure that both your LAN connection and TCP/IP stack are working properly.

Check TCP/IP's Performance

In the second step of troubleshooting you saw how to verify TCP/IP proper configuration. That's a bit different than actually proving that it is working properly. That's where **netstat –s** comes in handy!

Although it would be nice to have some way of directly measuring TCP/IP's performance, you have to satisfy yourself with looking at statistics of its recent performance. From these numbers, you can make inferences about how it is performing and where some problems might exist. Looking at Figure 14-15, you can see the wealth of information that **netstat –s** offers.

Figure 14-15 netstat TCP/IP Stats

```
Command Prompt                                                    _ □ ×
C:\Documents and Settings\Mark A. Sportack>netstat -s

IPv4 Statistics

  Packets Received                   = 40081
  Received Header Errors             = 0
  Received Address Errors            = 3
  Datagrams Forwarded                = 0
  Unknown Protocols Received         = 253
  Received Packets Discarded         = 39828
  Received Packets Delivered         = 36140
  Output Requests                    = 0
  Routing Discards                   = 0
  Discarded Output Packets           = 0
  Output Packet No Route             = 0
  Reassembly Required                = 0
  Reassembly Successful              = 0
  Reassembly Failures                = 0
  Datagrams Successfully Fragmented  = 0
  Datagrams Failing Fragmentation    = 0
  Fragments Created                  = 0

ICMPv4 Statistics

                           Received      Sent
  Messages                 61            1
  Errors                   0             0
  Destination Unreachable  61            1
  Time Exceeded            0             0
  Parameter Problems       0             0
  Source Quenches          0             0
  Redirects                0             0
  Echos                    0             0
  Echo Replies             0             0
  Timestamps               0             0
  Timestamp Replies        0             0
  Address Masks            0             0
  Address Mask Replies     0             0

TCP Statistics for IPv4

  Active Opens                       = 1817
  Passive Opens                      = 0
  Failed Connection Attempts         = 55
  Reset Connections                  = 390
  Current Connections                = 0
  Segments Received                  = 29313
  Segments Sent                      = 25337
  Segments Retransmitted             = 37

UDP Statistics for IPv4

  Datagrams Received    = 10452
  No Ports              = 63
  Receive Errors        = 0
  Datagrams Sent        = 10756

C:\Documents and Settings\Mark A. Sportack>
```

As you can see, this **netstat** option breaks out the statistics by protocol group: IP, TCP, UDP, and ICMP. Of these, the ICMP messages are probably the most valuable for troubleshooting purposes. All these statistics, however, indirectly measure the efficiency of TCP/IP.

That's quite different from the other tests you've seen. For example, you saw how to check if your browser was working by using it to browse your computer's hard drive. The **netstat** TCP/IP statistics aren't designed to tell you if TCP/IP is working. They are designed to tell you about the volume of data sent and received plus how well it's working; it does this by evaluating various aspects of historical performance data.

Some of the particular error categories that you want to keep an eye on include

- Source Quench
- Destination Unreachable
- Echo and Echo Reply
- Reset

It is important to recognize the differences between the Send and Receive columns for these critical datapoints. **netstat** only differentiates between Send and Receive for ICMP packets. A value that you might consider normal in the Send column might actually be a major indicator of trouble in the Receive column. To help you keep those differences in perspective, Table 14-2 organizes the important points.

Table 14-2   Important Send and Receive ICMP Statistics

Statistic	Send	Receive
Source Quench	Someone has established a connection with your computer and your computer is telling them to slow their rate of transmission. *You need to decide whether this is normal. Should people be connecting to your computer?*	You have established a connection with another computer and that computer is telling your computer to slow its rate of transmission.
Echo	If you are actively trying to test connectivity to a remote destination using any of the ICMP Echo requests (such as **ping**), a running tally of your efforts are kept in this field.	Usually, your computer is not the recipient of inbound ICMP Echo requests. Thus, this field should always be 0 or very low. There are, however, some circumstances in which your computer receives such requests. For example, viruses sometimes try to spread themselves by checking to see which IP addresses are active on the network. *If you see a large number of inbound Echo requests, you might want to make sure your antivirus software is up to date!*
Echo Reply	If someone is sending ICMP Echo requests to your computer, the number of your computer's replies is tracked here. *Under normal circumstances, a single user's computer shouldn't receive many Echo requests. Consequently, you shouldn't see many Echo Reply messages in this field.*	You have sent ICMP Echo requests to another computer in the network and this field counts the replies you have received. *If this number is less than the number of Echo requests you have sent, you can conclude that some network congestion has caused some of your requests to go unacknowledged.*

Table 14-2   Important Send and Receive ICMP Statistics (continued)

Statistic	Send	Receive
Destination Unreachable	Assuming your computer isn't set up as a gateway or configured to act as a content server, your computer shouldn't generate many, if any, ICMP Destination Unreachable messages!	Your computer tracks the number of times you tried to reach an unavailable server. The reasons for that unavailability can vary widely. For example, the server could be powered off, the service you are trying to access shut off, or the network could be having problems that prevent you from reaching that destination.
Reset Connections	If your computer is sending Reset Connection packets, it likely means your computer is set up as a server. That might be the case. If, for example, you have joined a peer-to-peer network for filesharing, your computer would be functioning as both a single-user machine and as a server. *If your computer is not set up as a server and you are seeing Reset Connection messages, it is possible that your computer has been hacked!*	As explained in Chapter 10, "Special Delivery for Special Messages," a connection gets reset whenever a computer loses synchronization of the TCP sequence numbers. Receiving Reset Connection requests is normal and indicates that TCP is working to overcome errors that inevitably creep in.

Many other nuggets of wisdom are waiting to be mined from **netstat –s**. In fact, an entire chapter could be written on just this command! For the purposes of this chapter—helping you understand a basic approach to troubleshooting connectivity problems in a TCP/IP network—I limit the exploration of TCP/IP performance statistics to those in Table 14-2.

Now it's time to move further down the stack in pursuit of isolating the source of the problem.

Check the LAN

After checking the operating efficiency of your computer's TCP/IP protocol stack, check whether your LAN connection is working. Figure 14-16 shows that you are now on the last of the potential sources of failure that can be isolated on your computer.

Figure 14-16 The Last Step: Check the LAN

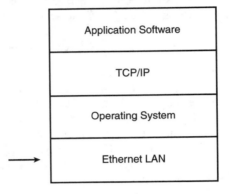

Running **netstat −e** on your computer's command prompt shows you exactly how well or how poorly your LAN connection is performing. Figure 14-17 shows you the results of just such a test. It is important to note that this test only checks the LAN connection on your computer! It is possible that the network itself might be having problems or that the server you are trying to reach is ailing. The purpose of **netstat −e** is to eliminate your computer's connection to the LAN as a potential source of failure.

 If you are seeing what appears to be a large number of errors when you run **netstat -e**, reboot and try again! Those errors might be old and just accumulated over time. Rebooting will clear them out.

Figure 14-17   netstat Ethernet Statistics

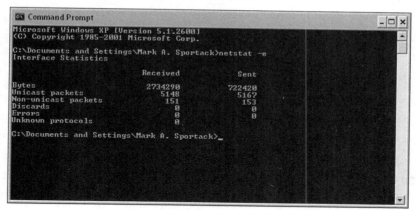

Looking at Figure 14-17, you can see that you don't get quite as much information as you did by running **netstat –s**, but what you do get is quite useful. The information is presented in two columns: Sent and Received. That should be fairly self explanatory. Your computer tracks Ethernet information based on what was sent from your computer and what was received by your computer.

The first line in this table is the total number of bytes processed by your computer. It is possible that, due to a wiring problem or other configuration problem, your computer might be sending but not receiving data. This is indicated by large numbers in the Sent column and 0s in the Received column. If that's the case, it's time for a call to your friendly neighborhood network administrator because there's not much you can do to fix this type of problem. Of course, if you really want to score points with your technical support person, make sure the wire is physically connected to your computer before calling!

The next thing to look for is a trend. Generally speaking, you receive far more bytes than you send. The **netstat** Ethernet statistics show you both the total number of bytes received and the total number of packets. Don't worry too much about the unicast versus non-unicast packets. A ***unicast packet*** is one that was sent to a single, specific destination. A ***non-unicast packet***, in this context, means packets that were broadcast to multiple machines at the same time. Remember: These metrics focus on Ethernet and do not count TCP/IP packets.

Sometimes Ethernet delivers packets (frames, really, but the **netstat** tool convention is followed) that are poorly formed or damaged. Those packets are discarded by their recipient and a running tally of those discarded packets is recorded by the machine. As you might have guessed, **netstat –e** shows you these under the heading Discards.

The last item of interest in diagnosing your Ethernet connection is the Errors row. Ethernet is subject to many types of transmission errors. For example, the data you send might actually collide with data sent by another machine on your network. When such a collision occurs, your computer keeps a running tally and displays that total in the Errors field. If your computer is displaying multiple errors or discards, there is likely something seriously wrong with your network or your network connection. All this information is invaluable to your network administrator in further diagnosing what ails your network connection.

One caveat: If your computer has been running for a while, you might be looking at an accumulation of errors that date back in time. These numbers get reset to 0s every time you reboot. Consequently, such accumulated errors might be completely unrelated to your current inability to access the web server. Many people leave their computers on forever because it saves the effort of rebooting. If you are one of those people, here's a great reason to invest the extra effort to power down your computer whenever you finish using it.

If your Ethernet LAN connection appears to be working fine and you can access other computers or resources, it is time for the next step: Is the problem somewhere beyond your computer and LAN? Such errors might well be beyond your ability to control, but that doesn't mean you are completely helpless!

Tracking Down Problems Beyond Your Control

The preceding section shows you all the tricks for tracking down a local problem. There will be times when a problem lies just beyond your reach. You might have seen indications of such a problem when you ran **netstat –s**. Unfortunately, there's not much you can do about such problems, but you can use some other tools to make sure that the problem lies beyond your control. This section shows you some of those tools as well as how to use them.

Back to ping

You have already seen how to run **ping**, so you're spared the repeat performance. However, it should be pointed out that it was gathering information earlier. Now you see how to use it to isolate the potential source of connectivity problems.

When you have satisfied yourself that your computer is working fine and that the inability to reach a specific destination lies beyond your reach, the next thing you want is to run **ping**. By using **ping** to reach that destination, you can immediately tell if the host is accessible. It is entirely possible that the web service on that computer is down even though the computer and its operating system are fine. When that happens, you won't be able to reach it using a browser, but **ping** returns some valid results. If you have successfully reached the destination using **ping**, you're done! You have isolated the problem to that destination computer's ability to run its web service.

The Trouble with ping

ping is a good tool but it is far from perfect. It is a simple, easy-to-use tool for checking the reachability of a destination using either IP addresses or domain names. One of its more notable drawbacks is that it uses ICMP for transportation. If you recall, ICMP enjoys the lowest priority of all TCP/IP protocols. Consequently, **ping** requests are often just dropped in a busy network or by a busy host.

The lack of a response might be interpreted as the host being unreachable when, in fact, it is either too busy to respond at that moment or it is connected to a busy network. Either way, you can get misleading results. Alternatively, a site or network might block all inbound ICMP as a way of increasing security. If so, that would prevent **ping** from working for you.

If **ping** didn't reach that computer, you don't really know whether the problem lies with that destination computer or the network that interconnects your computer with that destination. It is possible that the web server you are trying to reach is functional but unreachable due to network troubles. It is equally plausible that the server or its operating system is just not working properly.

In such cases, it is time to try one last trick to find out where the problem really lies. That trick is to track down the route your packets took in their ill-fated attempt to reach that destination.

Tracing the Route

If you still can't access that website and have successfully run through the tests shown here, the problem lies beyond your computer. The first thing you want to do is trace the path that your packets are taking. By following that route, you can also see exactly where in the network your attempted connection is failing.

The tool you can use to do this is **tracert** or **traceroute**, depending on which operating system you are using. Figure 14-18 shows a **tracert** session to the Cisco Systems website. You trace to the FQDN (www.cisco.com), but you could just as easily trace that route using an IP address.

When you start a **tracert** session, you are unleashing a flurry of ICMP Echo requests. Each router in the network is required by this protocol to decrement the *Time-To-Live (TTL)* value of the ICMP Echo request. In simpler words, what you get is a hop-by-hop accounting of the path that lies between you and your targeted destination.

The *hop count*, or number of routers that make up the route, is the first column on the left of the **tracert** results screen. The next three columns are running totals of the amount of time it took to reach that hop or router. The last column is just the name and IP address of the machine that responded to your **tracert** request.

Figure 14-18   Tracing the Route to www.cisco.com

```
Command Prompt                                                       _ □ X
C:\Documents and Settings\Mark A. Sportack>tracert www.cisco.com
Tracing route to www.cisco.com [198.133.219.25]
over a maximum of 30 hops:
  1     2 ms     2 ms     2 ms  192.168.1.1
  2    22 ms     9 ms     9 ms  10.19.80.1
  3    11 ms     9 ms    10 ms  ge1-0-0.gw2.atw.pa.rcn.net [208.59.249.2]
  4    10 ms     9 ms     9 ms  ge1-0-0.core2.atw.pa.rcn.net [208.59.89.67]
  5    12 ms    11 ms    15 ms  pos0-3.core2.phdl.pa.rcn.net [207.172.19.45]
  6    20 ms    19 ms    17 ms  pos6-0.core3.nyw.ny.rcn.net [207.172.19.11]
  7    16 ms    14 ms    14 ms  ge4-0.border3.nyw.ny.rcn.net [207.172.15.84]
  8    15 ms    15 ms    13 ms  4.78.132.5
  9    16 ms    15 ms    16 ms  ge-2-1-0.bbr2.NewYork1.Level3.net [64.159.4.149]

 10    91 ms   114 ms    90 ms  ge-0-1-0.bbr2.SanJose1.Level3.net [64.159.1.130]

 11    91 ms    89 ms    90 ms  ge-9-0.ipcolo1.SanJose1.Level3.net [64.159.2.35]

 12    92 ms    93 ms    91 ms  p1-0.cisco.bbnplanet.net [4.0.26.14]
 13    92 ms    91 ms    92 ms  sjck-dmzbb-gw1.cisco.com [128.107.239.9]
 14    97 ms    92 ms    91 ms  sjck-sdf-ciod-gw2.cisco.com [128.107.239.110]
 15     *         *         *    Request timed out.
 16     *         *         *    Request timed out.
 17     *         *         *    Request timed out.
 18     *         *         *    Request timed out.
 19     *         *         *    Request timed out.
 20     *         *         *    Request timed out.
 21     *         *         *    Request timed out.
 22     *         *         *    Request timed out.
 23     *         *         *    Request timed out.
 24     *         *         *    Request timed out.
 25     *         *         *    Request timed out.
 26     *         *         *    Request timed out.
 27     *         *         *    Request timed out.
 28     *         *         *    Request timed out.
 29     *         *         *    Request timed out.
 30     *         *         *    Request timed out.

Trace complete.

C:\Documents and Settings\Mark A. Sportack>
```

Looking back at Figure 14-18, you can see that Internet service providers (ISPs) try to use mnemonic names for their routers. This is quite helpful in understanding where your packets are going. The first two lines are the hops needed to get out of my home and onto my ISP's network. That ISP (RCN) carried my packets through Pennsylvania, into Philadelphia (yes, that's part of Pennsylvania!) and then into New York City. In New York City, RCN handed off the packets to Level 3 (another ISP), where it traversed the United States in a single hop. My packets literally went from New York City to San Jose in one hop! In San Jose, my packets were handed off to the BBN Planet network on which it appears the Cisco Systems commercial website is hosted.

If you see asterisks (*) followed by the words Request Timed Out, you might be seeing an error. As shown in the preceding figure, my **tracert** packets reached the Cisco.com domain, but that's where the information stopped flowing. Retries

were attempted with no success. This could indicate that the website you're tracing is unavailable. Or, as is the case with this particular website, the asterisks could indicate that security permissions have been defined inside the Cisco.com network that effectively prevent any additional replies to my queries.

It is for that reason that **tracert** is a good, but not perfect, tool. Use it to validate what you are seeing with other tools, but don't rely on it alone to diagnose connectivity problems. For example, having first established that any given destination was accessible by using **ping**, you might have gotten nothing but asterisks when trying to trace to it. When that happens, feel free to rerun **ping** just to make sure that the destination was, in fact, still accessible. If **ping** makes contact but **tracert** returns asterisks, you can rest assured that security permissions are generating the asterisks.

Please keep in mind that the Internet is a dynamic network and that routing decisions about the best path are continuously being reevaluated. Thus, you might run the same exact test just a few minutes apart and see different responses. If so, relax: That's the Internet hard at work picking the best route for you!

Chapter Summary

When you experience connectivity problems in a TCP/IP network, start at the top of the stack and work your way down to the physical layer using the tools described in this chapter.

Troubleshooting might seem like an advanced topic for someone just starting to learn TCP/IP. By following a systematic step-by-step approach, you can become more proficient with directly using TCP/IP and simultaneously grow in your mastery of TCP/IP and networking. In doing so, you can become what network engineers dream about: a well-informed and self-sufficient user!

Chapter Review Questions

The following questions reinforce the key concepts in this chapter:

1. What is troubleshooting?

2. What command verifies that TCP/IP is configured correctly on your computer?

3. Which TCP/IP utility tests the reachability of any given Internet destination?

4. Which tool determines if your computer's Ethernet connection is working properly?

5. Which tool determines if your computer's TCP/IP protocol suite is working effectively?

6. How would you find out if the computer you are trying to access (or the network it is connected to) is experiencing heavy congestion?

7. Which tool tracks the path your packets take through a network?

PART V

Appendix

Appendix A: Chapter Review Answers

Chapter Review Answers

Chapter 1

1. What is TCP/IP?

   Answer: TCP/IP is a complex set of mechanisms designed to enable communications between any two or more machines connected to a network regardless of what types of devices they might be, who made them, or their physical proximity to each other.

2. How are TCP/IP and the Internet related?

   Answer: TCP/IP and the Internet share a common heritage—a heritage that today is reflected in TCP/IP's status as the Internet's official communications protocol. The Internet is a physical network and TCP/IP is the logical suite of tools that lets you actually connect to and use the Internet. TCP/IP has gone on to become even bigger than the Internet—if you can imagine such a thing! Whereas the Internet is a global public network that interconnects virtually all the networks in the world, TCP/IP is used in even more networks than are connected to the Internet.

3. What five critical communications functions can TCP/IP perform?

   Answer: Some of the most critical TCP/IP functions include the following:

   - An addressing system that permits you to uniquely identify any given machine connected to the Internet. This system affords the ability to create literally billions of unique addresses.

   - A standardized packet that contains all the information needed for two or more devices to talk across a network and for that network to appropriately forward packets between those devices.

   - An ability to segment application data into manageable pieces. These segments are then placed inside a data structure known as a packet.

- Enables computers that receive a series of related packets to put the packets into the correct order. That way the reassembled data is exactly the same as it was before it was segmented by the sending machine.

- TCP/IP is smart enough to detect data that was damaged as it traveled through the network. Data that was damaged is discarded, and TCP/IP's mechanisms ensure that, when appropriate, the damaged block is retransmitted until it is successfully received.

4. How do you know when you are using TCP/IP?

Answer: If you want to use the Internet, you must use TCP/IP. All Internet service providers (ISPs) around the world have embraced TCP/IP as the standard mechanism for communicating through the Internet. Because of its success in this role, it has become much more widely used throughout the world. In fact, you would be hard-pressed to find any enterprise or home network today that didn't also use TCP/IP.

Although not all applications that communicate do so using TCP/IP, the vast majority do. Thus, if you surf the Internet or use it for instant messaging, e-mail, file sharing, gaming, or whatever else might strike your fancy, you are using TCP/IP.

Also, TCP/IP isn't just for the Internet. Since the Internet's commercialization, TCP/IP has been embraced almost universally and is the de facto standard networking protocol for the Internet, private networks, and even home networks.

5. What can't TCP/IP do? In other words, what communications functions must it rely on other mechanisms to do?

Answer: Despite its widespread acceptance around the world, TCP/IP is not a panacea, nor was it intended to be one. It is a communications protocol that provides a linkage between physical networks and logical tools such as application software and operating systems. Consequently, it is not a network nor is it an operating system or application software. It might contain some operating system elements, and even have some native utility applications, but its role is an intermediary between the user-facing software and physical networks.

Chapter 2

1. How can TCP/IP satisfy the network performance requirements of an unlimited number of software applications?

Answer: TCP/IP satisfies the network performance requirements of an unlimited number of software applications through the use of two mechanisms. First, it relies on open standards to ensure that everyone who writes software knows how to make their applications work with TCP/IP. Second, it doesn't try to work with each individual application. Rather, by analyzing the network performance requirements of applications, it merely supports two main applications types. Those two types are differentiated by their network performance requirements.

2. What are the two basic network performance requirements imposed by software applications?

Answer: Virtually all applications fall into one of two categories for network performance. Applications either require timely delivery or reliable delivery of their data.

3. Is TCP/IP a tool designed for business or pleasure?

Answer: Both. TCP/IP is a network communications protocol suite that supports literally every application that needs to communicate through a network. TCP/IP focuses on meeting applications' needs for network performance rather than on the applications themselves. Consequently, it is equally adept at supporting games as it is mission-critical business applications.

4. For what do you use TCP/IP?

Answer: Anyone who uses the Internet is, by default, also using TCP/IP. It's almost impossible to count all the ways people use the Internet, but surfing web pages, tracking stock portfolios, downloading tunes, e-mailing, chatting, and instant messaging are all popular applications that rely on TCP/IP. It also is used quite extensively in home and professional networks and can support filesharing, printing, and countless other business applications.

5. What does the term *reliable delivery* mean?

Answer: *Reliable delivery* is TCP/IP's mechanism that guarantees that application data will be delivered safely to its intended destination. That guarantee means applications can rely upon data being delivered, but no guarantees are made regarding when it will be delivered. Network congestion and other problems might force TCP/IP to try repeatedly before successfully delivering the data.

6. What does the term *best-effort delivery* mean?

Answer: *Best-effort delivery* is TCP/IP's mechanism to support applications that have timeliness requirement but do not require reliable data delivery. TCP/IP makes one attempt—its best effort—to deliver data. If it doesn't get delivered, TCP/IP and the application agree to move on to the next piece of data rather than waste time.

Chapter 3

1. What is the IETF?

Answer: The Internet Engineering Task Force (IETF) is responsible for developing and maintaining the Internet's technologies, as well as guiding its growth and development. Consequently, the IETF is frequently regarded as the guardian of the Internet and its technologies.

2. What is the difference between open standards and closed, or proprietary, technologies?

Answer: A closed or proprietary technology is one developed in secret. The details about how it is made or how it works are kept a secret. Conversely, an open technology is one developed publicly and whose technical details are shared freely with anyone who would like to know them.

3. What is interoperability?

Answer: Interoperability is the ability to build a functional networked computing environment by interconnecting products from different manufacturers.

4. What is the benefit of interoperability?

Answer: The benefit of interoperability across vendor platforms is that it makes products from different vendors compatible, thus encouraging price-based competition. The result is that it enables communications between dissimilar computer systems.

5. How do you create and maintain the technical standards that enable the Internet and its technologies to be interoperable?

Answer: The IETF creates and maintains the technical standards that enable the Internet and its technologies to remain interoperable. It does so by sanctioning committees to study problems and develop solutions. The solutions are documented publicly in Requests For Comments (RFCs). Products that conform to the standards set forth in the RFCs interoperate regardless of who made them.

6. What is a reference model and why is it needed?

Answer: A reference model is a logical framework that keeps a sequence of events in proper order. Reference models have been indispensable in developing open networks and systems by providing a neutral framework for all to follow.

7. Explain the concept of logical adjacency.

Answer: Logical adjacency means that two compatible applications function as if they are passing data directly back and forth between each other. For example, you use e-mail software to send e-mails to other people using similar software. In reality, the e-mail software packages communicate indirectly. They communicate directly with TCP/IP. Simply stated, the two e-mail packages appear logically adjacent, even though they physically are not.

Chapter 4

1. Name TCP/IP's major architectural components.

Answer: TCP/IP contains three major architectural components. Those components are described as tools for users, tools for applications, and tools for the network. Specifically, these translate into TCP (which encompasses user tools), UDP, and IP.

2. Which architectural components occupy the host-to-host layer of the TCP/IP reference model?

Answer: The host-to-host layer of the TCP/IP reference model encompasses tools for applications. The specific architectural subcomponents occupying this layer are known more properly as the Transmission Control Protocol (TCP) and the User Datagram Protocol (UDP). These two protocols include everything an application needs to communicate with an application on another machine.

3. How does IP relate to the other protocol components in the TCP/IP architecture?

Answer: IP is TCP/IP's network-oriented architectural component. It accepts data from application-oriented protocols (TCP and UDP) and packages them for transportation through a network. Both TCP and UDP must use IP for their internetwork mechanism.

4. What are the five most important network-oriented functions IP provides?

Answer: The five most important network-oriented functions provided by IP follow:

■ Provide a unique address for each device connected to the network.

■ Permit the network's routers to figure out how best to get from the source machine to the destination machine.

■ Set basic rules for communicating between hosts regardless of location. This set of rules is comprehensive enough that you don't have to know how many networks your data passes through to get to your computer.

■ Provide a packet that carries data between two or more computers through a network.

■ Impose a maximum Time-To-Live (TTL) for each packet.

5. What are the seven most important network-oriented functions TCP provides?

Answer: The seven most important network-oriented functions provided by TCP follow:

■ Assign a serial number, better known as a sequence number, to each segment of application data.

- Assign a port number that functions as the address of the application that is sending or receiving data.

- Keep track of the sequence of received data.

- Ensure that received data were not damaged in transit, retransmitting that data as many times as needed.

- Acknowledge that something was received undamaged.

- Ensure that nothing was lost during transmission.

- Throttle the rate at which the source machine sends data. This helps prevent the network from melting completely when it starts to get congested.

6. Which TCP/IP component is considered an unreliable, or best-effort, protocol?

Answer: UDP, the User Datagram Protocol, is a transport protocol. Unlike TCP, UDP cannot facilitate reliable data delivery. It is specifically designed to provide a clean, simple, and timely delivery of small quantities of application data. If data arrives late or damaged, the data is simply discarded and no attempt is made by UDP to negotiate a retransmission.

7. What's the difference between reliable and best-effort delivery?

Answer: TCP is a reliable transport mechanism that guarantees that transmitted data is a perfect copy of the original. UDP is a best-effort transport mechanism that makes no guarantees about its abilities other than it will make one good attempt to deliver that data.

8. Under what circumstances would you prefer a best-effort delivery instead of a guaranteed, or reliable, delivery?

Answer: Best-effort delivery is ideal for applications that generate small quantities of data in real time. For example, live voice or video communications can generate large quantities of data. The application segments that data into small pieces, typically in fractions of a second. Each fraction of a second's worth of data is passed to UDP for quick delivery to the destination machine. Because the data is being generated in real time, requesting a retransmission is impossible. Nor would you want to do so.

Chapter 5

1. What is a header and why is it significant to TCP/IP?

Answer: A header is a series of bits that is prepended to application data by TCP, UDP, and IP. These bits provide essential pieces of information that facilitate the communications between these protocol suites on the source and destination machines during a communications session.

2. What function is served by a port address?

Answer: A port address uniquely identifies the application in a communications session. Two port addresses exist in each communications session: one to identify the source application and the other to identify the destination application.

3. What's the difference between a source port address and a destination port address?

Answer: A source port address identifies the address of the application that initiated the conversation. A destination port address is the address of the recipient of that conversation.

4. What's the difference between a well-known, registered, and dynamic port address?

Answer: A well-known port address can only be assigned to system-level processes. Assignment of well-known port addresses is carefully regulated by IANA, as there are only 1,024 possible addresses. These range from 0 to 1023.

A registered port address is also regulated by IANA, but these numbers can be assigned to applications run by users. Registered port numbers range from 1024 to 49151.

Dynamic port addresses are selected on the fly from a pool of available or unused port addresses. The pool of possible addresses starts at 49151 and runs up to 65535.

5. What are the four most important network-oriented functions provided by IP?

Answer: IP performs four critical functions:

- Creating an envelope for carrying data through a network or internetwork.

- Providing a numeric addressing system that lets you uniquely identify virtually every machine in the Internet around the world.

- Enabling each envelope or data packet to be specifically addressed to its intended destination. This address is the packet's destination IP address.

- Enabling each envelope or packet of data to also tell the recipient machine who sent it. This return address is the source IP address.

6. What are the two most important network-oriented functions provided by UDP?

Answer: UDP's two most critical functions include

- Accepting data from an application and wrapping a UDP header around it. The combined structure of UDP header and application data is known as a *datagram*. Unlike TCP, UDP doesn't have to segment its data. The type of applications that use UDP are such that only small quantities of data typically are passed at a time to UDP. The datagram is handed to IP for further processing.

- Verifying whether the data in the datagram was damaged in transit. If the data is found undamaged, it is handed to its intended destination application. If the data appears to have been damaged, the entire datagram is discarded.

7. What are the six most important critical network-oriented functions provided by TCP?

Answer: TCP's top six functions include

- Chopping up application data into bite-sized chunks known as *segments*

- Managing the communications session

- Guaranteeing that data gets delivered to the correct destination machine and application

- Finding and fixing any damage that occurs to data when it traverses the network

- Ensuring that any data lost in transit is replaced

- Reassembling data received into a perfect copy of the application data that was sent

Chapter 6

1. What does an IP packet do?

   Answer: An IP packet wraps a user's application data into a neat package that protects and conveys that data through a network. This packet bears the user's "return address" (an IP address), the intended recipient's IP address, and other useful information as the packet gets pushed through a network to the destination machine.

2. How many stages are there in the life of an IP packet?

   Answer: Exactly three: The first stage is when the packet is created. Part of this creation process is adding all the necessary information to the packet's header to support bidirectional communications with the destination machine.

   The second stage occurs when that packet gets wrapped in the transport mechanism (known as a frame) of the physical network carrying the IP packet.

   The third and final stage occurs when the packet reaches its destination. At that point, the recipient checks the information contained in the IP header to ensure that the data is error free, and then strips the data out of the packet. At that point, the packet's mission has been accomplished and it is discarded.

3. Can an IP packet roam the network forever in search of its destination?

   Answer: No! IP packets have a pre-set Time-To-Live (TTL), and when that expires the packet is destroyed. Thus, an IP packet must reach its destination before it gets too old. *Old* is a relative term; for an IP address it is defined in terms of the number of network devices it can pass through rather than some arbitrary amount of time.

4. What is an IP address?

   Answer: An IP address is a 32-bit binary number that uniquely identifies both an IP-enabled machine and the network to which it is connected.

5. Why do you need IP addresses?

   Answer: Without an IP address, no machine could be uniquely identified in an IP network. Without a reliable means of identifying machines, you can't support communications between two or more machines.

6. Do you need those periods between the numbers in an IP address?

Answer: No, not really. The periods are there to make things easier for human beings. In its native form, an IP address is just a string of 32 binary digits, each of which can have a value of either 0 or 1.

Long strings of binary numbers are beyond the ability of people, so two things make IP addresses usable. The first is to chop it into 4 groups of 8 bits each. These groups are separated visually with the dots. Then, the string of binary digits represented by each group of 8 bits is converted to a decimal number. This allows you to work with relatively small decimal numbers rather than with lengthy binary numbers.

7. How do people use IP addresses?

Answer: IP addresses can be used directly by people to access anything connected to the Internet or any other IP network. Unfortunately, IP addresses tend to be difficult to remember. Thus, they tend to get used indirectly; people use friendly words such as www.cisco.com to access network-attached resources. These friendly words are translated to IP addresses behind the scenes.

Network administrators also use IP addresses as a way of organizing the resources connected to the networks they are responsible for managing. That organization is possible thanks to the two-part hierarchical structure of each IP address.

8. How does a network use IP addresses?

Answer: Routers, the communications devices that make up an IP network, use IP addresses as the basis for communicating known destinations and possible paths with each other. This behind-the-scenes process assures you that the network is constantly looking for the best paths between your network and any and all possible destination network addresses. Routers also must find each packet's destination IP address so they can forward the packets appropriately.

9. What's the difference between a host address and a network address?

Answer: An IP address has two parts: a host address and a network address. All the machines connected to one network share that network's address. In fact, that network address forms the beginning of the host addresses. Each host, however, must have a unique address. The host address portion of each IP address is where the IP addresses must differ.

Chapter 7

1. What is subnetting?

   Answer: Subnetting is a process by which a third level of addressing is created from IP's two-level address. The three address levels are network, subnetwork, and host address. A single network can be used to create several subnetworks, each of which can support numerous hosts. In very simple terms, subnetworks are just blocks of addresses reserved from within a network address. Each block of addresses can then function as a separate network-level address.

2. How many levels of addressing are possible in an IP address?

   Answer: There are three levels of addressing possible within an IP address. The first two, network and host addresses, are a native component of an IP address. The third level is the subnet address. The subnet address is created by borrowing bits from the host address field.

3. What are some of the benefits of subnetting?

   Answer: The three main benefits of subnetting are more efficient use of an IP network address, the ability to organize your resources within a network, and the ability to secure your resources by placing them into separate sub-networks.

4. What are two main drawbacks of subnetting?

   Answer: The two main drawbacks of subnetting are that it introduces some waste of IP addresses and greatly complicates the chore of managing an IP address block. The waste of IP addresses in a subnetted environment is caused by the allocation of two IP addresses per subnet for subnet identification and broadcasting within that subnet.

5. Can you see a subnetwork address in a dotted-decimal IP address?

   Answer: No. A subnetwork address consists of bits borrowed from the host address portion of an IP address. As such, it won't be readily discernable when you look at an IP address in its dotted-decimal form. You must first know the subnet mask and then convert the host's IP address to its binary form before you can see the subnetwork address.

6. What is a base address?

Answer: A base address is the first IP address in either a network address or a subnetwork address block. The base address typically serves as the address for that network or subnetwork.

7. What is an extended network prefix and what does it do?

Answer: The subnetwork address functions as an extension of the network address. The subnetwork and network addresses work together to form an extended network address. In fact, when viewed together, network and subnetwork addresses are known as an extended network prefix. An extended network prefix enables IP packets to be routed directly to your network but not to your specific workstation.

8. Name three types of masks encountered in an IP network. Explain what each does.

Answer: You will encounter three mask types in an IP network: decimal, network, and subnetwork masks. The decimal mask is better known as the dotted-decimal form of an IP address. It lets you avoid having to remember large strings of highly repetitive binary numbers, which is the raw form of an IP address. The network mask helps you see how large the network address block is by identifying just the bits used for network address identification. The subnetwork mask builds upon the network mask by adding the subnetwork address bits to the network address bits. The network and subnetwork masks can be used in either their decimal or binary forms.

Chapter 8

1. Identify the various stages of a communications session.

Answer: A TCP/IP communications session has three distinct stages: the startup, the conversation itself, and the end (which entails dismantling the session).

2. How does TCP regulate information flow between a source and destination machine?

Answer: TCP contains numerous mechanisms that ensure the rate at which information flows between a source and destination machine suit both machines. Those mechanisms also take into account network conditions, such as congestion, that might also affect the session. These mechanisms include negotiating maximum segment size and window size, and might include a dynamically adjusting window size known as a sliding window.

3. What is a three-way handshake and what is its purpose?

Answer: The three-way handshake is the process by which a TCP/IP communications session is established. The handshake starts with one machine sending a SYN request packet to another machine. That SYN request is an attempt to start a session and requires the sender to forward its TCP sequence number. The recipient must respond with a packet that has both the SYN and ACK flags turned on, as well as contains its sequence number.

The first machine (the one that sent the original request) then acknowledges receipt of that SYN-ACK packet with an acknowledgment packet of its own. After this is done, both machines have agreed to communicate and exchanged the initial sequence numbers that will be used in the session. They also have negotiated all the particulars that allow them to do these things.

4. What are the three uses for TCP sequence numbers?

Answer: TCP sequence numbers are the key to maintaining the integrity of a communications session. They are synchronized at the beginning of a communications session during the three-way handshake, are tracked by the source computer to ensure that all data sent was received and acknowledged, and determine to which running copy of each application incoming data must be sent.

5. What is a session?

Answer: A session is a coherent flow of information between two machines using the TCP/IP communications protocol. For information flow to be coherent requires a truly bidirectional flow of information. Application data might flow in one direction, but acknowledgments and other important protocol-level information must flow in both directions. That exchange of protocol-level data enables TCP to guarantee reliable delivery of data, to start sessions, and to gracefully dismantle a session.

6. How does a source computer tell a destination computer that the session is over?

Answer: A source computer signals the end of a communications session by sending a TCP/IP packet with the FIN or Finish flag turned on. This lets the destination computer know that it has received all the data it was supposed to and that the source machine is trying to gracefully dismantle the communications session between them. The destination computer must reply with a packet that has both the Finish and Acknowledge flags turned on. Lastly, the source computer, upon receiving this Finish-Acknowledge packet, must reply with an Acknowledgment packet (an ACK packet) that concludes the session.

7. What are the four special types of TCP packets that do *not* carry any application data?

Answer: The four session-management functions of TCP that do not need to be sent inside a data-bearing packet are

- Synchronize (SYN)

- Acknowledge (ACK)

- Reset (RST)

- Finish (FIN)

Each is constructed through the use of the TCP header's flag bits.

8. What is a datagram?

Answer: A datagram is a single unacknowledged packet of information that is sent over a network as an individual packet without regard to previous or subsequent packets.

Chapter 9

1. Which of the seven layers in the OSI reference model does UDP occupy?

Answer: UDP occupies Layer 4, the transport layer of the OSI reference model.

2. What is the relationship between TCP and UDP?

Answer: UDP and TCP are peers. They are both transport layer protocols designed specifically to work with the Internet Protocol (IP).

3. What is meant by the term *best effort*?

Answer: UDP's best effort is to make one attempt at delivering data. There are no guarantees nor any complicated mechanisms needed to fulfill any guarantees. The result is a spartan but fast and efficient transport protocol ideally suited to the needs of real-time applications.

4. What is meant by the term *connectionless*?

Answer: The term connectionless describes the loose, unstructured communications that occurs between a source and destination machine when using UDP. Unlike TCP, UDP does not establish a session, nor does it try to identify the sequential relationship between different packets of data sent.

In TCP, that was done using sequence numbers and the establishment of a session. With UDP, each datagram sent is essentially a standalone piece of data that does not require correlation with any other data.

5. What is the difference between TCP port numbers and UDP port numbers?

Answer: TCP and UDP port numbers are identical in size, shape, and function. Their only difference is that they are two separate lists of applications. Those two lists might have a lot of applications in common (to avoid confusion), but they remain separate lists.

6. Identify the functions performed by UDP on a source machine.

Answer: UDP on a source machine accepts data from an application, wraps a header around that data, and populates that field with pertinent information, including application port numbers. Next, UDP performs a mathematical process on the contents of the datagram it has just created and stores the resulting value in the UDP header's checksum field. Lastly, UDP passes that datagram onto IP for further processing.

7. Identify the functions performed by UDP on a destination machine.

Answer: On a destination machine, UDP gets involved after IP has received the incoming data from the local-area network (LAN). Its first task is to verify that the data contained inside the datagram is the same as when it left the source machine. It does so by performing the same mathematical process on the datagram and compares the results it received with the results stored in the UDP header's checksum field.

If the values match, UDP is satisfied with the integrity of the data. If the values don't match, the packet is discarded. The header is checked to identify the destination application (as indicated by the destination port address). That header is then removed and the data embedded within the datagram handed off to its destination application.

Chapter 10

1. What does the acronym ICMP stand for?

Answer: ICMP is the name of a component internal to the Internet Protocol (IP). Its full name is the Internet Control Message Protocol.

2. Which layer of the OSI reference model does ICMP occupy?

Answer: ICMP occupies Layer 3, the network layer, of the OSI reference model.

3. What is the purpose of ICMP?

Answer: ICMP was specifically designed to enable communications between the various machines that comprise a network. Computers that speak IP, as well as the devices in a network, can all communicate via ICMP and share news about problems within the network or within a single IP packet.

4. Is ICMP useful to end users?

Answer: Yes it is, just not directly. For one thing, ICMP enables a network's computers and other devices to operate more efficiently by sharing information about error conditions within the network. Users benefit indirectly from this by having a network that is more operationally effective.

Users can also benefit from some of ICMP's capabilities by using utilities that employ ICMP mechanisms. Two such utilities bundled into TCP/IP are ping and traceroute. They appear similar, but work in different ways and employ different ICMP message types. Consequently, they gather different data and perform different functions.

5. What are some of the tools you can use that rely upon ICMP?

Answer: Although ICMP gets used extensively in an IP network, it was designed as a behind-the-scenes communications protocol that only is used in system-to-system communications. End-user functionality just wasn't designed into ICMP. Having said that, two wonderful tools enable you to benefit from ICMP. These tools are ping and traceroute.

6. What does ping do and why is it useful?

Answer: ping isn't part of ICMP. It's a utility, bundled with TCP/IP, that uses ICMP messages. Specifically, ping enables you to check whether any given machine in the network is reachable. If it replies to your ping, chances are fairly good that it is alive and well and ready to serve you. If it doesn't respond to your ping, all you really know is you can't get there from here! The machine might be down or a network problem might prevent you from reaching that device.

7. Which ICMP message type does ping utilize?

Answer: ping actually uses two ICMP message types: Echo and Echo Reply. When you run the ping utility, you are causing an ICMP Echo message to be sent. The machine you are trying to reach is obligated by the ICMP protocol to respond by sending you an ICMP Echo Reply message.

8. What does traceroute do and why is it useful?

Answer: traceroute is another TCP/IP utility that takes advantage of ICMP's capabilities. This program doesn't generate an ICMP message, but it causes ICMP messages to be returned.

9. If you know what you are looking at, you can map out all the connections that make up your network and get a good perspective on how busy or idle each connection is at any given time.

10. Which ICMP message type does traceroute utilize?

Answer: traceroute works quite a bit differently from ping. Whereas PING employs two ICMP message types, traceroute uses just one—and indirectly at that! When you run traceroute you are not generating an ICMP message. You are generating series of IP packets with a short Time-To-Live (TTL) interval. As these packets expire during their journey through the network, network devices send an ICMP Time Exceeded message back to you. traceroute interprets the contents of these Time Exceeded messages and displays them on your computer screen.

11. Can using a system-communications mechanism such as ICMP make IP a reliable protocol?

Answer: No! IP was not designed to be reliable. ICMP makes IP more effective by enabling machines that speak IP to share information about either system- or packet-level problems in the network. That's not how you ensure reliable delivery of packets.

Besides, ICMP is the lowest priority of any IP-based protocol, so it is not uncommon to see network devices discarding ICMP messages due to the load they are experiencing. If ICMP is always the first casualty of a busy network, there's no practical way it could augment IP to ensure reliable IP packet delivery.

Chapter 11

1. What is a router?

   Answer: A router is a specialized device designed to push IP packets (or other protocols' packets) through a network. A router relies on routing protocols to actually apply intelligence to gather information about the network and make good decisions about where to send any IP packets it receives.

2. What does a routing protocol do?

   Answer: Routing protocols perform at least six critical functions:

   - Communicate information about known destination networks with neighboring routers.

   - Discover new destination networks automatically through communications with neighbors.

   - Compare different paths to the same destination.

   - Select the best path to each known destination.

   - Store all known best paths in a routing table for use in IP packet forwarding.

   - Send packets of data to their destination using the best known path as recorded in the routing table.

3. At what layer(s) of the OSI reference model does a router separate different networks?

   Answer: Routers separate networks at Layers 1 and 2 of the OSI reference model. Those layers are physical and data link, respectively. Physical networks, such as Ethernet, occupy solely these two layers.

4. At what layer(s) of the OSI reference model does a router interconnect different networks?

   Answer: Routers connect networks at Layer 3, the network layer. The Internet Protocol (IP) operates at Layer 3 and has become the world's dominant protocol for interconnecting networks.

5. What is a *hop* and why is it significant in routing?

Answer: A hop is the original distance vector. Each router in the path between a source and destination network counts as one hop. This basic mechanism is the foundation for distance-vector routing and continues to influence modern routing protocols.

6. What is a distance vector?

Answer: A distance vector is an arbitrary measure of distance in a network.

7. Why isn't hop counting a basis for efficient routing?

Answer: Hops tend not to correlate well to geographic distances in a network. Nor do hops take into account the amount of bandwidth available or other network conditions that might make certain paths undesirable. Consequently, hop counting is a rudimentary approach to selecting best paths in a network.

8. What is a potential problem with link-state routing?

Answer: Some types of link-state information are too volatile for direct routing decisions. Information such as a link's load level or the amount of delay currently experienced are too volatile to be useful in selecting best paths. Quite simply, the data would change many times before you could complete the decision-making process. Consequently, link-state routing has the potential to seriously disrupt a network's operation if it is not configured properly.

9. Which is better: distance-vector or link-state routing?

Answer: It is impossible to state definitely which approach to routing is superior. Rather, each approach to routing comes with its own strengths and weaknesses and, if you understand those qualities relative to your particular needs, you can't make a bad choice. Generally speaking, distance-vector routing is cruder and potentially ineffective, but easy to configure and use. Link-state routing is much more complex and powerful, but that complexity is its Achilles' Heel. If not properly configured, a link-state protocol can wreak havoc in a network.

10. When would you consider using policy- or rules-based routing?

Answer: Policy-based routing only works well when your primary goal is massive scalability. If you are not building a network the size of the global Internet, you are probably better off selecting a lighter routing protocol, such as a distance-vector or link-state protocol. Of course, if you intend to connect your WAN to the Internet, you might be required to use policy-based routing across that connection.

Chapter 12

1. Explain the relationship between TCP/IP and networks such as Ethernet.

Answer: TCP/IP is not a network. You run TCP/IP over networks, but it isn't a network unto itself. TCP/IP absolutely requires a network of some type to run over.

2. How many components are needed, at a minimum, to build a local-area network (LAN)?

Answer: All LANs consist of four primary components: two or more end-user devices such as computers, network interface cards (NICs) that connect those computers to the LAN, some medium over which to transmit signals, and a hub or switch that interconnects the end-user machines.

3. What is the difference between a hub and a switch?

Answer: A hub forces all devices connected to it to share the same bandwidth. A switch provides much higher performance by offering each device its own dedicated bandwidth.

4. Is coaxial cable obsolete or does it still serve a purpose?

Answer: Coaxial cable had verged on obsolescence but has found renewed life thanks to cable TV companies that use it to deliver high-bandwidth Internet connections. Today, home networks are typically constructed using either twisted-pair or wireless technologies and convert to coaxial cable only for Internet access.

5. What is a Category of Performance?

Answer: A Category of Performance is a speed rating given to twisted-pair cables. The higher the Cat-*x* number, the faster you can transmit over that wire.

6. What is the fastest speed at which a wireless network can operate?

Answer: The typical wireless network found in homes and small offices can run as fast as 54 megabits per second (Mbps) using either the IEEE 802.11g or 802.11a specifications. That technology is more frequently referred to as Wireless G and Wireless A, respectively.

7. What is the fastest speed at which an Ethernet wire-based network can operate?

Answer: Ethernet networks can run as fast as 10 gigabits per second (Gbps), but that speed is typically not used by end-user devices. End-user devices such as computers can connect to Ethernet networks at 10, 100, or 1000 megabits per second (Mbps). 1,000 Mbps is the same as 1 Gbps.

8. Which is more reliable: wire-based networks or wireless networks?

Answer: Wire-based networks are much more reliable because their signals are electrical impulses that travel through a copper wire. Those signals can suffer from certain types of interference, but they are less prone to such interference than wireless networks. Wireless networks can be impeded by a wide variety of forces, including other wireless devices and even microwave ovens.

9. What are the main drawbacks of wire-based networks?

Answer: Wire-based networks can't be as neat-looking as wireless networks. The amount of wire used to interconnect end-user devices to a network can become quite voluminous. Over time, that cable can become an unsightly mess, even in smaller networks. The second drawback is that the cabling is not at all flexible. You can bend it, but moves or changes more often than not mean you have to rerun new wires rather than being able to reuse the old wire.

10. What are the main advantages of wire-based networks?

   Answer: Wire-based networks are more reliable, more secure, and faster than their wireless counterparts.

11. What do wireless networks use to transmit signals?

   Answer: Wireless networks can use radio waves, microwaves, and even light waves to transmit signals.

12. What are the main benefits of wireless networks?

   Answer: Wireless networks are easy to install, save you the expense of network wiring, and offer a neat appearance. More importantly, wireless networks enable you to be highly mobile; you can literally pick up your laptop and walk around your home without losing connectivity.

Chapter 13

1. What is the Internet?

   Answer: The Internet is the world's largest and most successful TCP/IP network ever built. It spans the globe and functions as a public utility (even though it is privately owned), which means that access to it is not restricted.

2. What is the official network communications protocol of the Internet?

   Answer: The Internet's official network communications protocol is TCP/IP. One could argue that TCP/IP was made for the Internet.

3. What are your options for accessing the Internet from home?

   Answer: Typically, a home Internet user can choose between dial-up access or one of two dedicated, or always-on, access technologies. Those dedicated technologies include Digital Subscriber Line (DSL, which is usually offered by telephone companies) or broadband cable (which is offered by cable TV network operators). Unfortunately, the dedicated technologies are not as universally available as dial-up service; your choices might not be as complete as you would like.

4. Is the fastest access technology always the best choice for you?

Answer: Generally speaking, you want to have the fastest connection to the Internet available to you. However, depending on your confidence in your ability to secure a dedicated or always-on connection, a slower connection established by dialing up might be safer.

5. Under what circumstances might you find yourself still using a modem with a dedicated connection to a cable TV network?

Answer: Not all cable TV networks have been upgraded to carry data bidirectionally. Some networks in more rural areas might still have an analog-only network and be unable to carry the digital signals required for Internet service. Others might only be capable of delivering high-speed data but not accepting it over a cable network. In those situations, an asymmetric cable Internet service might be offered, which requires you to dial up the cable provider's network and receive downloaded data via the cable network.

Chapter 14

1. What is troubleshooting?

Answer: Troubleshooting is a systematic, step-by-step approach to isolating and testing components in a complex system. By testing components one at a time in a logical sequence, you can methodically isolate the cause of any given operating problem.

2. What command verifies that TCP/IP is configured correctly on your computer?

Answer: **ipconfig** is the tool to use to verify that your computer's copy of TCP/IP is configured properly. Of course, it helps to familiarize yourself with **ipconfig** and normal settings before trying to use it as a troubleshooting tool.

3. Which TCP/IP utility tests the reachability of any given Internet destination?

Answer: You can use two different tools to test the reachability of a destination on the Internet. Although both **ping** and **tracert** function similarly in this regard, **ping** was specifically built for that purpose.

4. Which tool determines if your computer's Ethernet connection is working properly?

   Answer: **netstat –e** is the specific command to run in a command prompt to see if your computer's Ethernet connection is working properly. Although it won't explicitly tell you if the connection is not working, you can surmise its status by examining the statistics that it presents.

5. Which tool determines if your computer's TCP/IP protocol suite is working effectively?

   Answer: The best tool for evaluating your computer's TCP/IP protocol suite's operating efficiency is **netstat –s**. That option shows you total volumes of data processed by both TCP and UDP and tracks send and receive data for ICMP messages.

6. How would you find out if the computer you are trying to access (or the network it is connected to) is experiencing heavy congestion?

   Answer: If you run **netstat –s** and see that your computer is receiving a large number of Source Quench messages, it is likely that whatever you were trying to do across the network was encountering congestion either at the network or host level. Either way, the message is clear: Slow down!

7. Which tool tracks the path your packets take through a network?

   Answer: **tracert** or **traceroute**, depending on your computer's operating system, is quite useful in tracking the specific path that packets sent from your computer take to any given destination on a TCP/IP network.

Glossary

A

ARPA   The Advanced Research Projects Agency (ARPA) of the United States Department of Defense sponsored critical research projects. ARPA sponsored the original Internet as a means of facilitating collaborative research among its supporting organizations.

ARPAnet   The original Internet deployed by ARPA was known as the ARPAnet.

B

base address   A base address is the first IP address in either a network address or a subnetwork address block. The base address typically serves as the address for that network or subnetwork.

best-effort delivery   The User Datagram Protocol is designed to provide a best-effort delivery. That is, it makes one attempt to deliver data and entrusts the network to get that data delivered. That is known as best-effort delivery.

bit   The term bit is an abbreviation for binary digit. A bit is the smallest unit of data and can have a value of either 0 or 1.

broadband   Broadband describes any of the modern, high-speed Internet technologies such as Digital Subscriber Line or cable modem service.

byte   A byte is a collection of bits, usually 7 or 8. The term, byte, is an abbreviation of **binary term**. A byte represents a single character.

C

checksum   Many communications protocols, including TCP, UDP, and IP feature a mathematical error-detection mechanism known as a checksum. Essentially, a mathematical process is performed at the source machine using the payload data as input. The output of that process is stored in the checksum field of the protocol's header. The receiving machine performs the same process and compares its results with the results stored in the header. If the two match, it is relatively safe to assume that the payload has not been damaged in transit.

CIDR   Classless Interdomain Routing, or CIDR (pronounced cider as in the apple juice drink), is the system that is currently in use for IP addressing. CIDR enables you to define a network address at any bit in the 32-bit address. Previously, boundaries between the network and host address were limited to every 8th bit.

D

datagram   According to the IETF RFC 1594, a datagram is "a self-contained, independent entity of data carrying sufficient information to be routed from the source to the destination computer without reliance on earlier exchanges between this source and destination computer and the transporting network." That definition is applicable to the data transported by UDP and not TCP.

decimal mask   A decimal mask is used to hide a raw 32-bit binary IP address behind something a bit more user-friendly. That mask takes the form of a dotted decimal number with four parts. For example, 10.1.2.128 is a decimal mask for 00001010.00000001.00000010.10000000.

destination machine   The networked device that receives a communications session.

Domain Name System   A Domain Name System, or DNS, is a database that tracks and correlates the user-friendly domain and host names used in the Internet with IP addresses. This mechanism allows you to initiate a communications session using a user-friendly name, even though an IP network uses only IP addresses.

E

EIA The Electronics Industry Association (EIA) defines open technical standards for the electronics industry. One of its more significant contributions to data networking has been the development of a series of performance-level standards for network wiring.

extended network prefix The network address plus subnetwork address forms the extended network prefix. This term is usually only encountered when talking with network geeks!

F

firewall Protects you from the Internet. Not everyone who uses the Internet has good intentions: Spammers, hackers, pornographers, and even marketers all use the Internet. The cumulative effect of these forces is that you can no longer leave open the metaphorical front door. You must secure your computer and home network from unwanted intrusions. That's the firewall.

A firewall lets you configure which types of communications you want to let into your network. You can write an entire book on firewalls and how to configure them. The more restrictive your firewall, the safer you are!

FLSM One approach to subnet masking is fixed-length and subnet masking (FLSM). Fixed-length features equally sized subnets. This approach is infinitely easier to manage over time than a variable-length subnet masking (VLSM) scheme.

fragmentation Fragmentation offset is the mechanism by which a destination machine figures out where the fragment fits relative to the beginning of the piece of data. This is different than the function used by TCP sequence numbers. Sequence numbers are assigned to data segments created by TCP as larger pieces of data (such as files) are segmented for transportation through a network. After segmentation, sometimes network conditions force further fragmentation of data than was done at the source machine. When a segment must be fragmented, the fragmentation offset tracks the sequence of fragments so that the fragments can be properly reassembled into their original segment.

frame   The data structure that transports IP packets through a local-area network or other physical network. The frame contains the source and destination addresses that are used by the physical network.

FTP   The File Transfer Protocol (FTP) is a utility built into TCP/IP that enables you to transfer files between two hosts on an IP network.

H

header   Network protocols prepend a data structure on each piece of data in preparation for transmission. This data structure, known as a header, bears all the information needed to ensure that the data gets delivered and, if applicable, for an acknowledgment to be returned.

hop   An arbitrary measure of distance used by distance-vector routing protocols. A hop is equal to one router. If there are 10 routers between you and your destination, you are said to be 10 hops away.

host   Any machine that can engage in a communications session using TCP/IP is known as a host.

hostmaster   A hostmaster is someone whose occupation is to design and manage an IP address block, including its subdivision into subnetworks. Although that might sound like a trivial job, I can assure you that a good hostmaster is worth his weight in gold. There is no end of grief that can be encountered in a network built using a mismanaged or unmanaged network address block.

I

IANA   The Internet Assigned Numbers Authority (IANA) regulates the assignments of numbers for use within and across the Internet and other TCP/IP networks. Numbers regulated include IP addresses, autonomous system numbers, and application port numbers.

ICMP   The Internet Control Message Protocol (ICMP) transports system-generated messages through a TCP/IP network.

IEEE   The Institute of Electrical and Electronic Engineers (IEEE or "I Triple E" as it is more commonly pronounced) is an independent, nonprofit organization that sponsors research and establishes the technical standards for a wide variety of electrical and electronic technologies. Its greatest contribution to data networking has been the standardization of many technologies, including Ethernet.

IETF   The Internet Engineering Task Force is a society of engineers dedicated to the maintenance and development of the Internet's technology base.

interoperability   Interoperability is the ability to build a functional networked computing environment by interconnecting products from different manufacturers.

IP   The Internet Protocol (IP) is the network layer protocol suite. It is responsible for carrying both TCP and UDP protocols across a network.

ISO   The International Organization for Standards (ISO) was chartered by the United Nations and founded in 1946. Its mission is to set global standards for virtually everything. Everything, that is, except for anything electrical or electronic. ISO developed a generic model for the interconnection of open systems. That model is known as the *Open Systems Interconnection (OSI)* reference model.

ISP   Companies that sell access to the Internet are called Internet service providers, or ISPs.

L

latency   The amount of time that it takes for a piece of data, such as a TCP or UDP datagram, to pass through a networked device or transmission facility.

logical adjacency   The layered approach to systems design enables applications or protocols on different machines to appear to be communicating directly with each other. In reality, communications flow vertically through the layered functions rather than horizontally between peer processes or applications. This concept is known as logical adjacency.

M

maximum segment size   The maximum segment size (MSS) is a field inside the TCP header that tells the machine it is sent to exactly how large of a TCP segment it can accept. This value is specified in bytes.

milliseconds   Thousands of a second. TCP/IP contains many tools for measuring the performance of a network, and those tools all use milliseconds as the standard measure of time elapsed.

modem   The word modem is an acronym of the technical functions of this device: **mo**dulator-**dem**odulator. A modem performs several functions. First, it establishes a connection on your command by dialing up the telephone number of another modem. Second, after that connection is established, it accepts digital signals from your computer and translates them into analog sounds that are transmitted across the telephone network. Your modem also accepts incoming analog signals and translates them back into digital signals, or data, that is handed to your computer's network interface.

N

Network Control Protocol   Before there was TCP/IP, there existed a collection of software utilities and protocols created and shared among the engineers that used the Internet during its early, precommercial days. This collection of software was called the Network Control Protocol (NCP).

Network Interface Card   Network Interface Card (NIC) is the device that enables a computer or any other device to connect to a network. NICs can come in many different forms including a port that is built into your computer's motherboard, a separate circuit board that plugs into your computer's motherboard, or even external devices.

network mask   A numerical way of identifying how many bits of an IP address constitute the network address portion. This mask can be expressed in either decimal or binary forms. For example, 255.255.0.0 is the decimal form of the network mask 11111111.11111111.00000000.00000000. The actual IP address could be

10.1.2.128, or any other IP address. The mask shows the network address bits using 1s, and the subnetwork and host address bits using 0s.

Network Time Protocol (NTP)   NTP is responsible for synchronizing time throughout a network.

O

open standard   Technologies that are developed in public forums, such as standards committees that consist of representatives from competing companies in the same industry, are known as open standards.

OSI reference model   A seven-layer logical model that organizes the necessary sequence of events that must transpire in a communications system between open systems.

P

padding   A field in the TCP header structure that fills in enough zeros to ensure the size of the entire segment is a multiple of 32.

payload   Generic term describing the data content of either a UDP datagram, TCP segment, IP packet, or Ethernet frame.

ping   The Packet Internet Groper (ping) is a text-based utility that helps you test the reachability of destinations through a TCP/IP network.

propagation delay   The amount of time required for a piece of data, such as a TCP or UDP packet, to pass through a transmission facility.

protocol   A small piece of software designed to perform one small, specific task.

POTS line   POTS lines are circuits that were designed to provide you with **plain old telephone service.** Although the full name might seem too cute to be a real term, that actually is what the acronym stands for! When you connect a modem to a POTS line, you can use a voice-grade circuit for sending and receiving TCP/IP data.

R

reference model   A logical framework that keeps a logical and necessary sequence of events in its proper order.

reliable delivery   The Transmission Control Protocol (TCP) guarantees that packets of data are delivered and can be put back into their original sequence after delivery. This is known as reliable delivery.

Round Trip Time   One of the many things that TCP/IP does for you automatically when you start a communications session with it is to keep track of the amount of time it takes to send a packet to a remote destination and to receive a response. That amount of time is known as Round Trip Time (RTT).

router   A specialized device that is designed to push IP packets (or other protocols' packets) through a network.

routing protocol   A software program designed specifically to continuously seek out IP network addresses that might be accessible indirectly through a network connection and assess the reachability of that destination. The protocol then compares different routes through a network to reach the same destination and selects the best one.

routing table   A listing of best paths to known destination networks. That list is correlated with the router's interface that must be used to get to that path. A routing table can also include routes to individual IP addresses but must be specifically programmed to do so. In normal operation, they track routes to IP network addresses.

S

segment   A piece of application data chopped into a transportable size by TCP and wrapped with a TCP header.

segmentation   The process of chopping up application data into chunks small enough to fit inside a TCP segment and IP packet.

sequence number   In order to ensure that the destination machine can correctly reassemble inbound TCP segments, TCP applies a serial or sequence number to each segment's header. The receiving machine can use this number to both reassemble incoming data correctly and to deduce which segments might have been lost in transit.

session   The flow of communications between two computer systems.

sliding window   A dynamic approach to controlling TCP window size. Rather than hard-code the window size, it makes sense to allow TCP to figure out what the right window size is, based on network performance. In other words, the actual size of the window can slide up or down in response to changes in the network's state. The window size identifies the number of octets or bytes that can be transmitted without having received an acknowledgment back from the destination machine.

SMTP   Electronic mail is carried through the Internet via Simple Mail Transfer Protocol (SMTP).

socket   The concatenation of the source machine's IP address and source port address together with the destination machine's IP and port address. Together they uniquely identify a specific communications session between the source computer and destination application. Unlike destination source ports, a computer can assign different source port numbers to accommodate the possibility of two or more copies of the same program running simultaneously. The ability to change the source port number guarantees that a socket can uniquely identify a specific communications session.

source machine   The networked device that originates a communications session.

subnet mask   A subnet mask builds upon the network mask by also indicating the subnetwork address bits with 1s. Just like the network mask, a subnet mask can be expressed in either decimal (which is most commonly encountered) or binary forms. Only the host address bits are expressed with 0s in the binary form of a subnet mask.

subnetting   Subnetting is a process by which the host address field of an IP address is split into two parts, thereby creating a third level of addressing. The three address levels are network, subnetwork, and host address.

T

TCP   The Transmission Control Protocol that operates at Layer 4 of the OSI reference model and enables guaranteed or reliable delivery of IP packets.

TFTP   The Trivial File Transfer Protocol (TFTP) is one of the many utilities built into the TCP/IP family of protocols. This mechanism enables you to transfer files between hosts with a minimum of complexity.

three-way handshake   Each and every communications session using TCP begins with a three-way handshake between the source and destination machines. This handshake enables the two machines to coordinate their activities and ensure reliable delivery of future packet transmissions.

TIA   The Telecommunications Industry Association sets open technical standards for the telecommunications industry. One of its more significant contributions to data networking was its collaboration with the EIA to produce performance-based categories of standards for network wire.

Time-To-Live   The Time-To-Live (TTL) field tracks the number of network devices that the IP packet passes through. When a certain threshold is reached, the packet is discarded.

tracert   A tool that uses ICMP to help you map out the actual path that your IP packets take when sent through a TCP/IP network. See also *traceroute*.

traceroute   Some operating systems name the ICMP trace utility traceroute. Traceroute is the same as tracert.

transmission medium   The transmission facility that connects your computer's network interface card to the network.

trunk line   A high-capacity telecommunications line that can carry multiple dial-up sessions simultaneously.

U

UDP   UDP is the User Datagram Protocol. It operates at Layer 4 of the OSI reference model and is a no-frills transport protocol. UDP makes one attempt to deliver an IP packet and that's it.

V

VLSM   One approach to subnet masking is variable length subnet masking (VLSM), which is infinitely more tunable than fixed length subnet masking (FLSM) to the specific needs of your network. The price of that tunability is complexity! It takes a mathematics wizard to keep track of a VLSM network address scheme.

VoIP   Voice over IP refers to an emerging family of products that replaces traditional telephone service with the ability to carry voice communications over an IP network.

W

Wireless A   The IEEE's 802.11a standard for wireless local area networking is more popularly known as Wireless A. This specification operates in the 5 GHz frequency range and offers 54 Mbps of bandwidth for distances up to 30 meters.

Wireless B   The IEEE's 802.11b standard for wireless local area networking is more popularly known as Wireless B. This specification operates in the 2.4 GHz frequency range and offers up to 11 Mbps of bandwidth for distances up to 100 meters.

Wireless G   The IEEE's 802.11a standard for wireless local area networking is more popularly known as Wireless A. This specification operates in the 2.4 GHz frequency range and offers up to 54 Mbps of bandwidth for distances up to 100 meters.

Numerics

I

M

W-Z

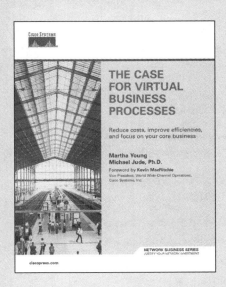

CISCO SYSTEMS

Cisco Press

Cisco Press

CISCO CERTIFICATION SELF-STUDY

#1 BEST-SELLING TITLES FROM CCNA® TO CCIE®

Look for Cisco Press Certification Self-Study resources at your favorite bookseller

Learn the test topics with **Self-Study Guides**

Gain hands-on experience with **Practical Studies** books

Prepare for the exam with **Exam Certification Guides**

Practice testing skills and build confidence with **Flash Cards and Exam Practice Packs**

Visit **www.ciscopress.com/series** to learn more about the Certification Self-Study product family and associated series.

Learning is serious business.
Invest wisely.

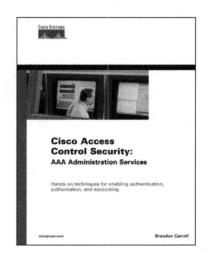

SEARCH THOUSANDS OF BOOKS FROM LEADING PUBLISHERS

Safari® Bookshelf is a searchable electronic reference library for IT professionals that features more than 2,000 titles from technical publishers, including Cisco Press.

With Safari Bookshelf you can

- **Search** the full text of thousands of technical books, including more than 70 Cisco Press titles from authors such as Wendell Odom, Jeff Doyle, Bill Parkhurst, Sam Halabi, and Karl Solie.

- **Read** the books on My Bookshelf from cover to cover, or just flip to the information you need.

- **Browse** books by category to research any technical topic.

- **Download** chapters for printing and viewing offline.

With a customized library, you'll have access to your books when and where you need them—and all you need is a user name and password.

CISCO SYSTEMS

Cisco Press

3 STEPS TO LEARNING

STEP 1

STEP 2

STEP 3

First-Step

Fundamentals

Networking Technology Guides

STEP 1 **First-Step**—Benefit from easy-to-grasp explanations. No experience required!

STEP 2 **Fundamentals**—Understand the purpose, application, and management of technology.

STEP 3 **Networking Technology Guides**—Gain the knowledge to master the challenge of the network.

TWORK BUSINESS SERIES

Network Business series helps professionals tackle the iness issues surrounding the network. Whether you are a soned IT professional or a business manager with minimal nical expertise, this series will help you understand the iness case for technologies.

tify Your Network Investment.

ᴸᵒᵒᵏ for Cisco Press titles at your favorite bookseller today.

Visit **www.ciscopress.com/series** for details on each of these book series.